Getting Personal

Books by Brian Masters

Molière
Sartre
Saint-Exupéry
Rabelais
Camus
Wynyard Hall and the Londonderry Family
Dreams about H.M.The Queen
The Dukes
Now Barabbas was a Rotter: The Extraordinary Life
of Marie Corelli
The Mistresses of Charles II
Georgiana, Duchess of Devonshire
Great Hostesses
Killing for Company: The Case of Dennis Nilsen
The Swinging Sixties
The Passion of John Aspinall
Maharana: The Udaipur Dynasty
Gary
The Life of E.F. Benson
Voltaire's Treatise on Tolerance (edited and translated)
The Shrine of Jeffrey Dahmer
Masters on Murder
The Evil That Men Do
'She Must Have Known': The Trial of Rosemary West
Thunder in the Air: Great Actors in Great Roles

Getting Personal

A BIOGRAPHER'S MEMOIR

BRIAN MASTERS

CONSTABLE • LONDON

Constable & Robinson Ltd
3 The Lanchesters
162 Fulham Palace Road
London W6 9ER
www.constablerobinson.com

First published by Constable,
an imprint of Constable & Robinson Ltd, 2002

A copy of the British Library Cataloguing in Publication Data for this
title is available from the British Library

1–84119–550–2

Printed and bound in the EU

For Caroline, Emma
and Victoria

Dr Anthony Clare, the psychiatrist, asked once if I was a man who had spent his life seeking forgiveness for some gross fault, or making amends as best I could for some deplorable defect of character. I either dodged the question or smothered it beneath generalities. I found it uncomfortable, and ought really to have examined why. After all, one cannot spend a great deal of one's professional life sorting other people out, through scrupulous and sometimes intrusive biographical research, without being prepared to have the lens turned upon oneself. I wonder if such self-examination is possible.

The art of the biographer is to probe beyond the façade which the subject has skilfully presented, to himself, as well as to others, over a lifetime, in order to discover the whole person behind the image; it involves both digging and building, archaeology followed by architecture. The notion that the biographer should be able to execute such work upon himself, at the same time as he, the subject, is busy deflecting such attention, seems absurd. Yet the effort is worth making, for in a sense the writer is always writing about himself, through the prism of other people; the way in which he considers their life stories, the questions he asks himself about them, the solutions he tries to knit together from apparent disconnections, all derive from what he himself deems important, significant, or crucial in life; another biographer must needs have another view. Thus what I have written, and the way I have written it, might both be oblique references to myself.

The biographical approach to understanding consists of sifting, selecting, and endlessly probing. What might there be about myself that I have not properly understood all these years?

CHAPTER 1

Nilsen's Boomerang

The temptation to entitle this memoir *My Life With Killers* has been easy to resist. There never has been such a life, of course, although it is sometimes assumed, because I have written three books on addictive murderers, that I think about nothing else. I was not predestined to dissect the motivations of these people, often erroneously called 'serial killers' (a mere mathematical observation, that), who murder and sometimes mutilate people entirely unknown to them, people to whom they are indifferent, people whose paths they have crossed at random and who then serve as props in their poisonous fantasies. I had known little about them, save that they were to be distinguished from multiple murderers, those who kill lots at the same time, such as snipers, military geniuses and terrorists.

My previous subjects had included studies in French literature, the history of dukedoms, an account of society hostesses in the twentieth century, and the biography of a Victorian bestseller. Why jump, therefore, from such relative calm into the muddy morass of Dostoyevskian gloom? And why, moreover, did I apparently turn out to be reasonably good at it? If the biographer in fact chooses his subjects, however subconsciously, because they offer him a way of looking at himself, then these would be worrying matters indeed. The idea that I should see echoes of myself in a repetitive murderer was untrue, but the idea that I might detect modes of thinking and habits of feeling within myself which might make it easier to *comprehend* (not 'understand') such a man was not so crazy. That, after all, would be the biographer's job.

I was aware of only two previous works that had treated the subject as worthy of serious reflection. Truman Capote's *In Cold Blood*, flawed by the author's insistence on inventing conversations without evidence, thus diminishing the psychology of the portrait and rendering it suspect. The other, Sybille Bedford's account of the trial of John Bodkin Adams, deeply perceptive but undermined by Adams' unexpected acquittal.

My own entry into this field was entirely accidental.

Dennis Nilsen was arrested at a house in Muswell Hill, a nondescript northern suburb of London, in February 1983. I read about it, like everyone else, in the newspapers the following morning. He was alleged to have murdered up to fifteen young men (he was eventually charged on six counts) at this address and at a previous flat in Cricklewood, making them drunk, strangling them, then keeping their bodies as companions to wash, make tidy, put to bed, talk to, and eventually dismember and burn (in the first flat) or flush down the lavatory (in the second). It was as clear an instance of madness as one could hope to encounter outside Dostoyevsky himself, and it immediately intrigued me. How could one possibly explain such conduct, if indeed it was true? And why did I feel so urgently that somebody *should* attempt to explain it? People would surely be content to enjoy the trial, despise the man, and pass on to other things. I was not so minded.

It was at breakfast with Juan (my companion at the time) that I first mentioned the possibility of writing about the case, the newspaper spread before me. I was my own most critical detractor, for I had no experience in the subject and knew that editors would be unlikely to trust me with it. I further felt certain that the Home Office, ever fearful of press accusations of helping criminals become famous, would refuse permission. It was Juan who pressed me to try, for he did not yet find my deep interest in the subject suspect. I did myself wonder why the case should make my antennae quiver. I told my agent, Jacintha Alexander, and she said she would make the proposal to the publishers of my two most recent books, Ben Glazebrook of Constable and Co., and Christopher Sinclair-Stevenson of Hamish Hamilton. Both eminent gentlemen, fastidious as well as professionally acute, turned the idea down immediately, as soon as it was mentioned, without wishing to hear any details of possible treatment or tone; they did not want their houses to be soiled with muck like that (not their words, I should add). Jacintha then thought we should try Tom Maschler of Jonathan Cape.

We went to see Maschler in his huge office on the ground floor in Bedford Square. Legendary in the publishing world, he was known to be quixotic, wild, a maverick who took risks. He certainly looked the part, hair like a spider's web and clothes from Oxfam, but he inspired trust by his translucent intelligence. He had never heard of me and had no inkling of my work so far. I was a tiro as far as he was concerned, but that would not deter him. He asked me to tell him exactly why I wanted to write this book. I had prepared no speech, no presentation, and stuttered away for about one minute, when he interrupted me. 'That's enough', he said, 'you have the enthusiasm for it, and I want to know why. The only way to find out is to read your book.' He commissioned me then and there. It was a lesson in the role of intuition in publishing. Tom was one of the last to be able to indulge it; there is no room for such fancies now that books are published according to accountants' estimates. I owe the publication of *Killing for Company* entirely to Tom's hunch.

Well, not entirely, for the book could not have turned out as it did without the co-operation of Nilsen himself. The first

thing I did was to write to Nilsen announcing my interest 'in
the case in which you find yourself involved' (for he was still
a man accused, not a man convicted), and declaring that I
would not proceed without his consent. This was honest. I
should have found it extraordinarily difficult to delve into
the character of the man if I knew that he did not want
me to, and I should have abandoned the project forthwith.
I addressed my letter to Brixton Prison, where every such
defendant was held on remand.

The letter I received in reply opened with ominous words
which are imprinted on my memory, even as they stood on
the page, etched in black ink, hard pressed into the paper,
and stretching from one border of the lined page to the other:
'Dear Mr Masters', it said, 'I pass the burden of my life on
to your shoulders'. It would be some years before I realised
just how true these words were to become.

The rest of the letter suggested we should meet, and invited
me to contact his solicitor, Ronald Moss, whom he would
alert. I had no idea, at that stage, how my letter and his
reply had passed through the scrutiny of censors. For, as I
later discovered, it was forbidden for authors to make such
an advance, which was why none of the Fleet Street criminal
correspondents had attempted to make contact with Nilsen.
Experienced professionals, they knew they couldn't. I got
away with it through ignorance.

I went to see Ronnie Moss, an ebullient cheerful chap, more
like a publican than a solicitor (he is now a magistrate), whom
Nilsen had instructed to be good to me. I think he was glad
to have somebody to talk to, for the crimes themselves were
so horrific, and Nilsen so unfathomable, that he felt soiled
and perplexed. No good talking to the police, who never
understand anything subtle, and Moss' secretary was sickened
by what she had to type out following interviews with the
accused. Ronnie told me that when he was arrested they had
found a head par-boiled on the stove, with human grease
caked around the edge, and the lower half of a torso stuffed
beneath the bath-tub. In the wardrobe were two black dustbin

bags which they had taken away to be opened and examined. In the police car on the way to the station, the driver had said over his shoulder, thinking himself deductive, 'Come on, now, are we talking about one body or two?' Nilsen simply said, 'Fifteen, I think', and the driver nearly went off the road into a tree. They had not the slightest idea what to make of him. Even worse, they liked him. He made them laugh! Ronnie, too, found him a pleasant enough person, straightforward and candid, talkative, not shy; intelligent, not dim. He would do whatever he could to help. But first, he said, he would have to find out whether the rules of his profession permitted his co-operation. 'Don't worry about that', I said, somewhat cockily, 'I'll get the President of the Law Society to call you.' (At that time it was Max Williams, fortunately a friend of mine.) Moss was so impressed his mouth hung open for a second or two, long enough to indicate that he would never have dared to telephone such an august individual himself.

On our next meeting, Ronnie told me that Nilsen had begun filling a prison exercise book with notes and reminiscences, specifically for my use, and he showed me drawings that the man had made in his cell. They were at once shocking and poetic. Under the provocative title 'Sad Sketches' (I was to learn that Nilsen enjoyed adopting the provocative role), he depicted neat, spare pictures of dead men, including the half torso found under the bath-tub, which he entitled, 'The Last Time I Saw Stephen Sinclair', another of a man lying on a bed, his head hanging to one side, blood dripping from his mouth, another of a man hanging inside a wardrobe. These pictures would eventually be reproduced at the end of *Killing for Company* and the originals are still in my bank vault. To my knowledge, they are unique in criminal history, both as a visual record of the murderer's own acts, and as grandly grotesque works of art. For they are not scribbles, and they are not apologetic. They are drawn with energy, with pride, with an odd kind of perverse affection. They alone tell one much about the killer's mind.

No lay person can visit a prisoner without an invitation.

It is simply not possible just to turn up during visiting hours, nor can one apply for an invitation. The prisoner himself has to submit names of proposed visitors to the authorities, who then presumably check records to make sure the name is not that of a man with a criminal record, or a manufacturer of escape equipment, and eventually pass the name as a permitted visitor. The prisoner then posts a V.O. (Visiting Order) to the person in question, who may use it on any visiting day within a calendar month. Nilsen put only one name on his list – mine – and presumably none of the searches revealed that I had written any books. I was grateful not to be famous!

We met for the first time at Brixton across a bare wooden kitchen table with a disposable tin ashtray in the centre. In the corner of the tiny room sat a bored warder, desperate to think of something rather than to have to listen to our conversation. He was there not to eavesdrop, but to ensure that I smuggled nothing into the prisoner's hands, and, I suppose, that the prisoner did not attack me. Nilsen had his arm slung over the back of his chair, in a studied position of nonchalance, too contrived to be natural, and spoke as if he were interviewing me for a job (he had, of course, been employed as an executive officer at the Job Centre in Kentish Town, and was experienced in such encounters). He obviously wanted to see whether I could be trusted to tell his story to the world, and I wanted him to understand that I would tell it in my way, not in his. We achieved these statements of position by indirection, for I was determined not to start questioning him about his crimes immediately, still less to ask him how it 'felt' to face such accusations, for that would have damned me as a prying reporter. For my part, it was important that he should understand I would approach the matter seriously. For his, that I should approach it without extravagant indignation. We both wanted that I should try to comprehend what had happened and why.

Nilsen told me that he had already filled three exercise books and would continue to fill more (there would eventually be over fifty of them). He said they contained childhood reminiscences and political views as well as accounts of murder, all jumbled in no especial order, and that I would be free to make use of what I needed and reject the rest. 'You're the artist', he said, (I'm afraid that was the word he used), 'only you can know what's important and how to select. I won't interfere.' He also volunteered, without any prompting from me, that it would be wholly wrong for him to profit by the arrangement, and that he should therefore receive not a penny from the publishers. 'But don't forget to bring a packet of fags with you when you visit. I'm allowed to smoke as many as I like while you're here, but you can't leave any behind.' I did also occasionally send him a postal order for £2 to help buy stamps for the letters he was sending me, sometimes two every day.

(While I am on the subject, I cannot resist the story relating to some eight years later, when Lord Longford had taken to visiting him. Frank did not smoke, and forgot to take a packet with him. Visits by then took place in a large hall, prisoners and visitors scattered at separate tables, a din of conversation crashing against the walls. In a loud voice calculated to tease, Nilsen greeted Longford with the words, 'I hope you've remembered to bring the drugs this time, Frank.')

For the eight months of his remand, I went to Brixton twice every week. For the two weeks of his trial, I saw him in the cells at the Old Bailey every day. And for ten years after his conviction, I went to whatever prison he happened to inhabit (in Yorkshire, the Isle of Wight, or Cambridgeshire) every month. Thus did Dennis Nilsen acquire from the bargain a benefit arguably more valuable than a cut in royalties.

I have often been asked since whether I liked him. I have to dodge the question, because it is based on a false assumption. I never knew the murder-less Nilsen, the man who talked the hind legs off a donkey, the man who wasted hours in self-opinionated bar chatter, the anarchist, the orator, the pamphleteer. I think if I had (and it is unlikely, because I loathe pubs), I should have found him a huge bore, incapable of listening, rigidly self-regarding. But the Nilsen I did know, the man on trial, the man facing his own deeds, the man without a future, was saved from being a bore by virtue of the strange, unnecessary nature of our acquaintance. It was a professional acquaintance, and it also became a friendly one. I admired his intelligence, and applauded his writing (though I often pointed out that it needed pruning and discipline, which typically he refuted; he was as verbose on the page as in conversation). I was grateful for his trust, and for a time he was grateful for mine. There were no awkward silences, and no moments of pretence. We both knew what we were there for. The differences between us were vast, but we shared one particular purpose. There are many who think, I know, that I was hoodwinked into serving his purpose alone, but I know this to be untrue, so am not troubled by it.

I was also frequently asked whether I was nervous in the presence of a murderer. The question appeared so strange to me that I was stuck for an answer, although I have to admit that it did not appear strange to those who asked it. So perhaps there was something suspect about my equanimity. All I can say is that I never felt the slightest unease. It did not cross my mind to wonder what he had done with those hands which shook mine in greeting (until now, as I write this sentence, and it feels distinctly silly to wonder anything of the sort), or to fear the Touch of Evil, or to make sure I was safe from attack. I could see that his threshold of anger was not high, but also that he would never be in a position to lose his temper with me, and would not want to. Addictive murderers are furtive midnight creatures, hurt by the light, scorched by contact. It would have been impossible to embrace the man, and even very difficult to lay a hand on his arm. He would have winced. The only human contact he ever positively welcomed was with a corpse. So the table between us was as much his protection as mine. He was the one to be afraid, in the deepest sense, not me.

What I am afraid of is my own senility. Once the police

knew what I was up to and agreed to help me, they thought I ought to be warned. Detective Inspector Jay was concerned that I might not have the stomach for the job, and before showing me the pictures taken by police of human remains found at Nilsen's flat, he casually passed over his desk to me a folder. 'That's the sort of thing we have to deal with on a daily basis', he said. 'Woman found in bed this morning, her head practically severed from her body.' I opened the folder and my eyes fell upon a black and white photograph of a young woman with a deep, frightening gash in her neck and terror in her eyes. For a split second – no longer – I envisioned the knife. 'Very nasty', I said, and pushed the folder back. But I had passed the test. Thereupon I was shown pictures in the order in which they were taken at Nilsen's flat. To this day I believe I am the only non-professional to have set eyes on these images, and I wish I had not. Of course, I only half-mean that, for it was important that I should see them, to remind myself of what this man, who made me laugh, had done, and try to enter obliquely into his soul the better to explain him; indeed, it was I who asked to see them. But those images, once entered into the brain, cannot be taken out again and chucked away. I saw the cooking pot with Sinclair's head in it, the lips boiled away, the eyes soft and gluey, the hair drifting to the side, and all that fat around the edges. I saw the reconstruction of his body on the floor of the morgue, five pieces placed together as in a jigsaw puzzle. I saw the jumbled contents of the black bags in the wardrobe, sad débris of what had once been vibrant, jumping life. I said that's enough, I do not need to see any more. 'I thought that's what you'd say', Jay told me, and closed the box. To me this was part of the archive that I had to study if I was to do the job properly. My old age scares me because those images might come leering back at me when I no longer have a mind to control them and keep them in their place, when they will have become, in a sense, my archive as well.

I take it this is what Nietzsche meant by his famous warning not to look too deeply into the abyss, lest the abyss enter into you.

I have said that Nilsen made me laugh. It is as well to throw the evidence in now, in juxtaposition with what has just been said, so that the reader may judge the taste of the man, and my questionable response in laughing at it. One story did find its way into the press somehow. It happened when there was talk of a film being made of my book. On a prison visit, Nilsen asked me to make sure that 'the cast be announced in order of disappearance.'

When his grandmother was ninety, his mother asked me if I would remind him to send her a birthday card. I knew this would be difficult, for I was not allowed to take anything with me into prison, and birthday cards were not a regular item to be sold inside. I explained my predicament to the governor, who agred to waive the rules on this one occasion. I bought a suitable card, and asked Nilsen to sign it so that I could post it on his behalf. He was very pleased. 'I really loved her', he said, 'she was always good to me. Trouble is, it's a bit difficult to know what to put when you've killed fifteen people. Shall I write, "Sorry for Any Inconvenience"?' Naturally, he wrote something kind and gentle, but he could not resist the joke.

When he was serious, Nilsen could come up with some challenging remarks. One such gave me awkward pause which I was not to resolve for days, and perhaps not even then. I told him frankly that intellectual honesty bade me admit that I, or anyone else for that matter, would be capable of murder in certain circumstances, that killing was among the human possibilities, and that in the face of all the historical and psychological evidence it would be ridiculous to deny this. I added, of course, that I prayed with all my heart that no such situation would ever arise, but the theoretical truth of the statement remained, whether it did or not. That part of his crime was within the boundaries of comprehension, and could be explained by imbalances in the brain or the emotions. On the other hand, I simply could not understand how he could treat human remains with cavalier contempt, how he could dismember people and throw the bits on to a bonfire like so much rubbish. Well, said Nilsen, if you really do have difficulty with that, then there is something seriously wrong with your moral thinking.

'The wicked thing that I did', he went on, 'was to squeeze the life out of a human being. That was wrong, unforgivable, and I am going to be properly punished for it. But what I did with a corpse is neither here nor there. A corpse is only an object. You can't hurt it, injure it, do it any harm whatever. It doesn't matter what happens to it, and I am not going to stand trial for abusing a corpse because the law recognises that it involves no wrongdoing. If you are more outraged by what I did to a corpse than by what I did to a living man, then your moral system is upside-down and needs overhauling.' I could immediately see the logic of this view, and briefly wondered why I had got the matter so fundamentally wrong, yet I still *felt* that the insult to a corpse was hideous. Why did I persist in feeling that, in despite of logic to the contrary?

The human experience is substantially more than a series of rational steps towards a purposeful conclusion. It involves reason, sequential thought, analytical decisions at every turn, but it also involves something deep and mysterious, a subterranean spring of intuitive knowledge which defies explanation. This is why, of course, there has always been room for religions in our various disparate societies, precisely in order to provide shape and certainty to truths which we feel to be diffuse and evanescent. We know these truths to be profound, but we also know our knowledge of them to be inadequate and unreliable. Religion plugs the hole.

I knew perfectly well that my response to Nilsen's treatment of dead bodies was deep-seated, in the bones and in the blood, not merely a product of the mind. We all feel a warm reverence for something that had once been alive and noisy, full of vigour and the pulse of a thousand potentialities. We see in the corpse a memory of what was and a reflection of our fragile tenancy of those potentials, and we behave accordingly, with sorrow and respect. If we were purely rational, we might dump the body in a field or chop it up for the dustman; it will, after all, partake of the eternal cycle of matter whatever we do to it. But we are not only rational, and that was what made Nilsen so separate from the rest of humankind. He did not *feel* any of this, and so was outside the human, was lacking in one of the essential ingredients of the human – that capacity for reverence without need. Certainly he was not on trial for this lack – he was right about that – but his crimes were the direct result of it. To look at death without grace is to throw dirt at life itself.

Once, in a casual remark which made me wince, he said, 'You'd be surprised how heavy a human head is when you lift it up by the hair.' There was the trace of a grin on his face as he said this, but no flicker of acknowledgement that it was terrible. He volunteered it as a curiosity.

In a sense, I was still pondering the dilemma of Nilsen's necrophilia when fifteen years later I came to write my one attempt at moral philosophy, *The Evil That Men Do*. I doubt whether he realised how much his logic had hurt.

As his trial approached and his co-operation both with the police and Ronnie Moss evaporated, I became the middleman, running errands from one to the other. His petulance arose from the appalling conditions at Brixton, where technically yet-innocent men awaiting trial were locked up for twenty-three and a half hours a day and treated like scum. In protest he first refused to wear prison garb and was clad, I gathered, only in a blanket. Then he withdrew all contact with his own solicitor and refused to entertain any further requests from the police, both useless exercises for neither Moss nor Jay could influence the governor at Brixton (for once Nilsen's logic appeared to be dormant). So if there was something Moss needed to consult him about, with regard to his defence, he asked me to pass on the question and take the answer back to him at his house in Pinner. The police, having brought charges against him, were not permitted to question him further unless he consented. He would not consent, but they still had matters they wanted him to elucidate. So the police inspectors and I would meet in pubs scattered across London (never the same one twice), as they told me what they wanted to know, and I reported back to them when I had spoken to Nilsen.

This devious clandestine behaviour was necessary to avoid the attentions of the press, which was by this time furious at my having sole access to Nilsen and tried to undermine my position in various ways. They sent reporters to the Queen's Theatre in Shaftesbury Avenue, where Juan worked in the box office, ostensibly to buy tickets but in reality to find out about me. They got messages through to Nilsen telling him that I was not trustworthy. Warders suddenly started to confiscate his notebooks, for no good reason. Nilsen decided to upset these efforts by planting a startling and sensational tale in one of these books, which was entirely invented and calculated to appeal to the minds of tabloid editors, then wait to see where it would turn up. As it happened, that piece of nonsense was not published in the Sunday papers, but it did temporarily derail the investigations of one of the psychiatrists engaged upon the case.

My own investigations produced a couple of surprises. Having access to all Nilsen's papers, including those discovered in his flat after his arrest and subsequently in police hands, I was intrigued to find a piece of paper torn from a pad, blank save for the first line, on which was written, in Nilsen's unmistakeable hand, 'It all started on New Year's Eve, 1978', then tapered into nothing. Since this piece of paper was already in the flat, the line was written before the discovery of Nilsen's crimes, while he was still a free man with a job and a pet dog. How long before, one cannot know, but the urge to confess, to unload a burden, was clearly present. Even more significant was the manner of his discovery. All the lavatories and drains at the house in Melrose Avenue were blocked, causing distress to all the tenants in all three flats. The landlords had said, on Friday, that they could not send anyone round to look at the problem until Monday. An angry letter was sent to these landlords insisting that none of the tenants should be expected to endure such conditions over a weekend and insisting that the problem be addressed urgently. It was, and human remains were found to be causing the blockage, thus leading to Nilsen's arrest. When I asked the landlords' agents to show me the letter, I saw that it was written by Dennis Nilsen himself. He had engineered his own arrest. (He was later to refer to 'the day that help arrived.')

I was blitzed with letters from him, and anxious about the pressure of his script, almost puncturing the page and filling every centimetre of space from the left margin to the right. There seemed to be something intense about this, something driven, and it made me uncomfortable. I took three examples of Nilsen's handwriting to a graphologist, taking care to select nothing which could reveal the writer's identity or give cause by its content to suggest abnormality. I left the specimens with her for a week, after which she would give me a full analysis and report. On my second appointment, she said, 'Before I tell you anything, I must ask you something very important. Have you ever been alone with this man?' I said I had not. 'Then please don't ever allow the circumstance to arise which might place you alone with him. He is extremely dangerous.'

Only four weeks before his trial was due to begin, Nilsen provoked a crisis by sacking his solicitor and counsel and making application to defend himself. There was no reason in law why he should not be so allowed, and he enjoyed creating a fuss and watching people scurry in obedience to his whim. I suppose that, at the very least, a mighty distraction was preferable to the suffocating boredom of Brixton prison. Besides, Nilsen was articulate and clever enough to have argued his case, and knew how to mug up on the law books in order to do so correctly. Nilsen was driven to the Old Bailey to state his case before Mr Justice Taylor. There was a moment when he declared his right to have an *amicus curiae* with him in the dock throughout his trial. This was to be a companion, literally a 'friend of the court', who would consult with him in whispers, but not be allowed to speak publicly during the trial. Something less than a lawyer, but more than an acquaintance up in the public gallery. The judge (who would one day be Lord Chief Justice) asked Nilsen whom he had in mind, but told him not to mention the name aloud; he was to write it on a scrap of paper and hand it to the clerk of the court. This he did, and the official ceremoniously carried the scrap of paper from one side of the courtroom to the other, passing it to the judge up on high. He managed to control his barely perceptible surprise as he read it, and announced, 'I am afraid you will have to submit this request to your trial judge; I am unable to deal with it.' The name on the paper was mine, and Peter Taylor was my good friend.

Fortunately, that idea evaporated, but Nilsen persisted in his intention to find a new solicitor, one who would be more energetic in fighting the antique system which obtained in Brixton, and this was to have powerful repercussions at his trial. The name of such a solicitor was suggested to him by another inmate. It was a Mr Ralph Haeems, with a practice in Peckham, south London. I was not professionally qualified to have an opinion on this matter, and to say anything at all would have been gross interference. So I kept mum.

Nilsen had intended up to then to plead guilty. He did not dispute that he had been responsible for the deaths of a number of young men, and saw no reason to drag out the proceedings and cause yet more distress to the families of his victims by having all the circumstances rehearsed in open court and repeated in all the newspapers. A guilty plea would have meant a very short trial, lasting perhaps one day, and would have spared the public the squalid details which they had no need to pore over. Now, however, Nilsen changed his plea to one of Not Guilty, and we all knew that the police evidence would have suddenly to be produced in full, and justified, that young men who had been nearly killed by Nilsen, or had escaped, or whom he had 'spared', would have to relate their terrible experiences in the witness box and suffer the fear all over again, and that expert witnesses would need to be called in the hope of establishing whether the defendant's responsibility for his crimes was sufficiently 'diminished' by reason of mental incapacity to render his plea acceptable to a jury. It would take up to two weeks in Court No 1 at the Old Bailey.

There was one serious consequence in all this for myself, if I chose to shoulder it. I had already been to Scotland on several occasions to talk to Nilsen's mother, a sweet white-haired old lady called Mrs Scott, who lived with her husband Adam Scott in a modest terraced house in Strichen, Aberdeenshire. She had always been warm and welcoming, ready with a cup of tea brewing as soon as I arrived, eager to cook a hearty lunch for me, cosy and talkative, and frankly bemused by the events which had enveloped her. The press had behaved wickedly towards her, descending in droves within an hour of her son's arrest and demanding photographs. Betty had gone upstairs to find what snapshots she could in her family album, and these had been snatched out of her hands, simply stolen in fact and sold to the world's newspapers as if by right of ownership. (It would take me some months to retrieve Mrs Scott's property and restore it to her, in the face of unbelievable reluctance from the plunderers.)

Betty's explanation to herself was that London was somehow responsible for setting her son on a wayward path. He would have been all right if he had stayed at home in Scotland. She knew that he had killed people, but wondered what his side of the story might be, what *they* had done. It could not have been all his fault! She knew nothing of the homosexual element in the crimes, nothing of necrophilia, nothing of dismemberment. There was no real need, up till then, why she should know. Her straight little life need not be contaminated by the horrors perpetrated by her son; it was enough that she should know he had sprung from her loins; that alone was painful to bear. Now that he was to plead Not Guilty, all these details would be aired, and she would read of them in the morning newspaper. I felt I could not allow that shock to descend upon her. So I went up to Scotland the day before the trial began to tell her everything – in my words, not the court's or the newspaper's – in order to prepare her for two weeks of turmoil.

It took me a couple of hours to get through it, measuring interruptions from the garrulous old lady, who seemed to rely on chatter and the busy-ness of cups of tea to protect her from too much reflection. But I could see the eyes forming images from time to time, and I myself threw in odd pieces of unrelated information to deflect her. The one immortal remark she made half way through was, 'Och, I hope he did it in a nice way', in response to which I had gently to remind her that there were no nice ways to throttle somebody. By the end she was resolved and strengthened, and much supported by her stolid, silent husband.

Only after the trial did I feel free to ask Nilsen about his choice of a new solicitor. His reply was so succinct as to deflect any further discussion. 'I reckon he's one of those lawyers with a tax-deductible heart', he said.

My own dealings with Mr Haeems were guarded. We both knew that the fifty-odd exercise books which Nilsen had filled would be valuable negotiating fodder for the Sunday newspapers. To prevent them being used in such a way, I informed Nilsen and he alerted the governor to the fact that I was to pay my last visit the following day, Friday, whereupon he would assign the copyright in all his prison notebooks to me. He would further instruct Haeems to hand them over to me at the end of the trial, as my sole property. Special permission was required for me to take the document of assignation into the prison and have Nilsen sign it. I had it drawn up by Michael Rubinstein on Friday morning, and handed it in to the prison for the governor to peruse in advance. Visiting hours were between two and three in the afternoon. There were no visits on Saturday or Sunday, and the trial was due to begin at ten o'clock on Monday.

I duly turned up at two, and could find no warder or official who was aware of our plans. Nobody knew anything about it, there was no document as far as anyone knew, and Nilsen had not sent a V.O. for me to gain entry. By twenty past two I began to realise that the copyright might be doomed. I asked to speak to the governor himself. Nobody knew where he was (they said!), and there was no telephone connection to his office. I flew out of the prison gates and ran down to Brixton Hill, where I knew there was a red telephone kiosk. I had to beg change from a passer-by, and I called the prison from there. I was put through to the governor, who could not understand why his instructions had been mislaid, and assured me that everything was ready. I flew back to the prison and was finally shown in to a room where Nilsen was sitting at a table, with ten minutes to spare. The document was brought in at five minutes to three, Nilsen signed it, and I took it away in my pocket. Juan was the first and the last person to see it apart from solicitors. It now resides in the vault of a lawyer's chambers, and the copyright in Nilsen's writing, up to the last day of his trial, remains with me to this day.

Nilsen's trial was undoubtedly a shuddering experience (I can still see the look of disbelief on a lady juror's face as she peered at the defendant looking for some explanation in his visage), but it was also, for me, an exhilarating one. I had never studied law, and now found myself deep in precedents and definitions, rulings and judgements. I had to learn all about *actus reus* and *mens rea*, to study the various acts of parliament which had struggled to work out what might constitute 'insanity' in the legal sense and what the 1957 definition of 'diminished responsibility' actually entailed. I had to study different psychiatric evaluations of madness, if only to see how their application in a court of law would confuse matters rather than elucidate them. Above all, I was captivated by the precision and clarity of legal language, and found myself enjoying the use of words as a tool for discovering truth. Before the trial I would have been disposed always to regard the psychiatrists as having the deeper, more subtle understanding of human nature, and to consider lawyers as prevaricators. I now came to see that it was the psychiatrists who trod their way stickily through approximations, and that they had to be rescued from their own semantic mess by lawyers with crystal-sharp minds. The finest, most allusive use of language might belong to the poets, but it is at its most proud, most honourable, and ultimately most exciting in a court of law, where the challenge is to present an argument so perfectly as to render dissent impossible.

I found myself regretting my tardy development from the cockney lout I had once been. For in Camberwell it would have been laughable to consider oneself fit to read law. Barristers were like gods, made of different mettle, begotten of different seed. Law was not an option to be dismissed as unsuitable – it was not even on the list.

When I had finished my book on the Nilsen case I decided to show the typescript to him and invite his comments. There might have been errors of fact in childhood or in the military which he could correct. As it happened, his recommendations were stylistic. In order to protect the families of his victims, I had given them numbers rather than names and scrambled the order in which they had died, for I was in possession of greater detail than had been given to the police or revealed in court. Nilsen's reaction was startling.

'I know it is nothing to do with me', he said, 'and I have always maintained that I should not influence the way in which you deal with the case, but I do have one reservation, if you don't mind. It's how you have treated the victims. You have robbed them of their identity, which is in a manner of speaking almost as bad as what I did to them. By restoring their names, you restore their dignity, and I really think you should, but of course it's up to you. It might be thought insulting to reduce them to numbers. When I was a policeman I always made sure that every person I cautioned had a name. They were never only numbers to me. And another thing, if you don't mind again. By mixing them up you make the narrative jumpy and clogging. The reader doesn't know where he is. He needs to be guided by some proper chronology.'

Tom Maschler read the typescript in a day. He was pleased with the way it had turned out, but had specific recommendations for improvement. 'You need to tell us who these people are', he said, 'give them back their names. And you need to put the events in proper order, not mingle them as you have done. The reader will be confused.' I did not dare tell him that his literary instincts were the same as the murderer's.

My connection with the Nilsen case did not terminate with his conviction, nor with the publication of my book. I continued to visit him for as long as he wanted me to, because it would have been unthinkable to stop simply because he could be of no further use to me. About ten years later he suddenly broke all contact, and I was freed from my obligation. And there was another connection, two months after the trial, which was almost haunting in its suggestiveness. Knowing full well that he would spend the rest of his life in prison, and being estranged from his immediate family, Nilsen decided to make me his heir. He accordingly instructed the police to deliver to me all the personal effects they had removed from his flat at the time of his arrest, and a small van duly arrived at Caithness Road bearing my booty. It included posters from the walls, a TV set, some clothing, a passport, a cigarette lighter, kitchen utensils, a radio-cassette player and headphones, and much else besides. The police did say that they would prefer to keep the large cooking-pot for their Black Museum, and I was more than happy that they should. But I felt the presence of these bits and pieces to be slightly threatening, weird, and I wondered whether objects could be infected by evil.

I decided upon an experiment. I began to use his radio-cassette, which resembled in shape and size any other, and was barely distinguishable from two others in the house. I still have it somewhere, but I no longer know which was his, which

I had before, and which I have acquired since. His notorious instrument has become anonymous. The clothing and TV set I gave to Madame Tussaud's in case they wanted to make a *tableau* in their Chamber of Horrors. The passport and personal things I deposited at the bank. One day, I suppose, they will form part of a collection. I can honestly say that I do not regard them as such. They are neither precious, nor an embarrassment; they are simply there until they go somewhere else. They do not matter.

What does matter is the possible insidious influence of Nilsen's personality upon my own. Critics chastised me with being 'sympathetic' towards the monster, but it was not sympathy I felt so much as bewilderment. He had done ghastly things, and his emotional response to them was arid. He did not think they merited such fuss, and I was, in contemplation, devastated by them. I wanted him to know why he had caused such offence to humanity, and, if possible, to watch him mend and repair his soul. I wanted him to renew himself, and firmly believed (erroneously, as it happened) that he could.

This does, of course, involve a subtle kind of identification. I do not mean that one needs to imagine oneself with the hands and mind of a murderer in order to write about such a man in an exploratory and explanatory way; that is the crude understanding of 'identification', which no real writer would recognise, for it would render writing redundant (one would simply have to 'be' the murderer in thought). What I mean is that one must be prepared to imagine what it would feel like to keep some essential aspect of one's character concealed from family, friends, acquaintances, one's entire social world, for a lifetime, and what a sustained effort in duplicity that must require. And if one succeeds in doing this, it follows that one is *able* to do it, and therefore that the habit of duplicity is likely to form at least a part of the writer's personality as it obviously does of the murderer's. So, in order to see Nilsen as he was, I had perforce to tap into that element within me which could cope with constant watchfulness and secrecy, that furtive solitary 'conspiracy of one' to hide from public scrutiny, to deflect curiosity. And it was something of a shock to discover that I had such resources, that by examining them with care I could explain a bit of myself to myself, and thereby help to explain Nilsen.

There are, perhaps, hidden boomerangs in all biographies.

Chapter 2

Tea Packets and Lust

My earliest memory of redemption, at least on a conscious level of understanding its purpose, relates to the age of about six years, in 1945. The war had come to a weary end, and with it my family's perpetual shifting from one bombed-out ruin to another. We were by then four, my father in the Home Guard, my mother bent and frail at home, and my little brother Colin, somehow conceived in the noise, dirt and fear of 1944 and born three months before the German surrender. Inevitably, my parents' love-making must have been in my presence, because we all three occupied one room, for every purpose, but I cannot pretend to have been aware of anything. Affective memories of those first six years are all self-regarding, visual memories are of the sparse decor, of an existence measured out in cups of tea. I can see a sink, a table, my cot, and the neighbour, Granny St John, with a pot of tea brewed especially for us (mugs did not exist in those days), held aloft in her right hand as she poked her bescarfed head around the door. I suppose she represents my first inkling of kindness, for though I had little to say to her, I knew that her attentions were benevolent, that she was a good soul, and that my mother was grateful for the comfort which she offered. So I must also have been aware that my mother needed comfort. Black and white snapshots of her taken at this time with an ancient box camera (which I cherish to this day – objects smell and feel the past more keenly than memories), show her thin like a stick-insect. I later learnt that she had shrunk to six stone after the birth of my brother. There had apparently been fears for her survival. Indeed, I recall all too clearly that I was myself taken to hospital with measles or chicken pox at the same time as she was taken to another place for her confinement, and that there was some kind of feeling, not precisely articulated, that this might be goodbye. I have a certain sense of separation, and of artless aloneness in the hospital bed. Did anybody come to see me? Probably not, if my mother was fighting for her life in childbirth and my father was desperate with worry for her. It was no doubt felt that I was in good hands, in the best possible place, and that, besides, I was dangerously infectious; children with communicable diseases were in those days kept in isolation. Even my collection of cigarette cards, my only real possession, was summarily confiscated, for which I was inconsolable, and which I still resent over half a century later. Obviously, I had done something which required this nasty, sobering punishment.

The room I describe with a table, a cot and a sink was at 1, Milton Road, in Herne Hill, up the stairs, on the first floor. It must be mixed with and glued to a lot of other similar rooms, for we lived at various times between 1939 and 1945 at Penge, Crystal Palace, another address in Herne Hill, Brixton and Camberwell. Some of these homes can surely not have lasted for more than weeks, and with each move no doubt the family's goods were progressively reduced. One of these rooms had the same small wooden kitchen table, but encased all around with metal bars down to the floor. We used to get under the table and close ourselves in when the sound of the bombs drew near. As these indoor shelters were replaced by underground ones in the back yard by the time the doodlebugs arrived in 1944, this memory must ascend to the Blitz, in 1940, when I was not much more than one year old.

I also remember my mother hurtling down the street with me in a dodgy pram, desperate to get under cover before the bombs, which were on their way, fell upon us; that also must be when I was a mere baby. Later memories, of huddling with my parents in a tight-knit ball beneath the frightening drone of the doodlebug, ascend to the age of five. The louder the noise, the closer was the bomb before it cut out; then we knew it was dropping; more than once we thought it was dropping directly above us, and Mum and Dad whispered hurried endearments lest we were about to be obliterated. I felt a diffuse fear on their behalf – submerged and terrible – but nothing for myself.

Still less did one worry, at that age, about the devastated landscape the morning after a night of bombing. My playmate of that year, a sad boy called Georgie, with eyes silted up by some congenital condition (or possibly malnutrition), lived in the house opposite. One day the house had disappeared, to be replaced by rubble, dust, and a smouldering smell. It was explained to me that Georgie was gone. Time to find another playmate.

A huge area between the Old Kent Road and Camberwell Road, lying to the east of Albany Street, had been flattened by bombs, the rubble still lying uncleared and inviting for curious children who had nothing else to do. Scores of prefabs were built on this rubble, and my parents were housed by 1945 in one of them, in Herring Street, opposite a rubber factory and beside a skin factory, each giving out noxious fumes which would now be termed an environmental hazard. But the lovely thing about the prefab, as I see in memory my mother's bubbling excitement (it was certainly the first time I had seen her visibly happy), was the refrigerator. She had never seen one before. Neither, of course, had I, and I found it quite magical. The cupboards, the clean sink, the hot water, the separate bedrooms, the bathtub, all were untold luxuries.

And next door, as luck would have it, between the prefab and the skin factory (one could see the sheep skins hanging inside), was a primary school. It was called St Alban's, because it was attached to and operated by a church, which was Roman Catholic. And that's where redemption first came in.

I was not Roman Catholic, was barely religious at all except in the most flimsy nominal sense, but the proximity of the school made it an obvious choice for my education. Whether I was placed there by local authority, or whether my parents applied, appealed, for me to be admitted, I have no idea, but the decision affected my life in every possible way, to fundamental and enduring effect. Every other child there was a Catholic. I was the odd one, the outsider, the one who did not fit. No child can tolerate this feeling for long. Either he must make himself fit, or he sulks and festers on the periphery for the rest of his life, occasionally shooting the poison of his contempt back into the laughing, confident throng. The Roman Catholic approach was hopeful, but if you rejected that hope, or even explored it, your fate was eternally awful. These were worrying notions to slot into the mind of a timid child. Alas, they took root within me.

The headmistress, Miss Bone, was a kindly, bosomy woman, elderly to me, but probably in her thirties. She was probably more maternal than my mother, whose fragile health always prevented her from bestowing energizing attention. Miss Bone took an interest in me. She spotted that I was clever, and encouraged me to shine, not to be conscious of being different, or ashamed of being a swot (I wasn't really, it just seemed that I understood things as soon as they were demonstrated or explained to me). She showed that I mattered in a rather special way by the simplest device of behaving like a woman instead of a teacher.

My pet dog, a cheeky mongrel called Rex who had been a stray before I begged permission to adopt him, would not let me out of his sight. He followed me to school, although the distance could not have been more than thirty yards, and left me at the gate when I went in to line up in the playground.

Then he would come into the playground and line up with me, not going home until we had entered the building. He would know precisely at what hour I was due to emerge, and was waiting there for me at the end of lessons. Not satisfied with these extraordinary privileges, Rex ventured to come into the classroom with me and sit by my desk. Miss Bone was aware of all this, and, more importantly, was intuitively aware also that had she banished the dog (who, by the way, always behaved with impeccable manners, and asked for the classroom door to be opened when he needed to relieve himself), she would have caused damage. Rex's welcome at the school eventually went so far as to give him entry into the headmistress' room, so that, when the bell rang for the end of the school day, I would emerge from my class while Rex would emerge from under Miss Bone's desk and we would be reunited for the short journey home. Of course, the beneficiary of this unusual treatment was not the scruffy mongrel, but the snotty schoolboy. (At this time I often had a runny nose and, not supplied with handkerchiefs because we had none, and paper tissues not yet existing, I would lick the stuff off my upper lip. Horrid memory, but I still recall the taste, and the reluctance with which I allowed my nose to be wiped, probably by Miss Bone.) She was a very wise woman.

She was also a very devout Catholic. As well as encouraging me to do well in class, and reporting my progress in glowing terms to my astonished parents (I still have a school report, aged eight, on which the word 'excellent' is marked against every subject), she made it her business to care for my soul. Not only was I the only child in school with a live-in dog, but I was the only heathen, the only non-Catholic. This was a worrying state of affairs which called for gradual but certain remedy. I attended prayers in church every day, for not to do so would have been to point to my exclusion, and I soon learnt the catechism as well as anyone else. I knew the rosary, and the number of Hail Marys the beads demanded. The ritual was soothing, providing a kind of togetherness in chant, and the deepest feeling I had ever had, up to then, of belonging to a community. I felt safe in the knowledge that I was loved by God. That must be what the love of God means, I suppose, because it cannot possibly mean what the words literally suggest, as one cannot be loved by an intellectual idea. I certainly felt warmth, even as much as a sensual glow, for being one of the chosen band of faithful; I was destined for Paradise, not for Hell. I became an altar-boy, doing God's work with the gladdest of hearts. To me, it was another subject of study, like arithmetic or grammar, at which I could shine, but with the added *frisson* that the reward for doing well was not praise from Miss Bone alone, but love from the firmament.

But wait a minute! Something was seriously wrong. By the time I was ten or eleven and the other children were preparing for their confirmation, I realized that I was still in essentials an outsider. My parroting the catechism better than anyone else would avail me nothing, for I was preparing for nowhere. I could not be confirmed, I could never be properly accepted. I could not go to Heaven without being confirmed in the faith, and that was an option which I soon learnt was closed to me as long as my parents persisted in remaining heathen. It must surely have been Miss Bone who pointed this out by degrees, unless I have heaped all memories of St Alban's on her overburdened shoulders. There was obviously a priest in attendance, but of him I have not the smallest memory – no face, no voice, no age, no word, nothing. He has been wiped clean, and I resist the silly modern notion that the very fact of his disappearance from memory is a sure indication of how important he was and with what fierce determination I have been able to block him out. No, he simply made no impression.

Unlike Miss Bone. The impression she made, coupled with my devotion and gratitude for her interest in me, was brought to a head one day in the prefab when I berated my parents for being messengers of the Devil and sought to save them from themselves. I cannot pretend to remember the words they used to defend themselves, but there was an atmosphere of quite unnecessary laughter. I was deadly serious. I wanted to convert to Roman Catholicism before it was too late, and for some reason I could not do it without their permission. The first job, then, was to convert them to my way of thinking, so that I could devote the rest of my life to saving all three of us (I did not spare a thought for young Colin, aged four, probably because I thought he could look after himself in time). It was my first attempt at persuasion, the first time (I think) that I had raised my voice, the first time I had had to marshal thoughts and the words that marked them in a desperate attempt to make my case. For I was desperate, I do remember that, mired in the fear of what would happen to me if (or when, for I secretly knew it couldn't work) they refused my pleas. I would be banished to hellfire for evermore, sunk, blown away, cast adrift, all my hopes of belonging smashed once and for all. I would no longer be able to join in. The love of God would be denied me.

They said something like, 'Don't be such a bloody fool.'

I fled to the local play area and sobbed my heart out for an hour or so, Rex by my side, peering up in concern and bewilderment. It was the first crisis, my first encounter with fear, and the fear was tied up with the removal of redemption, the impossibility of forgiveness, the certain promise of hatred from the angels and the church which was their home. I felt abject, absolutely cast out.

What is interesting is not so much that the Catholics were able to capture and poison a young heart so totally (nearly all religions make this their most divine purpose), but why I should so readily have succumbed. Whence this deep need for forgiveness? Why did the Roman Church offer such solace? What had I done? I think this is what Anthony Clare was driving towards when he suggested that the understanding I appeared to be seeking for the people I had written about was in fact an oblique appeal for my own redemption, still alive after all these years, unassuaged, and just as keen. There must have been something for which I felt a profound guilt which God alone could dispel.

My parents were good folk, not cruel, vindictive, negligent; not drunk, vicious, aggressive. They had drawn little from life, and were very supportive in pressing me to take advantage of the education which had been denied them (and which, by fortuitous timing, had just become available to children like myself by the Beveridge Report and the launch of the Welfare State, to which I owe everything). My father had left school at twelve to work as a kind of servant for his hopeless mother; he had never known his father. My mother had spent most of her school years in hospital, and had grown up with people whom she thought were her parents but who were not. Her mother and father had both died of consumption in their twenties. So I did not know any of my grandparents, and my traceable history goes back only one generation. More of this later. For the moment, I have good recollection of being sent to school, not dragged from it, like some others. School consisted of a room on a corner in Herne Hill with one teacher and about six children working with black slate and pieces of white chalk, pens and paper being so incredibly scarce. This must have been a charitable school of some kind. All I recall is the dustiness of the chalk and the hunger for learning. My parents saw that hunger and, unable to satisfy it themselves, made sure means were found for others to satisfy it. I could not be anything but grateful, yet there was something affective, unspoken and undemonstrable, which made me feel apart from them, and altogether guilty for so being. I was *wanting* in some regard.

I did not know why or in what regard, still less how to remake myself in order to deserve cherishing rather than merely tolerating. I existed, but I was not alive, and that I am quite sure is an accurate memory of an inchoate feeling, not a memory which in maturity I have invented to explain myself. I see myself as I was then, and feel again the emptiness of being stuck with no character which was valuable, or with the wrong character, which needed at all costs to be hidden in order to escape scorn. I shifted listlessly through the hours of the day, fearing ridicule more than anything else, knowing that I should be unable to deflect it, being too weak, and even more that it was correct and proper in the circumstances. I was indeed a ridiculous child, flabby and boring, with no immediately harnessable capacity for friendship. I must have spent many an hour thinking without end, but it would be wrong to pretend now that I can recall any of those purposeless thoughts.

But certain actions, silently pursued, were accompanied by feelings which I do remember. Two in particular. As I lay in bed waiting for sleep to protect me, I habitually took the corner of the pillow-case and stuffed it in my mouth, sucking for all I was worth, drawing on the material with hollow cheeks, until the corner, isolated from the rest of the pillow-case by my thumb and forefinger tightly clenched, was sopping wet. Now, it requires no great imagination to see that the triangle of wet cotton was a nipple-substitute, and that therefore I must have been deprived of my mother's breast very early on. It would not surprise me if I were, for she had not the strength. But what was odd was that I would then dab my nose with the wet material, almost punching myself with it, for countless minutes, perhaps even half an hour, before going to sleep. All the while, my other thumb was in my mouth, so that both hands were occupied. Very clearly, as if it had happened this morning, do I recall the wonderful sense of comfort, tinged with a slightly sexual pleasure, this strange ritual afforded me. I would often wake up the next day still clutching the pillowcase and would start thumping my nose with it all over again.

Unfortunately, at the same time I would wet the bed. This went on relentlessly until I was about thirteen, and must have driven my mother to despair. Another reason for guilt. A rubber sheet had to be placed under me every night, and after a while that was all that I had. There was no point in placing the rubber sheet under a real one, as the bed linen would have to be changed every day, so I slept directly on the rubber. Most of the time I did not notice when I urinated in my sleep, but occasionally I would become aware of it half way through, and could not stop it. The stickiness and the smell afforded me no pleasure whatever, merely unmitigated shame. It was a ghastly secret which I had to carry with me to school, hoping nobody would guess, or would see signs of the sin written on my face. *Mene, mene, tekel upharsin.* It is therefore no surprise whatever that, in adulthood, I have never been tempted by rubber fetish games or any sexual activity which involves sliding and slithering.

Which leads me straight to the other weird activity dating from those days. The bus terminal at Crystal Palace was in the open, not in a covered garage, and all the buses lined up one behind the other the whole length of the road. If I was lucky enough to take a journey which terminated at Crystal Palace, I had the ineffable joy of being at the front of a bus as it drew up deliciously close to the back of another. There was sometimes the barest number of inches separating us. It was for this reason that I always pestered Mum or Dad to let me sit at the front, and eventually gained permission from them to take bus journeys on my own. I was not interested in going anywhere, only in sitting at the front of a bus as it carefully drew intimate with the bus before it, as if in congress. Then I did have an erection (this solitary hobby began when I was about eight), and did not feel guilty about it. I did, however, feel apart and mysterious. Other people appeared to be indifferent to the secret sensual delight inherent in a double-decker bus, so perhaps I was the only person in the world to discover this pleasure. It was as private as masturbation, yet conducted in the midst of an unsuspecting public. That was thrill enough in itself.

Further, I took this private indulgence (which could not be called self-abuse, it was abuse of vehicles) even into the prefab, without my mother having any idea what I was up to. Tea-packets were oblong in shape then, as now, and roughly approximated to miniature versions of the Crystal

Palace buses. I think they were Brook Bond, and I somehow persuaded my mother to save packets as long as she could before opening them, so that I could play with them on the kitchen table. Round and round the table I would push them, bringing them ever closer together, and very slowly drawing the packet up close to the packet which preceded it. Of course, I had no idea at that age that sodomy was possible, and might not have believed it had it been explained to me. But there is no doubt that this game, apparently so innocent, so efficient at keeping me out of trouble, so helpful in keeping me quiet, contained a powerful sexual element. My attention was intense, I said not a word and must have seemed a curiously self-contained child. Closeness, intimacy, *quasi*-tactile contact, the union of two into one, the secrecy of an unsuspected *frisson*, these are feelings which predate sexual knowledge, yet are sexual in their nature. To this day, I long to engage the attentions of a *frotteur* in an Underground train, but in a long life it has happened only once, amusingly enough on the Central Line on the way to attend Nilsen's trial at the Old Bailey.

When, one day, my mother shouted at me to stop that silly game, I blushed in fear. She was no doubt rightly irritated that I should seize the packets when she would rather empty them into the teapot, but I wondered whether my secret had been snuffed out, and that was when a previously guilt-free exercise became a dangerous venture.

The seduction of the Catholic school was that, in church, all was forgiven, all these nasty, pasty, horrid little imaginings were comprehended by the One Who Knew and Understood Everything, so that one felt less alone, less peculiar, less excluded. For a time, I preferred the Church to my own parents. That is now an adult source of guilt, but at the time it was a resource of solace.

In *The Power and the Glory* Graham Greene writes that 'there is always one moment in childhood when the door opens and lets the future in.' In my attempts at biography, I have been been alert to that moment, on the *qui vive* hoping to be awake when it jumped out at me, and whenever it has worked, the life that I have been trying to reconstruct has suddenly sprouted a buttress which keeps all the subsequent messy meanderings in some kind of shape. With E. F. Benson it was the day that his father was appointed Bishop of Truro, or more particularly the moment a few days later when the family carriage had emblazoned on its door the new bishop's crest; young Fred was infected with an hierarchical pride which never deserted him and coloured his life and work thereafter. With John Aspinall it was the day he saw Guy the Gorilla at London Zoo, and felt the animal's communication of boredom, resentment, injustice, hit him squarely in the chest; thereafter the seed which would grow into Aspinall the animal protector overcame the seed which would make him a gambler. For Jeffrey Dahmer (subject of a later study), who as an adult killed seventeen young men, dismembered them, bleached their bones, and put them together again, that moment was the day when he brought home the body of a dog which had been run over on the wide Ohio road and asked his father how to dissect it. Lionel Dahmer, himself a scientist, was delighted that his son had found a worthy interest at last.

I well recognized the tense and tentative relationship between Dahmer *père* and *fils*, the boy's isolation and apartness, his solitary pleasures, his lack of overt speech, and his inability to please his father, who was always preoccupied with something else. Such feelings were in me, too. Fortunately, I was not keen on building skeletons; encouraging furtive friendships between tea-packets was sufficient for me. But it is interesting that one is able, as a biographer, to spot these moments in the lives of other people, yet ignore their significance in one's own. Until now.

Jeffrey Dahmer's life yielded another, even more crucial example. At the age of four he had been subjected to a double hernia operation, which involved the invasion of his most private self by foreign hands. Until that moment, he had not been touched. His father had been too shy to be tactile, his mother too self-absorbed with her pills and her pettinesses. He had not been a cuddly child, one to smile and bubble and invite caress. Now, suddenly, his innards were being caressed by human touch, and the unconscious memory of that intimate moment was never to leave him. Nobody at his trial in Milwaukee twenty-eight years later, not any of the lawyers, not the judge, nor even the psychiatrists and the doctors, thought that this matter of the hernia operation was worth enquiry. It was once mentioned and passed over in a single sentence, once in a trial of five weeks. Yet they all had the evidence that Dahmer's first act after killing was to open up the stomach of the corpse and plunge both his hands into the shining intestines and masturbate himself with them, and further, that the black table which he acquired specifically for the purpose of photographing and dismembering corpses was very much like the operating table in a hospital.

The defining moment for Dennis Nilsen took place at his grandmother's house in Fraserburgh, Scotland, when he was six years old. He, too, was a lonely boy. His one friend was his grandfather, a fisherman like most folk on the northern Aberdeenshire coast, at sea for weeks on end. Young Dennis looked forward more than anything in the world to his grandfather's return, which was always unannounced and therefore doubly exciting, and the grizzled old man would hoist him onto his shoulders, take him for long walks along the beach and tell him thrilling stories. That was love to him (his father had left soon after his birth, his mother was forever out dancing). One day he was asked if he wanted to see his grandad, which of course cheered him considerably. The man was in a box on the kitchen table, still and for the first time quite quiet. Nobody thought to tell the boy that this was death. From that moment the notions of love and death became inextricably entwined in his infantile mind, and he was nevermore able to disentangle them.

I am sure this is why Dr Clare asked me whether I was inclined to question my own motives and investigate my own history. Though I have always been as soft as marshmallow and quite incapable of ever hurting somebody, though I will spend an hour trying to rescue a spider from its frustration and set it free in nature, where it will probably be eaten within minutes, rather than squash it myself, despite my paralysing fear of all things which crawl fast, I seem to have been able to understand the minds and hearts of these cruel, merciless people. Why? Where is the echo? Try as I might, all I can find is the mute, dim suspicion that I *ought* to have been more assertive, both as a child and as an adult, that I have never had power, that I was always wimpish, grizzly, tearful, bludgeoned by others' indifference into an apologetic shuffle through life, not wishing to offend, not daring to draw attention. In a sense, I almost *envied* Nilsen and Dahmer for having got their own back. Readers probably sense this, and are understandably repelled by the implications.

My own volcano is still dormant, after all this time. It has never erupted. I hope it never will.

So, it would be superficial to say that the moment which let the future in was my admission to St Alban's Church School and to the benevolent interest of Miss Bone. True, but not enough. It is only slightly more probing to say the moment was my kidnapping by the Catholics with their certainties, their huge invitation to belong, and their wide, forgiving embrace. I should not have succumbed had there not been a yearning need to do so. It goes beyond, and before, either of these moments.

I have always found it virtually impossible to define my relationship with my father, whether at the time with a child's feeling for these things, or now with the adult's analysis of them. Perhaps there was no relationship at all, just a void where something should have existed and flourished but fell fluttering at first flight. I cannot tell. I have got to find out.

I remember him most as a stutterer. With simple round National Health spectacles strong enough to make his eyes owlish, a thick but well-trimmed moustache, three bumps on his head which poked through his lank, brown hair (cysts, I believe, and probably hereditary – I developed two like them in early manhood), the dominating impression was of a man struggling to make himself noticed. The stutter was but the manifest expression of this herculean effort to rescue from a timid outward form the would-be assertive personality that was cringing inside. He literally fought with words, several of them in each sentence, and one could see his muscles and mind concentrating on the effort to get them out, his eyes screwed up, his teeth clapping, always on certain initial consonants, usually the plosives. I even remember his giving up the ghost on occasion, exhausted, with a feeble 'T-t-t-tell him, Mabel' to his wife as he withdrew to a corner to light another cigarette. Obviously, the t was not so difficult to force out as some of the other doors into language which eluded him. The frustration was clearly intense, and the ceaseless cigarettes were not so much a prop, a comfort, or an aid, as a consolation prize for failure, which to him was commonplace and repetitive. He smoked immediately upon waking up, before his first cup of tea, and proceeded to continue for the rest of the day, getting through perhaps three packets. Of course, cigarettes were cheap after the war; I seem to remember about fivepence for a packet of Woodbines. Against which one has to remember that my father was earning about £5 a week.

Anyway, the cigarettes were as much a part of his character as was his stutter. Indeed, they were ultimately the same thing, a wretched protest at the fate which had stolen from him whatever self-confidence could have been his share. He spoke little about his own childhood, except, if I asked much later, to shake his head and mutter something about it being better I should not know. What he meant was that it was better he should not tell, because the scars were still too painful. I think that, had he obliged himself to talk, he might have disintegrated, and tears were what he feared above all else. The stutter served therefore yet another purpose – it drew a curtain over what should not be expressed by making it literally inexpressible, it was his protection.

Geoffrey Howard Masters was the third child of a woman

called Miriam Pink. His siblings were Cecil and Ruth, both fathered by a man called William Biggar, we believe. Albert Masters, my grandfather, seems to have married Miriam at some stage, because Cecil in adulthood took on the surname Masters in order to conceal his illegitimacy and became slightly respectable in Thornton Heath (that is, he wore suits and lived in a house with a garden). Cecil sought to rinse himself of the taint of Pink and Biggar, and looked upon my father Geoffrey with palpable contempt. I met him only twice in infancy, and my father would never have thought of inviting himself over to Thornton Heath for fear of rebuttal; he waited to be summoned. The most important circumstance of my father's childhood seems to be that he lived alone with his mother Miriam. There was never a family home, with three children living together. Cecil and Ruth were both sent to orphanages before my father was born, and Ruth eventually found herself shipped off to Canada at the age of nine, not to see her half-brother until more than thirty years later.

Geoffrey had limited schooling, and was made to work from the age of twelve. I could never entice from him what work he did, but I suspect it was looking after the house, cleaning, fetching and carrying, and covering up, for his mother Miriam, who was what was quaintly called a woman of loose morals. She may have been little more than a prostitute, and with no money, no prospects, and only disparagement to greet her as a single mother in Edwardian London, who can blame her? She can scarcely have had much choice. Of the man she married, Albert Masters, virtually nothing is known. The marriage may well have been undertaken as a favour, to rescue her from total disgrace, and may have lasted a matter of weeks. My father certainly never clapped eyes on him. The first and only time I ever heard his name mentioned was when, in 1949, a funeral bill turned up at our prefab. Albert, who had been a bus conductor in Leeds, had committed suicide with his head in the gas oven, and my father, as next of kin, was invited to settle the account. He returned the bill with fierce scorn. It was the only time

I had seen him proud enough to show his anger; it was as if that man's death had, to some extent, released him from the ordeal of a past he wanted to banish.

Thus I did not meet either of my paternal grandparents. Nor, as it would transpire, did I really know either of my mother's parents. I had no history, no template, no observable or ascertainable genetic inheritance which could predict the sort of person I was likely to become. I arrived without baggage from a distant port. My father, who joined the Home Guard (his eyesight and stutter prevented his going to the front), who worked in an aircraft factory and was subsequently unemployed after the war, who not only had achieved nothing but felt that nothing was achievable, whose self-esteem was fragile, was determined to be proud of me. The burden of that expectation was something I felt almost with my first breath, and because he could not articulate what he wanted, I could have no idea how to provide it. I recall an abiding sense of anxiety, an unvoiced hope that he would not ask anything of me, that he would simply leave me alone. I was not afraid of him; I felt useless to deal with *his* fears and ambitions.

It is only in infancy that depression grips. I was to suffer the usual adolescent silences and grapplings, and in adulthood have experienced unhappiness and misery in modest proportions, but as a little boy I knew what it was to be depressed, powerless to understand, isolated in an impenetrable personal space. Dahmer's fog of loneliness in childhood would certainly, nearly fifty years later, be no mystery to me.

Dr Lionel Dahmer was not without emotional responses; but his firm self-discipline prevented his ever allowing them to be seen. Not seeing them, the infant Jeffrey Dahmer could not know that they existed, and their lack of acknowledgement on one side, and lack of evidence on the other, created a mutual distance between father and son which the future could not remedy. In Jeffrey's case, the denial of emotion was so total that he formed a view of the world in which the emotional impact of words and deeds played no part whatsoever, and he was able to kill people with the curiosity and detachment with which one dismantles and reassembles a Meccano set.

My father's emotions simmered, invisibly but not insensibly. I was somehow aware that his immensely debilitating stutter was the cap on a volcano. The mystery to me, and the cause of my astonishing quietness, was that I did not know how to please him. No clues were offered, no guidance given, no hints dropped, or so I thought (perhaps I was blind to them). I have said that he avoided tears at all costs. His finest gift to me, and one that would have amazed him if he had known, was the one day in his life when I did see him surrender to desolate sobs. My brother Colin contracted a virus or a disease of some kind which none of the local doctors could understand. (This was hardly surprising, as not only was medical knowledge slim, but common sense was at a premium. For years my legs were covered in red spots which itched like mad and which I scratched to make hideous scars. I was variously diagnosed to have an excess of sugar in the blood or a rare eczema. Nobody noticed that they were flea-bites consequent upon my always sleeping with the cat, Tuppy, curled up under the sheet beside my leg, and that cat fleas found my flesh delightful.) Colin was about five years old, and I was therefore eleven. His condition deteriorated without reason or explanation, and both my parents were beside themselves with worry. This in itself was good for me to see, a revelation that they were not invincible and not cold, that they could experience moments of helplessness. My brother was taken to hospital. Doctors despaired. It seemed there was something attacking his brain. It was at that point, when his younger son was removed from his care and the future seemed bleak, that my father's humanity was made shatteringly clear. In the little sitting-room of our prefab his normally stern, unblinking, sterile face melted. He put his arms around me (that was shocking in itself, an unprecedented event) and wept loudly. He begged me to pray for my brother, to help him get better. Tears coursed down his cheeks, he had to take off his glasses to wipe them away (again, I had never seen him without his glasses; it was as if there were suddenly revealed a man behind them), he placed his hands on my shoulders, then he faced the wall and implored it, too.

My father's misery dismayed and disoriented me. Nothing had prepared me for such a display, and I was not mature enough to know how to cope with it. Here, at last, he was telling me that there was something I could do for him, that there was a connection between us, through my brother's plight, which we could tie and seal forever. It is commonplace to blame one's parents for each and every misunderstanding, because they are, or should be, better placed to resolve them. But for this lack of compassion on my part, I blame myself entirely. Geoffrey Masters was exposed for the first time, vulnerable and abject. He sought solace from the person whom he was meant to protect from harm. Thus he reversed the roles, and I was not up to accepting the challenge. I did feel that the man was in need, but I did not respond to that need demonstratively. I did it quietly, as I had always done everything. I went to the church next door and I did pray for my brother. I also wept by myself in bed that night, under the sheets. For once I did not feel sorry for myself. I felt sorry for my father.

Thereafter I was more at ease with him. I was still unable to be the son that he wanted, playing cricket against chalked stumps on the church wall, when I could never hit the ball and longed for the ordeal to end, but I was able to understand that it mattered less that I was not. The jealousy I had felt because Colin appeared to satisfy my father's wishes where I could not, shifted to a freedom from comparison and a delight in difference. The emotional release which I witnessed came just in time, before puberty's sinking into selfishness, while I was still capable of pondering its implications. My father was born for me that day.

One of the reasons that I was so susceptible to Catholic forgiveness, my being a disappointment to my father, was thereby gradually dispelled. Yet I was still damned for other sins, much more obdurate and tenacious. One was a cruel lack of sympathy for my mother, the other an indefinable but pervasive knowledge that I did not fit in with the rest of the world, and that this idiosyncrasy must be my own fault.

It surprises me now that I should use the word 'cruel' in relation to my love for my mother. I have consistently regarded her as a saint, a woman with crucifying disabilities and of heroic endurance, of whom I have already written in the final pages of my *The Evil That Men Do* as a glorious example of the good and the selfless. But to her I must have seemed the most bitter, demanding, unforgiving child.

The abiding image of her is a cough and a hunchback. The latter I hardly noticed in my infancy, but the cough was inevitably the first sound I heard, and the most repetitive. Mabel Sophia Charlotte Ingledew (I always delighted in the music of those ten syllables) inherited viciously damaged lungs which forced her to cough painfully for two hours every morning before she could utter a word. She coughed into my cot, she coughed as she summoned the strength to wash me, she coughed as she made a pot of tea and again as she drank it. I recall her gasping for breath in between spasms which shook her whole body, as if nothing but the expulsion of her lungs through her mouth would suffice to put an end to the suffering. Except that I could not have interpreted it as suffering at the time, and, as part of my own learning process, the first thing I learnt to do well was to cough. I even remember the sound I made, although it had no physical cause. It was simple emulation, but to her it might well have sounded like pitiless mimicry. What desolation she would feel in the recognition that while other mothers bestowed upon their first-born the precious gift of language, she was doomed to teach me only how to cough.

I have never forgiven myself for adding to her burden in this way. On the other hand, the memory has taught me how necessary it is always to be ready to forgive, since actions do not carry with them a label advertising intent, and motive can all too often be misconstrued. Obviously I, at three years of age and without judgement, could not be blamed for copying the most potent sound I heard every day, and the infant that I was should not need forgiveness. But the pain that I caused was acute, and the resigned sadness which I occasioned by my behaviour *looked like* the pale shadow of wickedness. To this day, I am only truly made angry by the bovine certainty of people who know what they think about others and brook no compromise in their opinion. I was once taken to task quite severely for writing that people who are sure how to interpret human behaviour with regard to others make me want to vomit. The expression was perhaps too vivid and physical, but the anger was real. I do not denigrate people who lack initiative, people who make mistakes, people with slack character or even people driven by circumstance and personality into crime. I do, however, detest the crass pomposity of thoughtless folk, who sweep aside subtlety, who will not see the terrible harm wrought by their certainties and will not dilute the absolute vengeance which those certainties demand. All of this derives, I think, from the mistake I imagine my mother made in thinking herself mocked by her child.

Again the church was able to intervene. The child was forgiven his faults because humans were mortal and fallible, and their certainties were dangerous errors of pride. Only God could be certain, because He knew everything. So that was all right!

The hunchback was more difficult to fathom. It did not seem odd that my mother should have a backbone shaped like a question-mark, until much later I pondered the real oddity – that other women did not. I then deduced that it must have been caused by the two-hour bout of coughing which launched every day, but it was not quite so simple as that. I was adolescent when I finally asked her to explain, and what she told me irrevocably shifted my impression of her and has never ceased to haunt my imagination.

Mabel had been brought up by Nobby and Lottie Clark, whom she took me to see for Sunday lunch once a month in a council flat in Brixton. I called them Grandma and Grandad, and even as a child was amused by the sly swopping of roles which their marriage demonstrated. Lottie was a robust nagger, treating her husband like a useless, errant brat ('Silly old bugger!' 'Bloody nuisance!' 'Silly sod!'), while Nobby sat there and laughed quietly, tolerant and unwounded; he had been a handsome sailor in his youth, and presumably their marriage had initially rested on his masculine conquest and her delighted acquiescence. What a difference the years made, I thought. We played a card game called 'Sevens' after lunch (which we called 'dinner' of course, there being no evening meal in working-class homes), and when Mum, Dad, Colin and I walked to Brixton Hill to catch the bus back to Camberwell Green, then the 42 down Albany Road, finally to walk through the bombed site to Herring Street, Lottie and Nobby went down to the pub for their daily Stout, which Lottie occasionally followed with a Port and Lemon. (The first taxi-cab I ever took, aged about twenty-four, was from the West End to the pub in Brixton, and I was so horrified by the cost, in excess of half-a-crown, equivalent to twelve pence today, that I almost cried with embarrassment and could not leave a tip. The driver was visibly miffed.)

Lottie and Nobby were not Mabel's parents. She bore the name Mabel Clark throughout her childhood, but her real parents had been Lottie's sister May and her husband Alfred Ingledew. May and Alfred had both died of consumption in their early twenties, shortly after Mabel was born, and the child had been shunted sideways to Aunt Lottie, which Nobby accepted on condition that Lottie's natural daughter by another brother-in-law should be kicked out to make way for her. Thus did Victorian families cheat the census returns, for none of this was ever recorded. The salient point was that Mabel's hacking cough became a great nuisance to Lottie, who resented her usurping her own daughter's place, and she would excoriate the little girl monstrously ('Shut up that damn noise, Mabel!'). As a consequence, in order not to upset her 'parents', my mother would stay in her room and press her head between her knees to stifle the sound of her coughing. Hence the hunch-back.

So seriously ill was she throughout her infancy and adolescence that she appears to have spent virtually half her time in hospital. She was constantly being admitted for observation and diagnosis (probably because Lottie wanted to be rid of her for a respite), only to be released after some weeks with glum looks from the medical men who could see little prospect of her ever being healthy enough to lead a normal life, nor to gain the strength to drag herself through even an abnormal one. She was weak and sickly, was made to know it, and as a result became uncannily quiet. She learnt never to complain, never to assert herself, never, as far as possible, to be noticed. That terrible cough grew into an embarrassment as well as a pain, for it drew attention to herself when she would rather be quietly ignored. Prolonged residence in hospital meant that she was not able to keep up with ordinary schooling. Whenever she resumed classes, she found that she was several months behind the other girls and could not catch up. Nobody took any special care to see that she should, and so she was routinely mocked. She used to boast that she would get her big brother to defend her, an idle fantasy which afforded some solace.

I have often wondered where, in the genetic soup, came those bits and pieces which have made me what I am – slightly creative, slightly intellectual, bookish, fond of music, fascinated by the history and structure of language, keen on clarity of thought and expression. There was nothing in the prefab to encourage any of this, the only reading matter being the *Daily Mirror* and the *News of the World* – not a single book – and the only conversation a bigoted, uninformed diatribe from my father. My mother would say nothing. She had no opinion about anything. Her function was to make do and get on with the tea. Yet the enquiring mind must have come from somewhere, and I like to think, without any proof, that had my mother benefited from proper education, with good teachers dedicated to releasing her potential, and had she not been confined so much to hospital beds when she ought to have been behind a school-desk, a quite different woman might have emerged. Both she and my father insisted that I should have the opportunities in education which had been denied them, which was the kind of banal benevolent attitude taken by most parents after the war. It was not until much later that I realized how profound, in their case, was this commitment to a future which they each knew, in different ways, could never have been theirs.

To return to Mabel's adolescence. On one momentous day when she was seventeen she was summoned by Lottie, with an acquiescent Nobby sitting in his armchair and darting the occasional smile of comfort, to the sitting-room in Brixton for a serious talk. The doctors had just offered their latest pessimistic prognosis, and Lottie thought it was the moment to tell Mabel the truth about herself. The announcement went something like this. 'Well, girl, it looks as if you're not going to live much longer, so you might as well know something. Dad and me, we're not really your parents at all. You're adopted, and your name isn't Clark. It's Ingledew. We took you in when you were less than two years old, because your Mum and Dad suddenly died, one after the other, with tuberculosis. That's probably why you're such a weakling. It's not been easy, I can tell you, you've been a handful one way or another, but we've done our best. Much good it did us, if the doctors are right, and I suppose they are. So now you know.'

Lottie was not subtle in thought or expression. Characteristically, my mother never told me how she responded to this astonishing news, whether she wept, or laughed, or said thank you, or gawped in disbelief. I think, secretly, it gave her the spirit to go on despite them all, and find her own route through life. For this was not the first, nor would it be the last, of her medical discouragements. The doctors informed Lottie, who told Mabel, that she would not live beyond the age of twenty. She did. They then said she should not stretch her luck, and would never be strong enough to marry (they meant that sexual demands would exhaust her). She married Geoffrey Masters when she was twenty-two. Finally the doctors said, with good reason this time, that she should never bear children, as the strain would undoubtedly kill her. She had two sons, and indeed, with the birth of the second, she very nearly slipped away. But in the end she outlived my father.

One more surprise greeted her on that day when she learnt of her mortality and her adoption. 'By the way', said Lottie, 'you've got a brother.' The kitchen door opened and there he was, a handsome, tall, fair young man of twenty, with a cheeky, friendly, mischievous smile, Joe Ingledew, the older brother of whom Mabel had foolishly boasted, as big as life itself. The children had been separated on their parents' premature death, and although Joe had always known of Mabel's existence, he had never been allowed to visit her, on Lottie's orders. He had been brought up by his grandparents on the Ingledew side of the family. The whole story sounds so fanciful, but I cannot see the point of making it up, and besides, it was eventually corroborated by Uncle Joe.

Mabel would never be told the other secret, that Lottie had her own daughter. This was Bertha, whom my mother had always to pretend, even in adulthood, was her aunt, despite having by then worked out her true identity.

Thus it happens that I knew none of my four grand-parents. One a mysterious figure who turns up only to impregnate, then to disappear and become a distant bus-conductor; another an immoral woman with a beguiling name; a third the soldier who contracted a deadly disease; the fourth his wife, who probably caught it from him and succumbed. When I say I have no history I mean that the roots of it are not detectable. In the same sense, I have no future because I have no progeny. I am in the present tense only.

The biographer is an architect. He must build a structure based upon the foundations of a past and shaped by discernible connections – the interpretations which are the biographical equivalent of lines, angles and harmonies –

which point convincingly towards a future which could hardly be otherwise. To write a biography without those connections to an ancestry, with explanations flapping only in the present, would be to miss the building blocks and see only the plaster caked to the surface. That is one of the reasons why, to me, biography has always been more of a pleasure than a chore, for I have delighted in tracing those connections and charting where they lead. In the most absolute sense, I am denied that possibility in charting my own selfhood. I am reduced to fumbling with feelings. Myself as biographer is faced with an historical blank in myself as subject. No wonder I find ancestry in others so beguiling.

There is some tiny shred of a link with the fourth of these shadowy figures. Mrs Ingledew had been born in a family called Court, on the outskirts of Chichester. She was one of five sisters and four brothers. The whole family assembled outside a small two-storeyed brick house with a central door, for a photograph on the occasion of the marriage of one of their number. At one end is Lottie, at the other is May, both very beautiful, slim-waisted, demure, utterly at variance with the coarse stout irritable woman Lottie became. They are all well dressed, either because they hired special clothes for a special occasion, or because they were socially a step or two up from the lowly servant-girls they would later be (Lottie and Nobby worked for a while as a live-in couple on a small estate at Coleman's Hatch in Kent, until they were dismissed when Lottie pinched a pair of Italian candlesticks. These are now my only heirlooms). I took my mother down to Chichester when she was about sixty, and found the house. We stared at it for half an hour, squeezing some essence of the past out of it, while the alarmed inhabitants watched us from behind twitching curtains.

Juan, the companion of much of my life, knew exactly who he was and where he had come from. The genes splashed around every word he uttered and burnt in his fierce eyes. Although his mother had frequently shouted at him, he never doubted that she loved him. There was, he said, *connection* in his family; they knew they were a unit, that they belonged to one another by blood and in fury. When he used that word I thought of E.M. Forster's ambiguous counsel, 'Only connect . . .' and suddenly understood, not with the head but with the emotion. For Juan intended that the word should be packed with personal reproof. 'I have never seen any love between you and your mother', he said. 'You say it's there, but it's not visible. You don't touch each other. You behave like casual acquaintances. You're not *alive*.'

Partly, habitual English reticence is to blame for this impression, the notion that it is vulgar to show emotion and brave to conquer it, a habit perfectly condensed amongst the nobility to such an extent that some of them cannot weep even if they want to, and either filtered down to the working class by example, or absorbed by them in emulation. But if Juan was right, there was something additionally frigid about our family, which is perhaps why my brother Colin and I always embrace, even though we are old men; we never did so as children, and we must make amends. We do not say it, but we demonstrate that we both recognize it. We held hands walking down the aisle after our mother's funeral.

Is it true? Were we frigid? I always supposed my mother did not cuddle much because she was weak, or because she was afraid of the coughing and the germs she was spreading. But perhaps she *couldn't*. Perhaps nature had been squeezed out of her, and left her coping as best she could in a world of pulsing, throbbing people she could not understand. She did once tell me (and only because I asked) that my father could not be affectionate, sitting on a sofa with his arm around her shoulder, without getting aroused. From his point of view, I suspect she might have seemed a cold fish, a source of frustration and rebuke. When Dennis Nilsen told me that he could not recall ever having been touched by his mother, he resurrected involuntary memory in me. I bearded his mother, Mrs Scott, with the remark. 'Och', she said, 'he was a strange wee child. I couldna pick him up.' I thought then, and sometimes wonder still, whose fault it was that they were estranged, his or hers? Standard wisdom holds that it must fall to the mother, with her experience and her duty to instruct, to offer tactile support. But perhaps I rejected any touch. I shall never know.

Jeffrey Dahmer did know. He recalled that throughout his infancy his mother had been so self-absorbed with her health and her pills and her diet and her sleeping habits, that she did not notice him, and he drifted further and further away into a solitary world ultimately fraught with danger. And yet her scrapbook yields conflicting evidence. She wrote of his progress with palpable joy, recording his first words, his first steps, his first toy. That she did not write what he felt like to hold in her arms was only to be expected; that sort of twaddle does not get recorded in scrapbooks, except by the self-consciously literate. She did not have to be explicit; the scrapbook itself is evidence of feeling.

Mabel was not explicit, either. Our trip to Chichester to look at the house outside which both her mother and her adoptive mother (her aunt) had been photographed, was my clumsy attempt, rather late in life, to demonstrate warmth towards her. I wanted her to know that her past was worth exploring, that she mattered, at least to me. But I did it in a literary way, as if I were researching for a book, as if we were feeding our minds with useful information. That was not the way. She had never shown me the way. I did not know quite how to cherish her.

Only once in my entire life did I do it properly. She was in her last illness, wherein I think she suffered far more than she let on because, as usual, she did not want to be a nuisance. Since she could not have withstood an operation, her breast cancer had been but superficially treated, and had spread. Her bottom lip was raw with biting, I suppose to negate the pain, and I, again as usual, seemed not to notice. She was blessed with one advantage, however. She always slept soundly and peacefully, waking to find herself in the same position as she had been when she had fallen asleep, and occasionally she dozed on the bed in the afternoon. I went to visit at her terraced council house in Cadoxton, Barry, and found her still asleep. It felt like curiosity on my part, as if I wanted to experience something other people took for granted, but there must surely have been something deeper behind the ordinary gesture which ensued. I sat on the edge of the bed and held my mother's hand until she woke up. I had never done that before. She smiled. I am very grateful that at least once she found me touching her, just being her son.

At the age of eleven I witnessed tragedy and did not recognize it. My mother's best friend, whom she had met very young when they were both in service as maids, and alongside whom she subsequently worked behind the counter at Parnell's in Victoria (I had been there once and had been thrilled by the system of paying bills by wrapping the money into a ball, and sending it inside a submarine-like object whizzing across the ceiling on suspended tram-lines with other submarines darting about in different directions, like bees criss-crossing), was called Ethel, and by me Auntie Ethel. I gathered she had been let down by men rather badly and very frequently. She had a daughter, Joyce, who also had a little girl, Janice, then five years old. So Ethel herself was a grandmother at about forty.

Joyce lived with her little daughter in a ground-floor flat by the railway at Herne Hill. I think it was called Milkwood Road. I only ever saw one room, at the front, because that was the only room Joyce occupied. It was her bedroom, and she was always bedridden. It was explained to me that she was 'not well', which need not mean more than that she had a cold. I had been far worse in my time, with measles and chickenpox and whooping cough and boils on the back of my neck which had to be cauterized with hot towels and burst like volcanoes, so I knew all about being 'not well.' The fact that Joyce coughed without respite, catching her breath only briefly from time to time to push words out, did not impress me as unusual, for the simple reason that I heard the same sounds at home, and had learnt to wait until my mother's coughing fits had subsided before she could let me know what she wanted.

On Christmas Eve, 1950, I was told that Auntie Joyce needed me to do something, and would I go round to see her at once. I must have taken the bus, because Milkwood Road was not within walking distance. I knocked at the door, and Janice opened it for me, reaching up quite high to find the latch. Joyce lay in bed, propped up on pillows, her long blond hair lying slack and lustreless across the pillow-case and a smell of sweat and effort in the room. Her chest heaved with coughing, and she kept putting a handkerchief up to her mouth as if she would eat it. When she spoke, it was with a voice weakened by strain and faint from losing the battle to subdue the rasping in her throat, which made noises like water going down a sink.

Christmas was upon her, and she could not get out to buy anything for anyone. Would I go to Brixton and get a little something for Janice, and for Ethel, and spend a shilling on something for myself as well. She fumbled in her purse to find coins for the errand, thanked me profusely, and slumped back on the pillow, exhausted.

I did the shopping at Woolworths in Brixton and returned within the hour to find Joyce very frail. I cannot remember what I said to her, but I recall the fierce panting, the pathetic glance of gratitude, and a paradoxical sense of urgency emanating from a woman who obviously had not the energy to urge anything much. She was worn out. I also remember feeling jolly pleased with myself that I had earned something for my errand, because I did not spend the shilling there and then, but saved it up. I think I told Joyce I would choose myself something after Christmas. When I got home, I told Mum that Auntie Joyce was 'not well' again.

She died later that day, stretched out on her stifling bed, her mouth open but freed at last from the hideous guest in the throat. She was twenty-two. Much later I was told that she had succumbed to that old bogey consumption, or TB, the tuberculosis which so ravaged the population when there was neither the knowledge to prevent it nor the money to pay for a cure. TB did not make waves. Everybody around me was very philosophic and resigned. Of course, they had all known that she did not have long to live, and were therefore not at all surprised when she didn't. You cursed fate and shook your head with sadness, but you went on with the next chore. Little motherless Janice came to live with us for a couple of years after that.

I had been the last person to see Joyce alive. Unwittingly, I had watched a woman die and done nothing about it. Nor had I felt anything much. Mum and Ethel were considerate enough not to draw attention to it, because they knew that I was too young to shoulder such a responsibility. On the contrary, they told me how lucky Joyce had been to have me run errands for her at the end. It was not until years later that I realized the truth, and found myself wanting (again). I still wilt with the guilt of it if I think and think and recreate that bedroom scene. I was not callous. I was not harsh or indifferent. I simply didn't know. If only she had said, 'Brian, I think I'm dying, will you run and fetch the doctor for me', or given me a message for Auntie Ethel, or done something to jostle me out of vapidity. I would not have shirked the responsibility; I would have welcomed it.

But she didn't. Like my own mother, she was attending to other people even *in extremis*. That was a lesson in itself. I think it finally freed me from the Catholic infection, that fervid frenetic saving of one's own soul. Indeed, the Catholics would have *blamed* Joyce for thinking of Christmas presents when she should have been preparing herself for God, confessing her sins, sweeping her mind clear of all anxieties and frivolities to enter the kingdom of heaven in a peaceful state. In *The Evil That Men Do* I included a chapter on the selfless condition, the habit of looking outwards from the self, the art of paying attention. That, I thought, was where goodness derived, it was the very essence of behaving well in the world instead of being locked up, as so many of my subjects had been, in the lightless, airless, loveless world of self-regard. Auntie Joyce had given me the first example of a good death, and I would despise any priest or vicar who said otherwise.

CHAPTER 3

Wilson's Grammar

Reading John Bayley's memoir of his wife Iris Murdoch, which contrives to be both distressing and uplifting, and at the same time grazing and munching through Proust's epic essay on human behaviour, I wonder which is the best route towards really understanding the past. The involuntary method – Proust's – is ever the most vivid, for it brings to the mind not only an event, but the colours, smells, fears and feelings which surrounded that event, and it must be by analysing those feelings, by re-experiencing them through the smells and sounds which accompany them, that one might know who one was, because one would briefly *be* that person again. And by briefly, I mean only a matter of seconds, or at the most a couple of minutes. During that short time one must make a supreme effort to hang on to the insights and truths which come cascading through one's head. The ability to do this was, I suppose, Proust's way of distinguishing between the artists and the donkeys.

Bayley is more direct. He grabs the past and cherishes it, holding it tight, not letting it escape into the evanescent world which gobbled up Iris, who dribbled away muttering in the

arms of Alzheimer. So his task is more urgent – driven by
love – and his past is more recent, more easily graspable.
I don't think he wants to analyse it, to tidy it all up, so
much as to perpetuate his present feelings, to keep them
going and thereby keep Iris going with them and in them.
Proust has no present feelings. He has present curiosity and
intellectual liveliness. His past feelings are a quarry in which,
with extreme diligence, concentration, hard work, he might
discover his past self and the view of life which he used at
some distant point to entertain. The implication is that this
strict cerebral discipline is more likely to attain the truth.

If I attempt to describe my fear, aged eleven, of going to
Wilson's Grammar School, where everyone wore a uniform
and there were big boys to stop one being little any more, I
am bound to say what I now think I must have felt, perhaps to
dramatize, certainly to turn the experience into proper words
and phrases, with sentences ending abruptly or effectively.
The truth was otherwise. It was not a question of being afraid
of anything in particular, but of a generalized, unfocused
terror, of being pushed and shoved unwilling towards the
future, of being robbed of oneself and having another 'self'
put in its place. Like shedding a skin, or rather having it torn
off one's back, and being forced into a new one which had to
fit immediately. I use a raw, cruel image, an image of flaying;
is that significant?

There was first the matter of the uniform, the 'new skin'.
My mother took me to a shop on the Camberwell New Road,
just round the corner from Albany Street, which specialized in
providing school uniforms. They were the appointed tailors,
in fact. Fortunately, Mum had a grant provided for the
purpose, as I had done well in the 11+ and was amongst
the first generation to benefit from free education in a welfare
state. There was no question of her ever being able to pay
for the uniform out of my father's weekly take-home pay
(which was usually gone by Wednesday, anyway). I can smell
the dustiness in that shop now, the odour of unworn new
cloth, of promise, of regeneration, of passing a rite, stepping

gingerly into a new world. My stomach was as empty and as dry as an old meringue throughout the whole performance, the man in the shop measuring my arm, taping the jacket in place on to my shoulder, getting the length of my first long trousers just so as to 'break' on my first black shiny shoes, my mother standing aside to look approval with hand on chin, though I suspect a trifle embarrassed at the onus put upon her to have an opinion one way or the other. My skin was hot, my face flushed, tears of ineptitude pricked behind my eyelids. I did not want anyone to look at me, and here it seemed everyone was engaged upon no other purpose than that. I could not endure it for long, and was mighty glad when we left.

Was I also proud? A little bit, perhaps, but largely I was smothered by tense apprehension. I had been made to feel special for once in my life, by Miss Bone, and I had shone to please her, coming top in everything. To abandon that cosy security and start all over again was overwhelmingly awful. I wanted to take Miss Bone to Wilson's Grammar with me. No more skipping-ropes with the girls in Herring Street, Dad bellowing at me to stop showing him up. No more chalking 'BM loves MC' on the pavement, and feeling heroically naughty before running away from the crime (that was a little hairless girl called Mary Cross). No more having Rex sit by my desk at school.

My mother did not take me to school on the first day, in that strange, itchy new clothing. I insisted on being brave, as it would be bad enough without having to stifle sobs on the threshold of prison. She escorted me to the bus-stop in Albany Street, where she spotted a 'big' boy in Wilson's uniform and delivered me to his tender care. I didn't know him, but I remember his name (now, for the first time in fifty years) as Bruce Goldstein. I was glad to have somebody to tell me what I could and could not do, for I was certain to blunder in to the wrong place or say the wrong thing without some guidance, but he never became a friend. A couple of years later I would come across him again in other circumstances, but for the time being he was my coach and companion on the 42 bus for a few weeks.

It seems scarcely credible, but the 42 bus, which went all the way to Camberwell Green, was an open top, with stairs outside, the kind of vehicle which had been in use before the war (the bus which now satisfies the tourist industry is a posher version – the original was like a giant Dinky toy). No longer did I derive any mysterious delicious thrill at sitting in the front seat; the journey was too laden with import to allow any pleasure. I sat at the back, brooding over what lay in store.

The rules were simple enough. 1. Wear your school cap in the street at all times. 2. Do not run in the corridors. 3. Defer to school prefects in every event. There were others, but it was not the rules themselves which worried me, so much as the fear that I might not retain them all in my head. The first day involved frantically fitting in and saying nothing. I was a scared mouse.

It was odd that Wilson's, although never a private 'public' school, shared much of the ethos of those patrician establishments. One characteristic was the fostering of healthy competition between rival groups, in order supposedly to build personality; thus I was assigned to Whiteley House, and our job, it was made clear, was to beat the hell out of the other five houses in every sport or endeavour. That was worrying enough, as I knew I could not hope to be much use in any sport and began already to think how I could contrive to avoid them, be passed over, somehow be forgotten amidst the assignations.

The other principle which smacked of elevated places was the ancient hierarchy of authority. The Headmaster, Mr Lee (we were all expected to refer to him out of earshot as 'Sid', although that had not the remotest connection to his name), shuffled about the place aimlessly, it seemed, licking his lips, appearing to mutter, hoping to find something to do. The individual housemasters had more authority, more 'clout' as it were, because they were heads of teams, leaders of the pack, who should command loyalty rather than obedience. Lower down the scale were the teachers, who were sometimes those same housemasters in different settings, whom one either respected or ridiculed according to the strength or weakness of their character. I soon picked up the fact that schoolboys *en masse* were merciless tormentors. This was wholly new, as there had been nothing but kindness in the air at St Alban's RC Primary. Last, but far from least, were the School Prefects. These were ultimate arbiters of behaviour, the final court of appeal, dispensers of punishment and humiliation. If a boy annoyed his teacher by gossiping during class, or throwing wet bits of paper across the room, he was immediately sent by the teacher to the Prefects' Room, where he had to knock politely on the door, wait for a post-pubescent authoritative growl of 'Enter!', then meekly declare who had sent him for chastisement and what had been the offence committed. The teacher would never condescend to make his case before this tribunal, of course; it was always left to the miscreant to condemn himself, then plead his own case in mitigation, or even denial. Looking back, I am astonished that it worked so well. No pupil ever failed to turn up at the door when sent, nobody ever lied about the reason for his being sent, everyone accepted punishment when it came, sometimes under protest but always with the tacit knowledge that there was no higher court to amend or reverse decisions.

It was also odd that the men who sent us there were grown-ups, married with their own families, yet perfectly happy to entrust the administration of law and order to five boys aged sixteen or seventeen.

And I am sure the prefects enjoyed themselves. It was part of the point of the system that they should, because by submitting to authority and then by exercising it one was expected to learn the principles of justice through experience, not through instruction. (It is true that nobody ever told a newly-appointed School Prefect what his duties were or how he should perform them; he was selected, enthroned, and left to get on with it. The assumption was that by that time he would know how to judge, evaluate behaviour, tease out the liars and the cheats, be fair towards the innocently accused without entirely letting them off, which was never a good idea, and if he was not quite ready to deal with all this, he soon would be. Thus older boys learned the responsibility of power by training themselves on the apprehensions and terror of younger boys. This may well be what happens in a thoroughly well-operated colony of baboons in the wild, and I know from my own observations that it obtains within the ranks of an extended gorilla family. In other words, it may be Nature's way). I now think it was admirably well evolved, and for the most part had the desired effect of a fast-track maturing process, both emotionally and intellectually. At the age of eleven, however, I thought it monstrous, because it made the air in the corridors tingle with fear, and the armpits sweat with the struggle of finding one's place in the hierarchy and nestling there.

As they learned how to behave at the top of it, the School Prefects refined their techniques of humiliation. Sometimes the growl of 'Enter!' would be delayed, so that one had timidly to knock on the door again, only to be scolded for impatience. The prefects had desks and chairs in their room, and did their own school work in there, with cups of coffee and the occasional cigarette – prestige and privilege indeed! So it was often a nuisance to be interrupted by a boy being sent for reproof, and his case might be heard in summary fashion, with little attention to those details which make all the difference to justice. Then one smarted with the pain of failure and ill-treatment. But again I say oddly enough, there was never at large a need for revenge. Some resentment, perhaps, but no fierce hatred or passionate desire to get one's own back. Rather did one feel that next time one would put one's case better and win the day. For the most part, the prefects encouraged this attitude and rewarded it.

There were five of them, comprising one School Captain and four lieutenants. They all wore flowing blue gowns, edged with a darker blue velvet, exactly like the academic gowns the teachers wore, but more glamorous. The four prefects could punish by keeping a boy behind at school after hours, giving him errands to do, making him write out the same promise a hundred times (the silliest and most useless of all punishments devised), and in the worst case, make a boy bend down and touch his toes while his backside was thumped up to six times with a slipper (we called them plimsoles, used in gym class; now they would be something like trainers). The School Captain alone had the authority to use not a slipper but a very flexible light cane, the swish of whose passage through the air was like a guillotine. The pain it inflicted was terrible, and the anguish acute. But it all depended upon who was wielding it, and there again one imbibed a very direct lesson in the observation of human nature.

Bob Cummings was a wholly reasonable School Captain, austere and aloof perhaps, but only to mask a very real shyness and to keep intimacy at a safe distance. He seemed not to have friends, and for this to be a self-imposed loneliness. He was afraid that if he came too close in a friendship he might betray affection, and that would be dangerous. Thus an encounter with Cummings in the Prefects' Room was a meeting of minds, a careful discussion as to what had happened and why one had been sent to see him, followed by an entirely acceptable punishment. Through the persuasion of well-chosen words and a nicely-crafted respect for you as a person, not just as victim, he convinced you that you deserved what was coming. And if the whacking hurt, it was not excessive. One did not feel that Cummings vented any ignoble wrath upon one; he simply did his duty. How vain and deluding are our little concealments! Cummings wanted the company of boys, and having told himself that affection was wrong, he made love to them by keeping them talking.

O'Rourke, on the other hand, was rough and bull-headed. He could not reason, and so expressed himself with summary frustrated anger, whacking boys with a ferocity which was little short of sadistic. As he brought down the cane his eyes screwed up, his lips pursed, his energies concentrated on that arc of pain. No nonsense with him about the company of boys; he wanted to whack them and get rid of them as soon as possible. Still, one did not mind even O'Rourke, for he taught one the danger of unreason, the meaning of rough justice, and the pathetic stupidity of sadistic pleasure, none of which could have been so well learnt in classes of philosophy or psychology.

O'Rourke was not, however, the chief sadist in school. He was more a clumsy amateur than one practised in the refinement of pain – a thumper rather than a thumbscrew. The really certifiable candidate was the only teacher at Wilson's who sent none of his victims to the prefects, but reserved the pleasure of punishment for himself. He was the geography teacher, and we called him 'Min'.

Heaven knows how he acquired the nickname. It meant nothing, although it certainly suggested something unpleasant merely by its thin, fleshless sound. His name was Mathews, he taught geography, and he must have been about forty (boys are notoriously useless at estimating age, everyone over eighteen being amorphously 'old'). Neither slim nor obese, but something like a tree-trunk, Min was always well-dressed, in a real suit and tie, punctilious, precise and sinister, his hair suspiciously black, probably tinted, and sleeked back with too much Brylcreem, his tight lips grinning like one of Giotto's devils, a nasty tongue emerging from them every few seconds, like a serpant's, to flick around and feel the air. He was licking his chops with enjoyment at the fear he created around him.

We would have to be in Min's class not just on time, but early, so that we were all seated, alert, ready, and as silent as the grave, before he came in. The room was last on the left down the huge wide corridor which ran the length of the great building, and which echoed with cracking voices and hurried footsteps. But not Min's footsteps; he wore slippers so that we could never hear him and anticipate his approach. Suddenly, he would be there, an apparition in the doorway, grinning, licking, glancing around to see whom he might catch whispering or staring out of the window or, heaven forbid, giggling behind his hand. The miscreant was summoned to the front, and publicly humiliated. Min used pauses for theatrical effect; he said less than any man, but spoke eloquently when no words issued from that mean little mouth, and the eyes glinted with hidden delights. The poor wretch who had been singled out for execution often waited a whole minute before a question was put to him, during which ghastly length of time he had to think, to imagine, to ponder what was coming next, and that was worse than the punishment itself. The rest of the class sat transfixed by fear. Min knew the power of suspense.

When the punishment came, it varied according to Min's mood, surprise or at least unpredictability being another very useful weapon of the sadist. When he was mischievous or whimsical (that was our interpretation at the time – Min having fun), he would slap the boy's bottom with his hand, the boy meanwhile placed with his head bent between Min's thighs, the professorial bollocks just above the nape of the victim's neck. When he was in serious mood, his jaw set against any hint of a grin, the tongue flicking out more quickly and tensely, he would require the boy to stretch out his hand as far away from his body as he could. Then he would take out his vicious cane, test its flexibility before everyone's eyes, and amidst a hush which turned the stomach, bring down upon the child's open palm, sometimes across his fingers, a furious downswipe. If the boy squealed in pain and withdrew his stinging hand, he was made to put it out again for further treatment. The best was to close one's eyes, grit one's teeth and not flinch; then one might escape with one stroke, and retire to one's seat to nurse the wound quietly, unobserved, weeping inwardly. But on occasion a boy would suffer three, four or even six of these because he was not brave enough to take the first. Of course, we did not spot the sexual impulses which fed this frenzy, because we knew nothing of such matters. To us, it seemed that Min was an instrument of our maturity, showing us how to be manly, robust, invulnerable to the shocks and pains of life; it was an essential part of our growing up, of our masculine destinies. We did not realize that we were witnessing a pathetic display by a man of perverted emotions, a man denied the usual joys of home pleasures, mutual love and soft affections.

The other teachers must have known, but chose not to interfere. Sid Lee was too weak to express an opinion anyway, and there was not one among us who thought to complain. We chatted about Min, shared our terrors and competed with one another to earn his approbation, but it never occurred to us to question his behaviour. Besides, he achieved results. We were consistently well-behaved in his class, polite, well-mannered, and we all passed with higher marks in geography and geology than in any other subject. It was a source of constant wonder that Min's classes produced such brilliant pupils, most of them achieving distinctions. I must say that his method of imparting information – simple, direct, organized, classified, repeated – was superb, but the ground had first to be laid to ensure our attention. He recognized that the good teacher employs personality first, facts only second.

I am firmly convinced that Min did us no harm in the end. Unwittingly, in my case, he was giving me an early lesson in the observation of aberrant behaviour, and in the psychology of cruelty, which returned to fuel my ruminations in later years. But he also presented me with an example of a problem I have never been able to solve. Jumping ahead five years to the time when I was myself School Captain and regularly administered punishment with the cane when called upon to do so (though I would always do my damnedest to avoid it), it was perfectly clear to myself and to every one of the boys 'run in' to place themselves at my mercy that I was utterly hopeless. I raised the cane as high as I could, I swept it down as fast as I could, I tried to do my duty and press force through my wrist, but something always stayed my hand at the last second, so that the blow itself was minimal, held little power to inflict much more than a tickle. I told myself it was because I was not a sportsman, and therefore had no biceps. But it was not that. The truth was, I was hugely uncomfortable with the notion of causing pain, to anyone or anything at any time, and so I could never have been moved by the attractions of sadism. The boys knew this in their hearts, and tried to present themselves at the Prefects' Room when they knew I would be present, and they could get off lightly. I imagined they may even have been laughing at me. But nothing could induce me to be cruel, not because I was thinking of the poor louts whose bottoms were being whacked (I was utterly indifferent to all but one of them), but because I could not let myself down, or contrive to be somebody that I was not.

I saw that sadistic needs must be so deep-seated as to be irresistible. The sadist was sadistic because that was an unconquerable part of his character which had perforce to find expression somehow or other, and being a schoolteacher was a way as efficient as any other. The corollary was that sadism could not be adopted, learnt, absorbed or grown into, because it would run counter to character. And yet there were the thousands of camp employees in Nazi Germany or in Stalinist Russia, themselves harmless greengrocers and fond parents before circumstances afforded them strange new opportunities, who *became* sadists, who learnt to behave in a way which had not, theretofore, been natural to them, and learnt moreover to enjoy it; in fact, they learnt how to alter their own selves.

In *The Evil That Men Do*, which I wrote forty years later, I devote some pages to the implications of a notoriously alarming experiment conducted in the United States in 1963 by Dr Stanley Milgram, which demonstrated beyond question that timid, kindly, decent souls could become monsters if offered the chance. Milgram presented them with a man shackled to a chair, his wrist attached to electrodes through which they could administer electric shocks of varying intensity; they should do this when the patient made a mistake in a text he was required to memorize. The experiment was designed, said Milgram, to determine the limits of tolerance to pain. Its secret purpose was to determine the length to which the forty experimenters would go in hurting a man whose cries for pity and evident anguish assailed their senses. (The man was an actor and there was no real electricity.) Over half of them went so far as to administer the largest possible dose even though, they were told, the man had a heart condition and might die. The horrible conclusion was that ordinary uncomplicated people could change into sadists if given sanction so to do from a higher authority.

My own tiny experience could not support this notion. I had been given every possible permission and encouragement as School Captain to hone any cruel impulses I might feel and give rein to them under the guise of law and order, of doing my duty. Yet I could not do it. I had to find other ways of exercising authority without inflicting physical harm, without being the cause of real distress. In short, I could not make myself into a person like Mr Mathews even if I wanted to (and part of me did want to, in so far as I thought I really ought to be a little more frightening, or I would be useless at the job).

I can no longer accept all the implications of the Milgram test. The man and wife with eight children in an end-of-terrace house in Gloucester, Frederick and Rosemary West, were separately arrested for murder in 1992, but due to be arraigned and tried together. The victims were girls and young women who had been tortured, gagged, restrained, murdered and dismembered in exactly the same manner, over a period of several years (the last being Heather West, their own eldest daughter). Frederick West committed suicide in prison before the case against him could be heard, and so his wife Rosemary faced trial alone. There was enough evidence adduced at that trial to demonstrate with crystal clearness that Fred was a sadistic character, and that Rosemary was not. He had endeavoured to indoctrinate his wife into the pleasures of inflicting pain, but she had resisted, and he had therefore to indulge them alone. He could torture and kill because he had no affective understanding of the impact of such behaviour; he was cold inside, he shivered at the heart. She was the kind of person – emotional, short-tempered and immediate, whose responses were sane, and who could not be part of an act of icy cruelty because she could place herself in the shoes of the other. (This is a minority view; Rosemary West was convicted of murder at Winchester Crown Court and is now serving a life sentence. I hold that there was no evidence against her, apart from 'similar fact', i.e. evidence which indicated possible offences other than those of murder.)

In a sense, Min the geography teacher was the first specimen of the sadistic nature I encountered. I would not fully understand his significance until I dug my fingers into the grubbiness of Frederick West's character some fifty years later. They both took delight in causing and looking at pain in others. Thankfully, watching humiliation in the weak sated Min's aberrant nature. West's was far fiercer, positively demonic. He wanted not merely to humiliate but destroy, to tear life apart. The one is a gruesome exaggeration of the other.

But I advance. In those first awkward, worrying weeks at Wilson's Grammar Mr Mathews loomed as merely a silent, inarticulate threat. One felt he was menacing, but one had no idea how or why; he was somebody to be kept well away from, an amorphous but solid enemy. Other teachers were approachable on a more human scale, and it was fairly astonishing how we, the first years, congealed quickly into a group with its own psychology and will, and summed these people up. There was no leader among us, nobody who suggested an idea which the rest of us followed, just a general insidious intelligence which pulled in all strands from all sides to become as potent as an ant-hill. This common denominator decided how to cope with the teachers, each in a different way. Mr Pitkin ('Peewee') was five feet tall and taught chemistry. He sometimes seemed as if he might fit into one of his own test tubes, with which he loved to play, mixing substances to make noxious evil-smelling smoke. Mr Shakeshaft ('Bullethead') taught biology of a sort. Languid, mischievous, lazy, he gave the impression he would much rather have stayed at home than come to supervise another shower of louts, but since we were there, we might as well learn something. His enthusiasm was lit only by the one obligatory lesson on the mechanics of human reproduction, at which he grinned throughout, watching to see if any boy would dare ask a question. Nobody did, although there was much guilty giggling behind furtive hands, which Bullethead also noticed, and enjoyed. There was nothing salacious about his amusement; he simply appreciated the absurdity of the exercise which he was bound, by custom, to perform, when most of his audience were already highly-practised masturbators.

The man who taught English, Jad Parr, had a crucial effect upon my future, the telling of which must wait until later, but he showed us all the attractions of quiet cynicism, the urbane refusal to take anything seriously, the polite, perfectly-worded verbal equivalent of two fingers. His name was John, and 'Jad' derived from his three initials. Witty, calm, he never raised his voice and showed, by contrast, that good manners were a splendid way to deflate antagonisms and deflect wrath. I often watched him win with a quiet word of grace, and marvelled at his ability to bring peace in his pocket, like God instructing the storm to abate. Jad was obviously a lonely man. I say obviously, as if boys discussed his private affairs and drew conclusions, which is far from the truth; we were not interested, could not be bothered, would not have had the imagination to intrude. Yet there was something effortlessly sad about this discreet and compassionate man which sunk into my soul without my ever acknowledging it, until much later in adulthood. Children do notice a great deal more than they let on, I am sure. He was one of the few teachers with whom one could have a one-to-one conversation, if one passed him by chance in the corridor. I remember his telling me that he was going to Italy for his holidays, and that he travelled light. How light? He took only his briefcase, the one he carried with him to school every day. What, no luggage?

'Don't you see, Masters', he said, 'that's all you need. Room enough for a spare shirt and socks, toothbrush and shaving kit. Why be loaded down?' That admission, though admirably sensible and right, betokened more of book-lined bachelor solitude than any remark I have ever heard, before or since. I reflected that, indeed, I had only seen Jad wear one suit on his rather stout body.

There were no female teachers. Indeed, there was only one woman in the entire building – the Headmaster's secretary, who had a tiny office next to the back stairs on the first floor. She was treated by all the boys as a kind of leper, not because there was anything remotely unpleasant or disagreeable about her, but simply on account of her belonging to an alien species. None of us had any idea how to respond to women, what to do with them, how to look at them, even how most efficiently to ignore them. The Secretary lived in a kind of lonely world surrounded by five hundred indifferent young males. I do not imagine for one minute that she minded; she was probably amused by our alternate shyness and brashness, indeed well used to boorish behaviour, paying it scant attention. I don't think I addressed a single word to her during my first four years at the school, until I felt grown-up and able to converse with her on terms of equality. Even that must surely have appeared impertinent to her. What a saint to put up with it all!

Being in an all-male society inevitably created emotional tensions. There were the boys who were just kids, with squeaky kittenish voices, and the boys whose grunts, growls and croaks revealed them to be incipient men. The former naturally looked upon the latter with innocent uncomplicated awe, while these struggled with the defining processes which were bursting their bodies and wrecking their personalities, all the time trying to appear utterly nonchalant. It was eternally farcical to watch, no doubt, but hideous to have to go through. The little boys were impatient to be big boys, long before they understood how awful that would be, and the big boys did not know whether they should be ashamed of the loyalty they excited in these nippers, as being stupidly sissy, or desperately worried because they enjoyed it. We were always told (by whom I cannot remember) that these were perfectly normal 'phases' that had to be endured, and from which we should each emerge unscathed in due course. The whole of adolescence was therefore concentrated upon that *one moment* when one would know that one had 'emerged', got through the ordeal and come out the other side. Presumably that would be the moment when one would feel free from all that wretched anxiety which seeped into the skin like slanting autumn drizzle.

My first friendship happened to me; I did not seek it, or encourage it, or even, in a way, welcome it. Friendship was like a fog which crept up on you unnoticed, and by the time it had enveloped you it was too late to prepare for and impossible to escape. Mine was with a boy called Fane, and it started in the second year, when we were both twelve, approaching thirteen. I knew something was different when it became a matter of imperative importance that we should sit next to one another at the same desk (all desks, with two ink-wells and two lifting lids, were fashioned to accommodate two boys sitting thigh to thigh on one bench, just as, at the swimming-pool, all cubicles were arranged so that two boys could dress and undress together – it was as if the entire system had been organized to test one's emotional strength). Fane wanted to be next to me with the same intense need that I wanted to be next to him, and we zoomed into the class together so that we might achieve our object before anyone else claimed one of our seats and upset the delicate arrangement.

Of course, we were soon the laughing-stock of the rest of the class, although, such is the ruthless cruelty of the male young, there were certainly other undeclared alliances being forged amongst some of the scoffers, who smothered their own embarrassment by re-directing it on to us. Good Lord, we might even be detected putting our arms around one another's shoulder (to be frank, it was more often my arm which slid round Fane's neck rather than the other way around), which occasioned loud hoots of derision, so we had to curtail demonstrations of friendship and learn to dissemble. Thus was it confirmed to me that emotions must be furtive, if not strangled at birth.

Being 'best friends' with Fane marked me out as some kind of freak, as had the incredible loyalty and softness of my dog Rex. Though Wilson's was a good three or four miles from home, at the end of a bus-ride and through major traffic; and though Rex had never been shown where the school was; and though I left him every morning at the bus-stop with the injunction to 'stay' when I got on the bus, and he looked miserable as he turned to make his way home alone; still he turned up one day at the school, wandering the long wide corridor, sniffing, dodging thousands of legs, looking up, anxious to find me. When he did, of course, there was much ecstatic wagging of tail, and redness of face from me. The other boys thought it all rather soppy, and typical of Masters to be so fawned upon. Rex came into class, and I had to get permission to take him home. The following day he turned up again, and was taken by one of the teachers to the police station in Camberwell Church Street, whence I had to bail him out at the end of the day. He must have been a miraculous dog, because when I explained to him the embarrassment he had twice caused me, and instructed him never to do it again, he desisted. It was as if he was satisfied at last to know where I spent the day, and was sufficiently content with that knowledge to make no further enquiry. Rex generalized from two instances.

My mysterious involvement with Fane (mysterious to me, that is, not for a moment understanding why his proximity mattered so much, though it aroused the same weird pleasure, somewhere at the back of the eyes, as had playing with buses on the kitchen table) was complicated by the fact that he had an identical twin in the same class. By genetic identification, therefore, the one Fane automatically shared some of the other Fane's emotional responses and affective calculations.

This meant that if anyone was going to thwart my friend's desire to sit next to me, it would be his twin brother. In this way I encountered, far too soon I think, the head-swirling turmoil of jealousy.

God knows how I was able to concentrate on maths or the Latin dative plural, or how any of us got any work done. The subtleties of assigning thoughts to different compartments in one's self-image, and keeping them separate, must have been amazingly quickly developed in the few months it took puberty to conquer. One had to learn very fast indeed. One rule I never broke in public was the use of the surname. Throughout my five years at Wilson's I never heard one boy call another by anything but his bald surname; to know a bloke's first name would have been too suspect, to use it would have been like a term of endearment, and therefore strictly taboo. So Fane was always Fane within earshot – it was a protection, a badge of normality. When we saw one another after school (which, astonishingly enough, we only did on about five occasions throughout our friendship), then I would venture to call him 'Bernie', and the use of the forbidden name forged a thrill of intimacy unlike anything I had ever felt before.

There was also intimacy on the sports field, of a rather more acceptable kind, because robust, rough, hearty, and physical only by accident. How many gropes occurred surreptitiously I cannot imagine, for it was the way in which self-consciously masculine boys could indulge their need to touch without the need being visible or the act detectable. Some very real affections gave strength to that loud, overt team-spirit, and obviously led to some fine victories. Boys were fighting to win not just for themselves, but for their chums, and not just to shine in their eyes either, but in order that their eyes should meet. Nobody ever explained to us schoolboys that the basis of team-spirit was love.

Not for nothing had the Spartan armies promoted the idea that pairs of male lovers would make the best fighters; no wonder they were difficult to beat! Nowadays we talk archly of 'male-bonding' as though love had nothing to do with it and the phenomenon were a mere echo of primal behaviour in the ancient tribe. It may well be, and the feeling of being in a school team may well have been descended from tribal loyalties, but it was a mistake to try to smother the 'feeling' aspect of it and pretend that loyalty was only won upon the corpse of the impulse to affection. Those poor boys who were happiest on the sports field had perforce to split themselves in two (yet another damaging psychological division, self-inflicted like the conflict between concentration on school-work and devotion to the friend), or even three on occasion. They had to convince themselves that their prowess was the fruit of self-discipline, the result of painstaking effort to rid themselves of the desire to love or be loved and devote themselves wholeheartedly to the game alone. Some of them surely grew into selfish, ungenerous husbands, whose sexual couplings were fitful and short, while their team-spirit continued to glow in disguise, well into adulthood, down at the pub.

My congenital aversions to mud, to speed, and to brute force, added to my certainty of failure if ever I strove to dismiss them, kept me well out of sports fixtures. Running was all right, both cross-country and sprint. I managed a creditable 100-yard run, often coming in second, and was up with the first six or so in that gruelling long-distance run which felt more like a punishment than a challenge; after that I knew what happened to my socks when I put them through the mangle. But that was really a solitary exercise, not a team-effort, so I was never part of that secret society of chums who were locked in collective embrace. In addition to all these time-wasting sporting events we had two sessions per week in the gymnasium, vaulting over so-called 'horses', climbing ropes, touching toes and swinging arms. The smell of sweat was overpowering, and the unspoken purpose of keeping boys out of mischief was constantly in the air. It is astonishing how quickly puberty hones the senses and makes the antennae alert, for it was clear to most of us, I think, that we were meant to get rid of our urges by doing all these ridiculous exercises in the gym twice a week. If a boy has to climb ropes and sweat it out for an hour, he won't be tempted to do vile things to himself when he is alone, so at least went the Victorian logic which was still hanging around in the 1950s. As it happened, it was in the gym that the medical examination took place every term, when a doctor visited to make sure we were all in good nick (shortly after the war there were still worries about malnutrition, and the free visits were part of the reforms of the Welfare State). Foolishly, he was accompanied by a nurse, usually a comely young lady. We lined up to appear before him, drop our trousers, and cough as he held our testicles in his large, pudgy hand, all in full view of the young woman. Tumescence was rife among the older boys, more than one of whom had to be sent to the corner to 'control himself'.

By the time I was twelve I found myself a job delivering morning newspapers for a shop called Wiseman's, next to the Thomas A'Becket pub at the top of Albany Street. This afforded me a minimal amount of pocket money, I think about 10/- a week (50p), which I used to escape the grey restrictions of the Old Kent Road. As a youngster I had devoured the 'Saturday morning pictures' which were offered free at the local cinema, then graduated to grown-up films once a week at the Regal. Now I was earning enough to venture forth into the world depicted in those films, the West End of London itself. To cross the River Thames was a psychological and social barrier fraught with complications and almost too overwhelming for most South Londoners to attempt. My first visit to Trafalgar Square and Piccadilly Circus was heady, intoxicating, and to taste it properly I determined to meet the people to whom these were familiar sights. This meant film stars and celebrities, and so I quickly became one of the select band, about five or six altogether, of London autograph-hunters.

I and another boy from Ilford, Ray End, spent our weekends stalking the famous, for which I have no doubt we were unpopular with some (and which today fills me with a kind of bashful shame), but which lifted our lives far above the humdrum. We were expert sleuths. We chatted up chauffeurs to find where people were staying, and even at what time they were due to emerge from the Savoy or Dorchester hotels for appointments; we discovered private addresses; we were informed of broadcasting schedules, and we made thorough nuisances of ourselves. I collected over two hundred signatures, some of which are probably very valuable today. The books languish at the top of my wardrobe.

It would be tedious to attempt a list. I mention only the most interesting encounters. We discovered where Winston Churchill dined every Thursday, and lay in ambush to catch him leaving from the servants' entrance in a happy state. We caught Joan Collins at her top-floor flat in Hanover Square, knocking at her door after breakfast and finding her in dressing-gown. We jumped in a taxi and uttered the immortal words 'Follow That Car!' (aged thirteen, mind you) to pursue Doris Day, who had declined to be gracious, trapping her finally in an underground garage. We were insulted by Katherine Hepburn and charmed by Sophia Loren, quite the nicest and most unaffected film star one could imagine (I am told that she is still sweet-natured). I had brief conversations with both Marilyn Monroe (who asked me the way to the nearest drugstore, giving me the delicious opportunity to correct her – she meant a chemist's) and Charlie Chaplin, who said I should be at school. Humphrey Bogart was tiny, Stan Laurel and Oliver Hardy grateful for the attention (they were at that time has-beens, long before their rediscovery as comic geniuses by a subsequent generation).

Collecting signatures was in itself undeniably silly, but it was, in my case, possibly a prelude to a need to discover. To be dazzled by the shiny surface was only the initial, overt effect. I wanted very much to know who these people really were beneath the glitter, to discern real personality behind dark glasses, to ferret and reveal. A ludicrous ambition, of course, but it would one day transmute into more useful form. The biographer also nags at his subject, bothers and perseveres beyond the casual, and is finally as big a pest as the autograph-hunter. The difference is in degree; the motives are not so very far apart.

There was one celebrity with whom I was infatuated. Zsa Zsa Gabor was so glamorous, so far removed from standard beauty as to be a kind of masterpiece of confection. She was young, slim and exotic, not a great actress but with a noble bearing which I intuited despite her being the subject of constant trivial gossip. She often visited London, usually on the arm of Porfirio Rubirosa, a South American playboy reputed to be oversized in member, and I was so often in attendance that she grew to recognize and greet me. I could not allow her to come to London without at least a nod, until I outgrew the autograph habit and was no longer at the hotel door. She evidently noticed my absence, for I received through the post (I must have rather grandly given her my address) a signed ten-by-eight photograph with the inscription that I should 'hurry up and finish your studies, so that you can be again my bodyguard.'

More than forty years later I was assigned by a London newspaper to cover the O.J. Simpson trial in Los Angeles for a week. The editor, keen on getting value for money, asked that I should combine this with another piece. What would I like to write about? I said I should like to spend a day with Zsa Zsa Gabor, and he agreed. While I was still in London I found her telephone number and called her from the Garrick Club. 'You have a *vunderfool* accent', she purred, to which I replied, 'You should listen to yours sometime.' 'Nonsense', she said, 'I am an American citizen.'

True, no doubt, but she was also a Hungarian aristocrat, as I discovered when I went to see her at her house in Bel Air; my juvenile intuition had not been mistaken. The resulting article pointed this out, amongst other details previously ignored by the press, and the editor placed Zsa Zsa's photograph on the front cover of the magazine section. She told me later that it was the best and kindest article that had ever been written about her. I am not surprised – it had been germinating for nearly half a century. (There is an old school exercise book of mine packed with bits and pieces about her – my first attempt at narrating a life.)

When I reminded her that I had met her before, that she had been my antidote to school chores and grim bombed-out terraced streets, and that I had based my drawing of the female figure in art class upon her handsome breasts and tiny waist, she roared with laughter. 'So it was you, my little bodyguard!,' she exclaimed. 'And you', I said, 'were my Helen of Troy.'

CHAPTER 4

On Gilbert Harding

My progress through Wilson's Grammar was intended to culminate in freedom and loot. All my contemporaries were planning to leave at the end of the fifth form and O levels in order to earn money. Necessity, not greed, impelled them, for their parents could hardly afford them to remain non-productive members of the family for much longer. The traditional route in the Old Kent Road was to go into 'the print', a subsidiary but essential off-shoot of the Fleet Street newspaper industry, and several boys who did exactly that are now multi-millionaires. I, too, wanted to earn some money. I recall a very precise ambition, reached on the top of a bus as I passed new Wates flats for rent on Denmark Hill, that I would eventually have to earn as much as £20 a week to get myself out of the bomb-sites; I calculated that my father's wage of £5 a week was what was keeping us there. I also shared the ambition to take girls to the cinema and perhaps snog at the front door afterwards, on the expectation that once I tried it and learned how to do it well, the desire to repeat would rescue me from unhealthy erotic fantasies involving other boys. So I was all set to claim my freedom at sixteen.

It was not to be. Schoolmasters ganged up on me and advised my parents that I was bright enough to cope with sixth-form work and that they would earnestly desire that I should benefit from every educational opportunity. Mr Massey, my Housemaster, told me it was my duty to stay on, and that I was destined for university (the thought had never crossed my mind). Sid, the Headmaster, joined in and promised that I would be made one of the School Prefects. They all managed to make me feel that I would be letting them down if I insisted on leaving. Selfishly, I did not recognize that those I would be letting down were my parents, who had both been denied schooling and were prepared to sacrifice their own interests (a second wage-packet) to give me a better chance than they had had. When I realized I was doomed, indulging misery drove me to contemplate running away from home, but I lacked the courage and was too fond of the comfort of being provided for. Besides, a secret curiosity tickled within: would I not enjoy being part of the elite?

Another crucial circumstance intervened. Jad Parr, the English teacher, had somehow discerned that, although I was top of the class and did all the work required of me, I was ill-at-ease with it, for I did not enjoy it. He was right. Milton was a bore, and Shakespeare so impenetrable that I longed for a translation. Understanding was a chore which I merely had the knack of possessing.

Jad suggested I take a bus one Saturday morning to the distant suburb where he lived, beyond Lewisham, and meet him for a cup of tea and a sandwich. It was an odd request, but I was flattered by the attention and had always marvelled at Jad's apparently inexhaustible intelligence. I took a Greenline bus, the single-deckers which served rural communities surrounding London, and was met at the bus-stop by Jad in weekend tweed jacket with leather elbow-pads, and the inevitable pipe. He said he wanted to talk to me about my work, and my future, but in the event he did both less and more than that. We walked into the woods, and for two hours this meek, lonely, book-infested man talked to me about Shakespeare, illuminating defining moments in the plays, proposing insights into character which he invited me to challenge, searching for my intuitions. He went off on several tangents, about the craft of acting, the potency of words lying in their shape as much as in their use, which led to philology and the way words change their meaning over centuries, which led to the philosophy of mathematics. Jad's enthusiasm overwhelmed me. I felt changes taking place in my head and in my pulse that very Saturday morning, which nothing would ever be able to reverse. I was not being told things that I must learn, but invited to share the fun of knowledge, to enjoy myself, to permit fresh air to blow through the mind and quicken it. I was given one-to-one education in a couple of hours, as education ought to be, pulling things out of me which I did not know were there. (As Jad would have said, perhaps did say, from *educare* – 'to lead out'.) At the same time I was astonished by his kindness, that he should take such trouble with me, make a special effort for one person, with the result that my memory of that morning is not only of a new life of books opening up in front of me, but of the gentle warmth of human goodness. One word we examined was 'courtesy' – its root, its purpose, its powerful layered subtlety. Well, what Jad Parr bestowed upon me that day was unparalleled courtesy, the demonstration of respectful attention; he treated me as if I deserved the attention, and I was bound thereafter to show myself worthy of it.

Many memoirs talk of the Great Teacher, the one person who lifts a boy or girl from the numbness of childhood and points the way towards realization of his or her potential. Jad Parr was mine. I could not have done without him, and without the experience of that Saturday I might have won my rebellion and gone into 'the print'. Did he know what he was doing, what effect he was likely to have? I'm sure he did. At one point he questioned me about my plans, and likened my mumblings to Hamlet's pained hesitations. He felt he had to do something to stop me going in the wrong direction, and I have ever been grateful to him for spotting the danger.

Thus I went into the sixth form, where my subjects were Latin, English, French, Geography and History, and I was assigned the blue velvet-edged cloak of the School Prefect, with the right to go down stairs which everybody else could only walk up, the right to punish, the right to lead school assembly, and the inestimable privilege of showing off. I found every possible excuse to float down those stairs, exhibiting my status and allowing the gown to flow out behind. Classes became adorable feasts of intellectual discovery, with only three or four pupils in each, and to translate English prose into Latin verse for Mr Opie became as perfect a pastime as the most challenging crossword.

At more or less the same time, another crucial event helped cause a change of direction. We had all grown up in London well accustomed to the famous annual fogs, the so-called 'pea-soupers' which so astonished foreigners, for they cast a blanket over the city which almost throttled it. The fog swept in at least once a year, and lasted for two or three days. If we were lucky, it might be severe enough to let us off school, especially if we lived sufficiently distant to render travel impossible, but we were nonetheless required to make the effort; more than once I walked the three miles to Wilson's by radar, knowing where I was going because I knew where the streets should lead and where the walls should be. Trams continued to operate, being on lines which did not depend on visibility, but buses could only run if the conductor walked in front of them carrying a torch. Progress was witheringly slow, streetlights shone dimly through cotton wool, all sound was muffled. Sometimes one wondered how a city ever came to be established in such an accursed spot prone to regular burial in mist, but for the most part one got on with it cheerfully; it was something to talk about.

The mist which invaded in 1956 was, however, something altogether different. It was a killer. The word 'smog' was first formed that year to describe the mixture of natural fog with the effluent from a couple of million domestic chimneys. Smoke, unable to escape and be diffused into the cosmos, was trapped, circulated, infiltrated, poisoned our eyes and filled our lungs. There was fog *inside* the house, nothing could protect one from it, and for the first time I was rather apprehensive. To deliver newspapers that morning I had to get down on my hands and knees to feel the road beneath me and grope until I found the kerb. I could not see below my waist or beyond my elbows, and the paper-round, instead of taking half an hour, stretched to three hours of painstaking terrain-touching. The silence was frightening, the chill so eerie it was like being stroked with a brush dipped in ice.

The point of the story is that my mother was made wretched by this awful invasion. She could scarcely breathe. Her weak lungs were unable to fight for themselves, and she was mostly in bed, trying desperately to hide from the insidious, slinking enemy. The doctor who was called to see her recommended the only cure that would offer her a chance, and it was drastic; she would have to leave London, or perish. My father knew at once that this was no exaggeration, and when I learnt later that 20,000 people had died in London that autumn as a direct result of the smog, I realized that my mother's life had been seriously at risk. Immediately plans were made to swap homes with a family living in a more healthy climate, and I think it must have been the doctor himself, and through him a government department, who organized everything. A family was found in Barry, near Cardiff in South Wales, on the edge of the sea, with fresh air and healthy winds, who were anxious to find their fortune in London, and so while they inherited a prefab, we took over a small terraced house in a strange land.

It was a monstrous upheaval for my father. He had recently taken a job at Smithfield, the meat market, training in every aspect of the butcher's trade and starting, aged nearly forty, at the bottom, as a heaver of crates. He was planning to go into business himself, and he had now perforce to change into fast gear so as to establish himself in Wales on what little experience he brought from London. For Colin it was a release. He hated Wilson's (because I was there) and had not yet completed one year, so the prospect of a new school in Barry, and of being himself, far removed from my shadow, was doubtless exhilarating. But for me it was quite otherwise.

I had just begun my own new life, the liberating tonic of sixth-form study, and I was, moreover, destined (so it was hinted to me) to be School Captain in my final year. It would be madness to throw all that up in order to be with my family in South Wales. Besides which, the house was tiny, and there would not be room for me as well as my brother. It was absolutely obvious, thank God, that I could not, *must* not go, and I do not recall any argument about it. I would have to live alone, at the age of sixteen and a half, and make the best of things. Bob Cummings, who had just gone up to university, offered me a room with his family in Dulwich. His father was a retired policeman, his mother a busy, neurotic housewife, an older sister had married, and a younger sister was in the house. I would have my own room, and take meals with them. To me the house appeared vast – indeed I think it still might, as those Dulwich residences were built for bourgeois families who wanted to advertise their success. But I was happy enough in my own room, which boasted a real bed with wooden headboard and footboard, as well as wardrobe and desk. Independence came to me early, and for that I was very grateful.

The Head, wishing to encourage me for being so brave and taking the decision to stay on despite great personal hardship (or so he thought), entered my name to represent the school in a competition run every year by the London County Council for a Rhodes scholarship. This Rhodes has nothing to do with the more celebrated American Rhodes scholarship which sent bright, earnest American students to spend a year at an Oxford college. This Rhodes was a successful businessman passionately keen on the future of Canada and anxious to make Canada's great qualities more widely appreciated. (Then, as now, it was peculiarly difficult to work up any enthusiasm for the country, which seemed like America asleep.) To this end, he determined that the best, most inquisitive and searching minds among Britain's youth should go to Canada at his expense and, when later they were rich, successful men of business, they would remember the experience and fight for Canada's interest. Schools all over the country sent one delegate each for interview at County Hall, and from all these, forty boys were chosen to represent the country. I was one of the lucky forty, a prize won, I suspect, on cheek and precocious charm, flirting my way forward.

It was a magnificent adventure, combining a passage on the Cunard liner *Sylvania,* escorted up the St Laurence by dozens of smaller ships, welcome committees in Quebec, Montreal and Toronto, with speeches from the mayor, red carpet laid out down the steps of the Town Hall, and motorcycle escort each side of our bus through the city, jumping every traffic light. Heady stuff for adolescents longing to be noticed. The high point was a weekend in a Red Indian camp in northern Ontario, in those days barely accessible to the outside world. By train for hours, then transfer to buses for a few more hours, and finally, when there were no more roads, by canoe through the wooded, hooting lakes to the tents made ready for us. We were up at five in the morning, we shaved at the lake's edge up to our knees in icy water, crossed rivers and burnt hundreds of leeches from our white skinny legs, and were sent off by the Chief in magnificent head-dress. We felt we were treated almost as royalty.

But I had a personal connection, which I asked permission to honour. There were cousins whom I had never met in Toronto, and whom I should visit for one evening. My father's half-sister, Ruth, had been dumped in an orphanage and packed off to Canada at the age of ten. She had survived, flourished, married and given birth to five children, of whom the youngest, Carole Anne, was three years my junior. This was the clan to which I should be yielded in Toronto.

They had all assembled in one house, and spilled over into the backyard. My Aunt Ruth was facially so like my father that for the first time I felt the magic of the genes, the romance of descent from generation to generation. We did all come from the same tree after all. I did have a past, mysterious though it might be (Ruth and I only shared the line of Miriam Pink* her mother and my grandmother; her father was somebody called Frederick William Biggar). These reflections no doubt created a mood which was detected, and everyone became very fond of me as I of them. They took me to the station to reconnect with the other boys on the night train to Ottawa, and there were tears on the platform.

No sooner had we arrived in Ottawa than there was a telephone call for me. It seemed a matter of some importance, I was told. I took the heavy receiver a little gingerly, and discovered my Aunt Ruth in a state of some agitation. 'You've got to come back', she yelled, 'Carole is in a terrible state.' I explained that I was not free to break the programme whenever I felt like it, and I didn't feel like it anyway. I had to continue. 'Brian, I'm afraid for Carole if you don't come back one day. Just tell me you will. After England. I've already spoken to the doctor and there's no real objection to your being cousins, it'll be all right.' The penny dropped. This fifteen-year-old girl had convinced herself that she was in love with an eighteen-year-old stranger and would do herself a mischief if he did not promise to marry her. I was very relieved when the ship sailed eastwards across the Atlantic two days later.

Three years afterwards, when I had my degree and Carole Anne was a young lady, we went together to Paris and Berlin for a holiday, crossing the newly erected Berlin wall and getting lost in unlit No-Man's-Land on the eastern side as night drew in. We were nearly shot dead by a nervous East German guard who initially assumed we were his countrymen about to escape (*Achtung, Achtung. Was tun Sie da?*) and pointed a shaking rifle at my chest. The poor boy was no older than Carole herself, and there was sweat on his brow. Overcome with happiness, he escorted us to Checkpoint Charlie and our exit to the West. 'That was a close shave',

---

* actually Edith Marianne Pink according to records

said Carole, 'almost as dodgy as your shotgun engagement to me four years ago.' I had avoided all mention of her mother's telephone call, and was now grateful for her light reference to it. We have remained in touch ever since.

In Paris we stayed in the cheapest possible hotel for down-and-outs on the Left Bank, where to save yet more money we slept in the same room. One night a cosy cuddle took place, though I was still terrified of any close encounter and certainly did not want to *look*. The resulting chaos caused her to doubt her appeal and me to question my ability, and finally both of us to collapse in laughter. The following day, however, I was less ready to laugh at myself. The fact that I was taking so long to mature was a serious matter, and made me wonder whether I might not be queer in the end. I had been waiting for some years already to 'grow out of' the narcissistic hand-held addiction, and to be stuck with it still at twenty-one was no cause to rejoice. I was worried, not only because it would help me plan the future if I knew what sort of man I was, and because the life of a queer was extremely solitary in the 1950s, hedged in by fierce hatred and prejudice, both of which were supported and encouraged by the law. The young today would scarcely believe it possible that the word 'homosexual' was never seen fit to print anywhere, save in a medical journal; the newspapers talked only of 'unnatural acts' and to propose such an act was to 'interfere with' somebody. Until the law reforms of 1967 policemen had the right to demand your address book and scrutinize the number of men mentioned therein – an above-average total was suspicious; they might then sift through your correspondence, and any letter from a man signed 'love' was likely to lead to questioning at the station, arrest, imprisonment, and the pursuit of your friends to their ruin. It was nightmarish. No one wanted to be queer (the word 'gay' was not in currency), and I clung fervently to the hope that I would not be.

A full account of sexual trial and error is unnecessary. Tony M. offered me his sister Joan's mouth for fellatial purposes in the air-raid shelter when I was seven and she about five, and I shrank from that. There was a ludicrous attempt at penetration when I was ten, behind a lorry in Herring Street, which lasted until somebody came round the corner and both I and the girl ran away in opposite directions. A man sat next to me in the cinema when I was twelve and proceeded to produce an enormous member, shielded by his coat, which he invited me to touch. Again I ran as fast as I could. Fumblings at school were never more than that, and during my friendship with Bernie the delicious novelty of an arm over one's shoulder or thighs touching on the bench awoke feelings far more mystical than sexual arousal could ever match.

There had been, however, one involvement which surely set the pattern, though I did not recognize it as such until it had vanished. When I was School Captain I made something of a joke of the power invested in me. The Prefects' Room, over which I presided, I repainted in red, as near the colour of blood as I could manage. Over the door I inscribed *Abandonate ogni speranza Voi ch'entrate*, which boys were invited to translate to escape punishment. And I tended to give tedious lines rather than physical punishment because I knew that I did not hurt anyone, yet did not know why my arm was drained of all strength. The boys knew it was worthwhile to find me alone, when they would not risk being beaten by one of my more muscular subordinates. One boy in particular went much further.

His name was Roy, a cheeky, self-possessed, argumentative fourteen year-old. He was always in trouble, and delighted in spending up to an hour with me in the Prefects' Room debating whether or not he deserved punishment as we together analysed his crime, his character, his capacity for mischief, the likely consequences of his being pardoned, and eventually my character, my suitability for the position I held, my feelings of foreboding whenever I knew that he was about to be sent to me. We each gave the other the enormous flattery of attention, and quietly, in utter ungoverned ignorance on my part, we were falling in love. I was seventeen by then, and should have known better. Roy, the youngster, seductive, coquettish, knew exactly what he was doing, and I do not think for a minute that there was any ignorance on his side. He was determined to capture me, whether I was aware or not of what was afoot, and he was perfectly single-minded about it.

On Sundays I worked at the Express Dairy opposite Victoria Station for eight hours, with a break on the top floor for lunch, for £1. My job was to clear the tables, stacking the dirty crocks on a trolley which I then emptied in the kitchen. It was a big cafe seating up to 100 people and it was important to keep the tables moving, i.e. keep them clean and ready for the next lot of customers. (Once I was put behind the counter to pour out tea, and instructed how to get twenty cups of tea out of a single teaspoon by constantly topping the teapot up with water.) Somehow Roy found out where I worked, and turned up to see me. I asked the manageress's permission to sit with him at his table when I had cleared all the others, and we sat talking for three hours without a break. It was only when the kitchen reported that they had no crockery left that I looked around and saw every single table piled high with dirty plates and cups, knives and forks, dried egg, cold bacon, a hopeless nasty mess. It was enough to put anybody off going to the Express Dairy again, and I wonder I was not sacked on the spot. The Manageress must have been a very intuitive lady. Anyway, that was the moment I realized I was besotted. It was an uncomfortable as well as a thrilling sensation, rather like being under siege.

For weeks thereafter we visited one another in the evening, sometimes spending every Saturday and Sunday together, and keeping up the pretence of indifference by his calling me by my surname at school. We seemed unable to spend a moment apart, as if we were being melted and fused. It was both an exhilarating and a frightening experience, quite new to me, and it inevitably sought tentative sexual expression in time. Whereas Fane's had been an affectionate friendship, Roy's grew insidiously, before I could notice, into an obsession. I did anything to ensure his favour. He dumped me as soon as he had drained me of self-respect, and turned his flirtatious attentions elsewhere. He taught me how to smoke, how to distrust, how to despair. He also ought to have shown me who I was, but I persisted in refusing the image in the mirror, pathetically clinging to the assumption that I would 'grow out of' this nonsense. Thus when, three years later, I found myself inviting my cousin Carole to take a holiday with me, it was in the hope that we might, after all, somehow become a couple. I expected 'normality' to flow artlessly from 'ordinary' circumstances. But I lacked the will for it. She must have been perplexed and befuddled. I think now, even more than I did then, that it was very good of her to laugh about it.

Before I take leave of Wilson's, there is one other event which curiously knits together all these disparate meanderings, although it was not related to any of them directly. It has to do with my pursuit of the famous, with my abandonment of London, with my intellectual ambitions. It, too, changed the course of my life forever.

Once I was established in the sixth form I conceived the plan of launching a new school magazine. The existing one, naturally called *The Wilsonian*, was an unmitigated bore, with leaden accounts of football matches and uninspiring posed photographs of cricket teams. There was not a single sentence of fun or amazement. I approached Sid Lee, who, never having had before to cope with an initiative, fussed for a few minutes and finally assented because he could think of no good reason not to. 'But you'll have to produce the thing yourself, Masters', he said. 'I mean, the school cannot afford to subsidise this venture of yours, however worthy. The most we can do is let you use our Roneo machine.'

The Roneo machine was in the secretary's office. You typed on a carbonated sheet which left impressions on plastic which could then be run through the machine once for each copy. It was laborious and had to be done after school hours, but at least it felt akin to printing a real newspaper. I commissioned poems and travel pieces from other boys, but I knew that in order to recover the costs of the Roneo and the paper and the staples, I would have to provide something of interest to the teachers, and they were manifestly hard to shift. The magazine, to be called *The Speaker*, was priced at 3d (just over 1p in today's money), and could not survive solely on boys begging from parents, especially as the number of boys who would even bother was sadly limited. So the staff had to be woken up somehow. I thought a celebrity in-depth interview might do the trick, and it would have to be a celebrity who never gave interviews in the normal course. I had to make the magazine a subject of discussion.

My experience hunting for autographs in the old days made me less likely to be shy than somebody trying it for the first time. So I wrote boldly to Gilbert Harding.

I am certain that anyone under fifty reading this will not know who Gilbert Harding was. Even a fifty-five-year-old might have to scramble his memory to see why the name rings a bell. He died in 1960, but in the two decades before that he was the one person whom everybody in the country knew; even those who forgot the names of politicians, band-leaders, film stars, war heroes, soldiers and popes all knew, and in their differing ways, cherished Gilbert Harding. You would have to be without a wireless (radio) not to be aware of him. Every morning after nine, he started the day's broadcasting with a programme of record requests called *Housewife's Choice* (there were no early morning news programmes, it being assumed that the public would never stand for their breakfast being spoilt by *news*). Twice a week he could be heard on a general knowledge quiz programme called *Round Britain Quiz*, or another – *Twenty Questions* – of which he was Chairman; and in the infancy of television six years after the war, he was one of the team of four on *What's My Line?* who had to work out the occupation of a contestant based on a piece of mime and their own deductive questioning.

All of which sounds depressingly trivial. Indeed, he called himself a 'tele-notoriety' and secretly despised the way he earned his living. He was truly the first ever Television Personality, a man celebrated for being himself. But with all radio and television programmes going out 'live' in those days there was an immediacy of contact between Harding and the audience 'out there' which tapped into deeper wells than the entertainment provided might appear to justify. Everyone felt he knew what kind of man Harding was, since his qualities could not be disguised by editing or direction. He was affectionate and soft, but with a gruff, impatient manner and a voice so authoritative and stentorian that he commanded sudden silence and respect. He seemed to be extraordinarily well-educated, with a knowledge wide in scope and rich in memory and allusion, a man intellectually far above the role he was condemned by fame to play. He could also be very short-tempered, appallingly rude, and quite often drunk. It was said that contestants on *What's My Line?* trembled with fear of what he might say to them, and it took all the Chairman's tact to keep them from bursting into tears. When he was drunk on the air he insulted everyone within earshot, bumbling on about their stupidity or crassness, with distraught producers not knowing how on earth he could be stopped. He might be withdrawn from his programmes for a few weeks by way of punishment, but the clamour for his return could not be resisted. He was phenomenally popular, because he was honest and unpredictable; what you heard was what you got, the real thing, not a blown-up confection. He was remorselessly genuine when the age of the fraud was just beginning. Just as producers did not dare contradict him, so the public at large knew better than to get in his way.

It was thus tacitly understood that in the whole country the two people whom one could not ask for interviews were the Queen and Gilbert Harding. In writing to him, I committed a monumentally reckless act.

Two days later, I was in the Lower Sixth doing Latin when the Headmaster's secretary knocked on the door. She came in and announced that there was a telephone call, for Masters. All heads turned, and I blushed to the point of eyes pricking with embarrassment. In Camberwell in the mid-1950s, nobody had a telephone, and no schoolboy ever received a telephone call. There was nowhere to take it anyway. Except, that is, for the Headmaster's study, for his was the only telephone in the building. I marched up to his room, and held the heavy black receiver in my hand as I stood in front of the seated Mr Lee, who thus heard half of the following conversation:

GH: Well, boy, when are you coming to see me?

Self: Whenever you say, sir.

GH: What about tomorrow afternoon, for tea? That do?

Self: I'm sure, sir. Yes, sir. Thank you, sir.

GH: Podge will tell you how to get here. 4 o'clock.

Podge was Harding's personal assistant, secretary, trouble-shooter, soother and punch-ball, Roger Storey, who proceeded to give instructions as I wrote them down on the back of my exercise book. I was to go to a flat in Weymouth Street, in the West End behind BBC Broadcasting House, which I could get to on a Number 12 bus.

When I put the phone down, Sid Lee tapped his fingers together and looked at me sternly. 'Am I to understand', he said, 'that you have chosen to represent this school with Mr Gilbert Harding without my knowledge or permission?'

'Well, sir, I didn't really think he would telephone, and I was going to tell you afterwards if he did.'

'*Tell me*, Masters? Don't you mean *Ask me,* and that *before* the event?'

'You might have refused, sir. Sorry, sir.'

'Of course, you have to keep the appointment', said Sid, pondering. 'I will not have it said that a Wilson's boy lacks manners, even when, as in your case, he lacks respect. I shall write a personal note to Mr Harding, which you will show him before your interview begins.' He then wrote a letter and allowed me to read it before he sealed the envelope. It said *This boy comes to you without the consent of his Headmaster. If you choose to show him the door I shall heartily concur.* With this bomb ticking in my pocket, I left the Head's study convinced that I should be soundly humiliated on the morrow.

The West End was no longer a total mystery to me, and I had known Broadcasting House since the days of catching people who were *In Town Tonight* as they emerged from the whimsical art nouveau building. But I had never explored the posh streets behind, part of the Portland Estate in the possession of Lord Howard de Walden and including such resonant names as Harley Street, Wimpole Street and Cavendish Square. Gilbert lived in Weymouth Street, almost on the corner of Great Portland Street, and thither I went, nervously clutching my school cap and that rotten letter. The entrance up some stairs from the street revealed a hall into the centre of which descended a magnificent slow old lift, of the kind Katherine Hepburn inhabited during many scenes of *Suddenly Last Summer*. The flat was on the third floor. I clanked my way out of the lift and found before me a highly-polished, imposing mahogany door, with brass knocker and letter-box. Absurd to reflect, I had not seen mahogany before, and that bold, proud door seemed to be making a personal statement to me. First, it told me that I was going to have to be careful what I said once I had crossed the threshold. Second, it promised a new direction. Something was about to happen.

The door opened and there was Mr Storey, an agreeable, fey young man, efficient yet also protective. He wanted to reassure me that I would not be eaten in one gulp, and did so with a smile and grace that made me know, without words, that I should have an ally. He took me into the sitting-room, where deep comfortable chairs and the most gigantic television set indicated comfort and status. On the other hand, there was nothing pretentious or especially valuable to be seen; it was the room of an unimaginative Oxford don, pleasant, soothing, slightly soporific. Roger offered me a cup of tea. 'Mr Harding won't be long, he's on the telephone at the moment, so I'll leave you here.' The tea came, on a tray, with a little jug for milk and a little pot for sugar, all matching, and all, to me, frightfully special, and I had the impression that Roger would get into trouble if he didn't immediately go back to wherever Harding was and attend to him; I also thought he would be quite able to stand up for himself and would not easily be bullied. He was the sort of man who would terminate a row with the remark 'There'll be tears before bedtime', and walk away. All this was clear in the first ten minutes, as I sat alone sipping my tea and watching the announcer Sylvia Peters filling in gaps between programmes on the television. I could hear the deep rumble of Harding's presence, the bassoon drum voice and its earthquake potential, coming from a room nearby.

Eventually the voice was raised. '*Boy!*' it shouted. I started to arrange myself, position my tie, stroke my hair, and prepared to follow the voice, when Roger came in to summon me and lead the way. I entered a dining-room, dominated by a mahogany table (again highly polished) laden with four telephones, a budgerigar in a cage, a plate, a toast-rack, cup and saucer, paper and pen, three or four newspapers. At the end sat Gilbert, almost occupying the width of the table, talking on one of the telephones and, at the same time, studying me with a beady eye through heavy spectacles as I stood there. Without interrupting his conversation, which was packed with anger and vituperation, he waved at me to come and sit in the chair on the long side of the table, to his left and at right-angles to him. I did as I was told. He pushed the toast-rack towards me and motioned that I should help myself. Thinking it polite to refuse, and not feeling remotely hungry, with a dry mouth and tight stomach, I motioned back, and he looked so furious that I forced myself to nibble a slice. He was in a dressing-gown, and I suddenly realized that this was his breakfast. It was four in the afternoon.

When he finished the telephone conversation, he turned to me and immediately related a piece of high-positioned gossip, which he must have known would impress and flatter me with confidence. It was also rather dirty, though I forget why, and Roger, standing by the door, threw me a glance of complicity and reassurance. Then Gilbert made the first of his magnificent gestures: he took all four telephones off the hook. 'There', he said, 'now we shall not be disturbed, and the next hour is all yours.'

The second gesture followed. 'I take it you do not write shorthand', he said, eyebrows raised in half-questioning mode. I admitted that I did not. 'In that case', he said, 'I shall dictate my answers very slowly, so that you can get every word, and you can stop me when you like if you need to catch up.' That this man with the fearsome reputation should be so solicitous and considerate endeared me to him right away. But he had not finished. I told him that it was my duty to give him a letter from my Headmaster before anything else, and handed it to him across the table, mindful of the fact that he had been a schoolteacher before becoming a broadcaster, and wondering whether the content of this letter might change his conduct towards me. He read it to himself, not knowing, of course, that I already knew what it said. Then he placed it back in the envelope and pushed it aside. He looked me straight in the eye and said, 'Your Headmaster tells me you come here entirely on your own initiative. I congratulate you.'

Relief relaxed me, and the graciousness of the man conquered me there and then. I knew that he could not be the ogre of public legend, I felt there was a sweetness and vulnerability in him somewhere, and I knew that he would have my loyalty; at that time I had no idea I should ever see him again, but he could ask anything of me, and I would do my best to serve.

The interview was doubtless banal (I still have it in a drawer somewhere), but Gilbert made it as important to him as a meeting with Winston Churchill or the editor of *The Times*. More so, for he would not have taken so much care to put either of those gentlemen at their ease; they could look after themselves. When it was over he told me some more funny stories, some of which were over my head, and he could see that I was struggling to fit in, to tune myself on a wavelength utterly foreign to me. The best thing he did was not to ask me to tell him any stories, as he knew that I would flounder and disgrace myself. That was the teacher in him, as I was subsequently to discover more deeply – his was the role of imparting, mine the role of listening and learning. I mentioned that my parents had moved to Wales and that I was living in digs. 'That's good', he said, 'you can come and see me again. Call Podge, and he'll arrange it.'

This was difficult to resist, but resist it I did. It would have been importunate of me to take him at his word too soon, yet the enticement of exchanging Dulwich and digs for a spot of glamour at the BBC would eventually pull me once more across the river. I waited four weeks, then sent Mr Harding the account I had written of our conversation. When I telephoned from a call-box on Camberwell Green, ostensibly to check that he had received it, Podge answered with audible enthusiasm, saying that Mr Harding would consider it an honour if I would visit again. This happened three or four times, until I realized why Podge was as enthusiastic as Harding himself. He told me in confidence one day that he was devoted to Harding and dealt with all his mail as well as his appointments, professional engagements, and health, but that it was an exhausting job, without respite for seven days, and he sometimes didn't get home until after one in the morning (he had a flat in Great Tichfield Street, a hundred yards away) because Gilbert was so demanding. He needed to talk, and craved company. He also needed somebody to be close at all times to administer oxygen, which was carried in a huge orange cylinder, four feet high and eight inches across. This was to rescue him from attacks of asthma or what sounded like emphysema, because Gilbert smoked incessantly and drank enough to keep a battalion merry. I later found out that he did both on purpose, precisely because they were harmful. Anyway, Roger would welcome a week off, and I was the only person Gilbert would put up with to take his place. It was therefore arranged that during the holidays I would move into the guest room at Weymouth Street for up to a week and take over Roger's duties as far as possible, excluding the typing of letters, which would be allowed to accumulate. (I did, however, send out his standard postcard to all fan mail, which said 'Dear Blank, I wish I thought as much of me as you appear to do. Yours sincerely, GH'. I also saw him receive a Christmas card from, say, Richard Attenborough, and scribble 'and GH' at the bottom before sending it off to somebody else.)

I was meant to answer the telephone and confer with Gilbert before passing it on to him. I could not disturb him when he was asleep, usually until midday, no matter who it was wanted him. I made cups of tea, occasionally cooked breakfast, and accompanied him to lunch at the Grosvenor House or the Savile Club, where he would embarrass the world, and nobody more than me, by insulting the waiters, refusing the wine, gossiping loudly about people present, and finally falling down. I did not know how to stop him, and any suggestion from me, still only seventeen, that he might not want another whisky would cause him to order two and glare at me defiantly as he drank them. And there was always the cylinder of oxygen, which accompanied us in taxi-cabs and to television studios. More than once, coming home from the studio after *What's My Line?*, Gilbert would say he was going for a pee and would I get glasses ready on the kitchen table, and I would wait five minutes and begin to wonder, then find him collapsed in the corridor, his face blue and gasping. Having given him oxygen, he then wanted only to go to bed, but I could not lug that mighty carcass, like a stranded walrus, any further than the bedroom door, and would wait there with him until he summoned the strength to haul himself upwards and help me get him on to, if not actually in, the bed.

It was of course intoxicating to be in a television studio and to be greeted by the regulars, once having a brief chat with the great Tony Hancock, but the real treat of the evening, and the lasting influence on my life, came afterwards at the kitchen table. There for perhaps two hours the most distilled and precious part of my education took place. He sat perilously on a kitchen chair which I always feared would break under his tormented and inebriated weight, and would instruct me, first, how to make eggs and bacon (the clue, which I have never forgotten, was to fry the bacon in its own fat, which had to be cut off first and fried longer). While I was cooking, he was opening a fresh bottle of whisky, which it would take him the allotted two hours to drink, and washing down an alarmingly high number of sleeping pills, one of which would have been sufficient to knock out a normal man. They did not work on him as they should have done, so he would take another, and another, until they finally did. As he sank progressively into torpor, his mind was paradoxically freed from restraint (I suppose the effects of alcohol and depressants fighting for supremacy, the alcohol winning). I would sit opposite him, also with a small whisky, and listen.

Gilbert was a teacher of genius. His enthusiasm for the subject under scrutiny transformed his voice and his manner, like a great actor warming up for a part. Indeed, he reminded me at times of the great Donald Wolfit, whom I think he knew and admired, stomping the stage and crashing chandeliers with his vocal power. Gilbert's neighbours had to thump on the wall to warn him of the disturbance, which he treated with disdain. There was a huge element of showing-off in this, but I am convinced that a teacher who does not have the knack of showing off is a teacher without wit. It requires panache to recite the whole of the first act of *Hamlet* from memory, as Gilbert did, taking each part himself, then to reduce one's power for the tender, controlled sadness of A.E. Housman's verse, and to lift it again for a magisterial account of the coronation ceremony of Elizabeth II, which had taken place only two or three years before, and which he had witnessed (perhaps even commentated for a radio programme) and committed to memory. I swear on that occasion there were trumpets in his voice and cymbals in his eyes. Unforgettable. He had a rare appreciation of the modalities of poetry, the point of scans and emphases, the music of the word, the broad fluidity of the phrase, and being something of a ham, his lips would tremble at the right moments. But a ham is not a fraud, he is an exaggerator. Exaggeration may demonstrate the architecture of a sentence, the rotundity of a vowel, the crisp clip of a consonant, the beauty of the whole structure. Listening to Gilbert Harding at his kitchen table night after night was like a crash course at the Royal Academy of Dramatic Art coupled with private tuition from the Oxford scholar Maurice Baring.

The question arises, why was Gilbert not himself a great scholar, since he had such breadth of knowledge and enjoyed sharing it? I think his tragedy was a determination to fail. He told me that he had not worked at Cambridge for the three years he spent there ('frittered my life away', he said ruefully), and only mugged up for the exams in the last week. He came away with a miserable Third Class degree, which was shameful for a man with a First Class mind and sad for his mother, who had worked herself to illness in order to pay for him to go there. He could never see himself as worthy of such sacrifice, and therefore made himself unworthy, in accordance with just deserts. He became famous in spite of himself, in spite of a measured route towards nonentity. By the same token, I realized my value to him. He wanted more than anything in the world that I should not waste my time as he had done, that I should work for a good degree, that I should succeed where he had failed. I was to be his redemption.

The kitchen table seminars were supplemented by tiny tips and reproaches throughout the day, insignificant in themselves but pregnant with the potential to embarrass. I once answered the door to find Marlene Dietrich, who was coming to tea, and I was so confused I hardly knew what to do or say. Somehow I stammered the accursed banality, 'I'm very pleased to meet you', which infuriated Gilbert, looming down the corridor behind me. 'You're nothing of the sort', he boomed. 'You cannot be pleased because you don't know the lady. You might be pleased to have met her, but you must wait to find out. Don't anticipate. Say "How do you do?" and be done with it.' I could have done without such a lesson in front of such a person, but it worked. Gilbert used discomfort to latch on to a memory and hold it fast.

I had the afternoon off. 'Where are you going today, then?' asked Gilbert, in benevolent, gentle mood. 'I'm going to see a relative.' The mood switched abruptly, a frown darkened his brow, his eyes flashed and his moustache bristled. 'Don't talk to me in that slapdash manner', he said.

'Sorry, Mr Harding, but I am. It's my Aunt Ethel in Brixton.'

'I don't care what her name is', he thundered, 'nor where the wretched woman lives, but I do care that you should speak of her correctly. Whatever else she may be, she is certainly not an adjective. You cannot visit an adjective, whereas you can, and will, visit a noun. She is your *relation*.' That, too, is lodged in my head, unbudgeable. With these and countless other instructions, sometimes hurled like the lash of a whip, sometimes whispered with an avuncular twinkle, Gilbert taught me to be precise in language, the better to convey true meaning rather than an approximate impression, to be careful, to be spare, to be resonant. Merely to hear him speak, with the panache of Dr Johnson and Gibbon's rich rotundity of phrase, made one long to make music with words, to carry conviction by matching harmony of sound and balance with acuity of expression. Words jumbled in sense or syntax were such an affront to him that he would physically flinch, and when I did offend, I felt I had hurt him.

Gilbert Harding wrote nothing of value himself. Some newspaper columns in the less demanding tabloids, usually dictated to and typed out by Roger Storey, an introduction to an anthology of verse, a lightweight autobiography entirely ghosted by someone else, were all that he managed to leave to posterity, and I would be surprised if any of them were ever consulted today. Such study would yield little. Yet his mind was brilliant, his understanding perceptive, and even if he was by no means an original thinker he was certainly an interpreter far more inspiringly robust than any host of television book programmes today. Had he applied himself, he might have been the Melvyn Bragg of yesteryear, with less verbosity. But application was what he lacked above all things. He was essentially, lamentably lazy.

The laziness was not wilful, however; it was the result of an emotional blockage, a psychological rampart thrown up by that same self-loathing which made it impossible for him to succeed in anything vital. He felt he did not deserve to, and therefore made sure that he would not. Sadly, the audible manifestation of this self-loathing was, as so often happens with displacement, its opposite – an apparent contempt for people less clever than himself. This is why he was reprimanded for his rudeness to defenceless contestants on the radio, why he shockingly abused frightened waiters and telephone operators, why finally, in the famous *Face to Face* interview with John Freeman (about which more later), he was accused of sadism.

Gilbert did enjoy his verbal assaults and appeared to pay so little heed to the injuries he inflicted that he might be supposed to enjoy the pain he caused as well. But he didn't. He was mortified when he realized, in sobriety, what he had done, and being a Roman Catholic (convert, I believe), he enjoyed the mortification even more than the sin. I was staying the weekend at his Brighton home, a Queen Anne villa in Montpelier Terrace, when Hector Bolitho, then a prolific popular historian, came to dinner. (Gilbert never cooked, by the way, and Podge was never asked to, besides which Podge guarded his weekends as far as possible for himself. The cook in Brighton was called Joan.) As we went into the dessert, Gilbert was warming up. He devoted almost twenty minutes to berating and humiliating me in front of Bolitho, whom I had not met before, until I was fit to collapse. 'This boy here has the temerity, the cool upstart effrontery, to imagine that he can go to university, when he can barely write a sentence. I've told him that university is for men of proven intelligence, not for cockney louts, but the message will not get through. He is stubborn, petulant, ignorant and cocky, and he ought to stay in the Old Kent Road where people of his level belong. But we now have education for the masses, and here is the result, sitting with us at this table. Do you know, he has never heard of Molière, and he has the cheek to say he is going to study French Literature? French poppycock!'

There was much more in this vein, on the face of it a heartlessly cruel attack. He was sophisticated and well-known, sitting with a friend of his own age, equally sophisticated and successful. I was an unformed, socially inept, partially-educated, shy and leaden seventeen-year-old. The frustration welled up in me until I had to make an excuse to leave the table. I went into the next room, leant my forehead on the mantelpiece, and wept copiously. Bolitho found me there shortly afterwards and consoled me. 'Don't take it to heart', he said. 'We have all seen Gilbert behave badly, and all too often, I'm afraid, but we know he is punishing himself more than anyone else. He means you no harm. He wants you to do well. Try to put up with it, for his sake.'

He did not need to tell me. Even as I stood there racked with sobs, knowing rationally that I was not a prisoner, that I need not stay and tolerate such treatment, that I had a return ticket to London in my pocket, I knew that I would not desert this tormented and derelict man. I was not forced to like him – on the contrary he seemed to do all he could to ensure my distrust – but despite all evidence I knew that he needed loyalty. It would have been cruel on my part to make him face the enormity of what he was doing, using his position and weight to undermine the confidence of a growing boy.

At breakfast the following morning (it may have been a different occasion, but the script was similar), I sat opposite Gilbert at the round table in the window with its sunny view of the whole back garden, and he looked unbearably contrite. After some bluster about the toast (directed at Joan) and the folly of politicians (directed at the wall), he lowered his voice and said, looking straight at me with piteous mien, 'I know how I behaved. You do not have to say anything to remind me. But please, always, remember one thing. Whenever you are disposed to despise me, remember that nobody could despise me more than I do myself.' The word 'despise' has ever since carried for me a particularly powerful spell. It is a word I use very rarely indeed.

There were occasions when Gilbert would rescue me from a social gaffe instead of relishing it. One such was the day when I committed my most awful *faux pas*. There were to be three of us to lunch, Gilbert, myself, and Peter Daubeny. 'Now let me tell you about Daubeny', he said as we waited for him to arrive. 'Peter is a theatre producer, what is nowadays called an impresario, which means he puts plays on in London. Married with three children, very nice man, good-natured, easy to get along with. He won't frighten you. Only one thing you must not mention.'

'What's that?'

'His arm.'

'Why not?'

'Because it's not there, that's why not. Shot off in the war. Feels so bitter about it that he refuses to have a false arm fitted, and won't even roll the sleeve up. It hangs there empty, dangling in the wind, as a permanent reminder of his loss. So please don't refer to it at all.'

'No, of course. Thank you for warning me.'

Lunch was enjoyable for me as long as I sat listening. These two men knew everyone of consequence and much that was happening behind the headlines in the newspapers and in the theatre. They had a lot to say of interest. But gradually, as the minutes ticked by, I became aware that I would be expected to contribute something or other, even if I had nothing to say of interest and knew nothing of the subjects under discussion. Gilbert would be furious if I stayed mute. I waited for a pause in their conversation, which was a long time coming, and when it did come I knew it would offer me barely a few seconds in which to strike. I thought quickly. What does he do? He's an impresario. I know. I'll ask him the name of the play he is going to put on next.

'Oh, Mr Daubeny', I said, feeling worldly and nonchalant. 'What have you got up your sleeve for your next production?'

I have no idea what else happened that day. As the words slipped out of my mouth, I could hear them and knew at once that they were wrong, but I could not gather them up and plop them back down my throat. I felt myself falling overboard. Gilbert jumped in quickly and said something innocuous, diverting, and I knew he was saving my skin, and I felt profound gratitude for that. The story causes me to blush in recollection even now, and I did not tell it to Daubeny's widow, Molly, until forty years later. She roared.

When we were alone, either there was an impromptu lesson in Shakespeare or philology at the kitchen table, or Gilbert would become lachrymose. His devastating confession that he despised himself was both true and theatrical; he did believe he had been worthless, and he knew the admission would have a stunning effect. Like many a Roman Catholic he attached almost as much importance to effect as to substance, and his religion also encouraged copious use of his most useful prop – self-pity. He was much given to tears and self-abasement, and though they were not sham, his indulgence of them was exaggerated, for his own purposes and to his own benefit. He needed to chastise himself, and to be seen to be so doing. This is not to say the self-pity was unjustified. It was.

Gilbert had been born in a workhouse in Hereford where his mother was a cleaner. Widowed at twenty-seven with a daughter and son to bring up on virtually nothing in the lean years of the First World War, her difficulties were made more acute by the knowledge that her boy was unusually bright and ought to be given a proper education. She took in extra jobs and saved every penny to see that he got all the opportunities available to the better off, and even managed to pay for him to go to Cambridge when he was sixteen. Hence Gilbert's acute remorse at having wasted his time there and having let her down. But his guilt went deeper than that. His mother was always the person in the world whom he treated the worst, the one whom he insulted in the most dreadful language, the one who most bore the scorn of his rapier tongue. It is a truism that one saves one's worst behaviour for those whom one loves best, knowing that it will be forgiven. Gilbert was a prime illustration. He told me a story so distressing that it sounds contrived, yet I know it was wholly in accordance with his character.

Mrs Harding became smitten with cancer. Gilbert was devastated, and had her well looked after in hospital, visiting her daily, surrounding her with flowers and sweets and everything she might like. He made sure she had the best possible attention from the country's foremost experts, but she sank nonetheless, until the doctors felt it better to advise him not to visit. He arrived at the hospital one day to find his way barred. 'She won't recognize you', he was told, 'it will only upset you, to little avail. She is unconscious, and we do not expect her to be conscious again. It is better for you, Mr Harding, to retain your image of her as she was.' Gilbert was a big man, in size as well as reputation, and it was impossible to prevent him doing what he wanted. 'Get out of my way', he yelled, as he barged his way past the medical men and to his mother's room. There she lay breathing fitfully, her face already slightly black, a body waiting for the light of the soul to turn off. Gilbert was beside himself. 'Mother, mother', he shouted, 'Please don't die. You are all I have. You can't die now and leave me all alone, you can't, you can't.' At which point she unexpectedly opened her eyes slightly and looked at him. 'That's right, Gilbert', she said, 'you will think of yourself until the last.'

Those were her final words to the son for whom she had sacrificed her health, and I never began to imagine how he could have lived with them ever afterwards. By telling people, I suppose (I may not have been the only one to hear the story from his lips), and by flagellating himself with the words. Yet again, I saw why it was important to him that I should not undervalue the chances I had and the self-denial of my own parents to make those chances available. I was to relive his life, and do it better. I was the surrogate son.

It was general knowledge, especially within the BBC, that Gilbert's mother had died, and that Gilbert felt the loss acutely. And it was this very matter which made the 1958 *Face to Face* interview one of the most riveting in the history of television, as well as one of the nastiest examples of journalistic prurience. I was with Gilbert in the studio that day, carrying his oxygen. I saw his wounds being picked at in public, and travelled back with him to the flat in Weymouth Street afterwards. I think, in the end, he was glad it had happened, for he felt his punishment was now visible to all.

Freeman framed his questions to suggest that Gilbert Harding was a sadist whose various professions of school-teacher, policeman and television bully afforded him opportunities to demand obedience and inflict suffering upon those who resisted his authority. Gilbert deflected this with suave dignity, although the distinct tremble in his voice betrayed his discomfort at being probed in this manner; it was a novel situation for him. The shock came with Freeman's question, 'Have you ever seen anyone die?' Gilbert could not articulate a response. His lower lip shuddered, his voice was strangled, he muttered the tiniest sound to signify that he had, indeed, had that experience. His distress was patently obvious, yet Freeman went on. 'Only once?' he asked. Again Gilbert, close to breaking down, grunted something. Freeman pressed again. Finally Gilbert forced a shattered voice, plangent with grief, to say, 'Yes, only once, yes.' The whole country found it painful to watch, and impossible not to. John Freeman ever after claimed that he had not known that Mrs Harding was dead. Few believed him.

The *Face to Face* interview, which is available on tape, was the only time the public caught a glimpse of the real Gilbert carefully concealed beneath the blather of omniscience. They also heard a surprisingly sympathetic narrator in his recording of *Peter and the Wolf*, wherein the wolf was by no means the hero. One intimate corner of his life was rigidly sealed off, yet even this was touched upon by Freeman, rather boldly for that age, and honestly answered by Harding. Freeman asked him why he had never married. Instinctively, he found himself framing a banal answer to the effect that he would not have wished himself upon anyone, but then he hauled himself into the light, as if prodded by distaste for evasion, and came out with a momentous sentence. 'My mother', he said, 'was a widow at twenty-seven. My sister never married, I never married, and as we all lived together under the same roof, we set up a cloud of sexual frustration sufficient to blot out the sun.'

Gilbert's homosexuality was never acknowledged in his lifetime, and in any case it would have been somewhat of a misnomer. He was impotent and quite incapable of a sexual conquest of any kind. Largely the result of alcohol and pills, I am convinced that he secretly welcomed even this affliction as another measurement of the castigation he decided he deserved. I never felt threatened or anxious in his company. The most he ever asked was to sit on a wooden chair in the bathroom as I took a bath, and sometimes hand me a warm towel afterwards. He did not pounce, and I found his attention rather endearing.

The frustration that he admitted to the world on television was not the subject of any conversation between us. I believe he felt that would have placed a burden upon me which I might not have been able to deal with, and also that my admiration for him would have diminished (he was wrong at least in that). But it was implicit in all his dissatisfactions and regrets, in his weariness and impatience, in his terse dismissal of popular values and myths. He did not like life, and looked forward to the final consolation of God's embrace. One evening he told me that he had been to consult his doctor, who I think was Moran, Churchill's own doctor. 'He tells me that if I go on drinking and smoking at my present rate I shall drop dead of a heart attack, and he says I must cut down by half. Well, I'm not going to. I shall double it.'

He collapsed outside Broadcasting House as he was waiting for a taxi following one of his radio broadcasts. I am told he was dead before his body hit the ground. It was exactly as he would have wished. I was sorry only that he did not live to see that I got a First in French and Romance Philology a few months later. He would have teased me about it, he would have deflated any pomposity on my part, but he would have been happy.

My parents were bemused by this connection, which surely would have dribbled out in the normal way had they not moved to Wales. My lingering in London after their departure gave me that independence which made possible the continuation of what would otherwise have been a simple interlude in life. Dad was distrustful and suspicious, but too embarrassed to say anything. Mum only remarked that I had begun to 'talk posh'; she was, perhaps, afraid that I might become a stranger. They were often very much like the Garnetts in the TV series *Till Death Us Do Part*, grunts and shrugs being substituted for real communication. What my father really meant was that I had fallen into the clutches of the rich (everybody north of the river was 'rich' to him), and what my mother longed to say was that she did not want to lose me.

My acquaintance with Gilbert Harding spanned only the five years before his death at the age of fifty-three, and was not continuous. I would see him perhaps twice during term-time, then for a week or two in school holidays and university vacations, when we would coincide at the London flat for his broadcasts on Sunday and Monday, and he would go to Brighton on Tuesday, leaving me behind. His influence upon me was, however, far greater than these sporadic visits might suggest. He taught me precision in the use of language and respect for its grace and power. He taught me the glories and sweetnesses of great literature. He taught me that pride was self-defeating and demeaned the personality. He taught me the gentleman's virtues of restraint and polite social intercourse, and the wise man's gift of tolerance. And if this latter seems absurdly paradoxical in one who was famed for his ill temper, one can only say that a man's faults may not be his description. That, above all, is the lesson which endured – the recognition that each human being is a jumble of inconsistencies and contradictions, and that judgement of character must not isolate one trait of personality and ignore all the others. They blend sometimes, they conflict sometimes, they whirl around and fly off the edge, they are confusing and confused. But they represent the whole. If I was able to approach the job of biography with that spirit of detachment which made me want to comprehend both grace and wickedness and place them as part of the whole, it was partly because I had seen in Gilbert Harding that the easy, facile, superficial assessment is never the correct one.

CHAPTER 5

Montpelier

My mother once made a shattering statement. 'Do you know, Bri', she said, 'for three years you didn't say a word to me, no more than yes or no. You completely clammed up.' Taken literally, it seems scarcely believable that I should have been so crass, but I cannot deny that I was, for part of my teens, particularly surly in my behaviour at home in the prefab. There cannot be a reader who does not recognize the symptoms of adolescent introspection, an absorption so total that the world outside is practically cancelled unless it impinges upon the central matter of self. The emergence of personality, the acute awareness that one has become an object to be watched, scrutinized, found wanting, all combine to make getting through the day without mishap a major undertaking. I was forever nervous of being misunderstood (more properly now I realize I was afraid of being understood, of being laid bare), suspicious of being prevented from doing something or forced into obedience, resistant to advice, and above all convinced that my parents could not possibly know me, and that I certainly did not wish them to. The privacy and secrecy of this weary passage into manhood are absolute.

So, it is true, I mumbled and was ungracious, looked at the floor, shook my head, pouted, shrugged and was generally tiresome. My father grew restive as he came to recognize that I was likely to be more stubborn than he, and that he could not shift me or master me easily. It made his stutter significantly worse. He began to panic. My mother, more resilient, more philosophical, and better able to reserve her resources rather than waste them upon a boring, self-regarding young man, ignored me unless I was actually rude. Home life became a struggle of wills, and my heart used to beat faster as I approached the front door, wondering how I should be questioned and how I should best be able to avoid answering. The family's move to Wales, and my taking digs in London, came as a release from tension, all generated by me and my sulkiness, me and my gloom, me and my arrogance. It was not only my education which benefited from this unplanned independence, but my father's self-esteem, my mother's health, and my brother's future stability.

The year I spent as School Captain of Wilson's polished my self-image as somebody who could, despite shortcomings, assume some dignity and integrity of purpose. It went to my head far too quickly, and dear Jad Parr had to whisper a gentle warning. It was to be Sid Lee's last year as Headmaster, so I conceived the pompous and rather unkind idea of giving him a send-off so emotional that he would find it hard to find a way of responding. I wrote to every School Captain who had served under him, some twenty men, by then scattered across the world, and asked them to send a word of greeting. I also organized a collection from the whole school to buy Sid a farewell gift, and we gathered enough to get a handsome piece of furniture which contained radio and gramophone. On the last morning assembly, I had this draped with a Wilson's flag, and, announcing that the Head was to retire, before allowing him to see his present, I read out all the messages from all his former boys. It was a kind of *This is Your Life* without the red book or the excitement. The poor old man was nearly reduced to tears, and I am sure he must have known that the cheers from the boys in front of him were alloyed with some hearty ridicule.

The new Head was to be a man called Norman Friskney. Although I should have gone up to university by then, I had some time free in September before term started, and volunteered to stay on at Wilson's for two weeks to help him get used to the place. Though I was allowed to stay on (I don't think I *asked* anybody whether I could, I *announced* that I would), Mr Friskney very sharply told me that he did not need any advice.

To be a first-year nobody at a distant university would do me a lot of good. I had by this time (after two years) grown tired of living in somebody else's house, and applied for University College, Cardiff, so that I could live with my family in Barry, a short way to commute, and be a little pampered. It was then that my mother made the observation with which this chapter opened, shocking me into a considered rumination which has never really stopped from that day.

There were only eight of us in the French and Romance Philology class at Cardiff, and we were very privileged. The Chair was occupied by Professor Heywood-Thomas, a frail, precise, kindly gentleman who made his department the most admired in the land. It was the only French department where every class, whether it be on literature, language, semantics or translation, was conducted in the French language. The corrections of a passage of prose had to be explained in French, and for three years we never once submitted an essay written in English. Not even Oxford and Cambridge demanded such a rigid absorption of cultural building-blocks.

Heywood-Thomas himself offered the best illustration of its value. He shuffled into the lecture-room, his gown hanging droopily from his elbows (we were naturally all required to wear black academic gowns at every lecture and in every class), visibly old in gait and diffident in manner, stooping, slightly shaking, thin white hair, white moustache, pince-nez spectacles. He did not appear to have the energy to get through an entire hour of talking. But as soon as he began, he underwent a startling metamorphosis. His back straightened, his hands raised high in the air, waving, gesticulating, or pointing like Kitchener out in front of his suddenly rejuvenated body, his eyes aglint, voice powerful and above all French. In fact, he became a Frenchman before us. 'Eh bien, aujourd'hui on va parler de Jean-Paul Sartre', he said, almost shouting, his lips pursed in the French manner, his enthusiasm intoxicating. There followed a wonderfully vivid exposé of Existentialism, painstakingly explained, packed with allusion and quotation and personal reminiscence, delivered with verve, vigour and panache. At the end, he would pour himself back into the old man's frame, resume his stoop, lower his voice, and shuffle out as if he did not quite know where he was going and would need help in getting there.

Bill Sullivan taught philology, Gallo-roman, the architecture of language, the history of words. Again, he was so enthusiastic about his subject that he was as thrilled to explain as a little boy might be to show off his train-set. He was also something of stand-up comic whose material, instead of mother-in-law jokes, was the surprising structure of words. After Jad Parr and Gilbert Harding, Sullivan contributed the final fix which made my interest in etymology an addiction. I never forgot the revelation that the word 'nice' derived from the Latin word *nescius*, meaning 'nasty', 'harmful', 'inimical', and that the highest rank in the French cavalry, *maréchal*, was originally the name given to the boy who held the horses. Bill Sullivan was almost a contemporary, no more than five years our senior, which made for an unmatched geniality in our sessions.

Then there was a woman, Thelma Morgan, unmarried, in her forties, an authority on Voltaire and given to what we thought was eccentric absent-mindedness but which turned out to be epilepsy. She might begin a sentence, then start moaning quietly, her eyes settled on some secret spot, her hand scratching the table rhythmically, the moans getting louder as if she would explode or collapse in front of us.

We always met in a seminar room rather than a lecture-hall (I realize now, so that she would not fall), all of us seated around a table with Thelma at the head. It did not take long for the others to make sure I was sitting next to her because they thought, erroneously, that being from London I would know what to do. They were alarming experiences, for we did not know how to help her, and gradually realized that help would not have been welcome. She would emerge from these ominous chanting trances after a few minutes to go on with her talk on Voltaire. All I ever did was make sure that she did not get up from the table to leave the room until she was fully recovered. Christine Spackman, today the wife of the United Nations expert on the fate of Venice, cowered in a corner.

There was an active political nest, as one would expect with the radical Welsh, and the Labour Party branch recruited a firebrand orator in my year called Neil Kinnock. I heard him speak, with flourish and verbosity, but we only met once, and that briefly, for I did not join any of the political clubs. My interests were still largely literary, and I proposed myself to the college magazine *Broadsheet* as a contributor. Yet again I relied on the editor's falling for the famous, and said I would get an exclusive interview with Bertrand Russell, then at the top of his popular reputation both for the constant reprints of his *History of Western Philosophy* and for his courageous support for those campaigning to get rid of nuclear weapons, which involved his being arrested and imprisoned despite his frailty (he was something over ninety). Russell held the view that as long as nuclear bombs existed it was only a matter of time before some demented or foolish human being would use one and put an end to the world we knew. (This is still true, though widely ignored.) In promulgating this view he wrote to and consulted with leaders in the Soviet Union, which at the time was construed as tantamount to treason, but he held to his conviction that reasoned argument must prevail and that one could hardly expect such a commodity, without help, from politicians. The students who controlled

Broadsheet did not think it likely that I would be allowed to interview him.

Through Gilbert Harding I got hold of Lord Russell's telephone number and called him from a box in St Mary Street, Cardiff. So passionate was he to warn the world against the disaster which loomed that he would disdain no opportunity to make his voice heard. He invited me up to his home near Penrhyndeudraeth, North Wales, about four hours' drive away. One of my colleagues in French had to go north that weekend and he dropped me in the village. Russell lived in a beautiful, rambling rustic house at the end of a long lane. He greeted me himself at the front door. 'You are living a very long way from London', I observed, thinking that perhaps I should commiserate with him, as if he had been exiled to this abandoned corner of the island. 'That is the whole point', he said, 'here I can think and work. In London one worries, but unproductively.'

Russell spoke with a mellifluous fluency which was beguiling. His voice was thin and high-pitched, and his vowel sounds came from another era when 'tea' was pronounced 'tay'. One was immediately aware that he was still a Whig, a left-over from the Whig ascendancy, for he spoke like a Whig and had the exquisitely polite manners of the landed aristocracy. His grandfather was the Prime Minister Lord John Russell, and his godfather was John Stuart Mill, born in the eighteenth century. It was an eighteenth-century voice I was hearing, with eighteenth-century emphases and intonations, and it was John Stuart Mill's sharp, precise prose to which the voice was giving expression. As Russell had sat on Mill's lap, in two generations we were leaping across two centuries.

I quizzed the great man about epistemology as the basis for moral perception in a way which I now find embarrassing to admit, but he was unfailingly obliging and answered every question as if it were important to think it through. After a pause of some six seconds, there would issue from that reedy voice a paragraph so perfectly framed and balanced, with subject, exposition, verbs beautifully placed and predicate pounding to an irresistible conclusion, that left me breathless. He talked in sentences, not in staccato jabs, in a way that I have only heard since in the conversation of Enoch Powell, and there but dimly by comparison. No wonder he had written so many millions of words, they flooded out ready-formed, they did not have to be dug out of an unwilling brain. Eventually I asked him if he worked hard on his books. He said all the work was done in his head over the years, getting the thoughts straight, but the writing was easy. 'I have been doing it for so long, I have acquired the habit, you know.' He could write a book of 30,000 words in little more than a weekend, and it would be a gem of perfect prose. He also could not prevent himself from thinking logically. Having offered me a cigarette, which I declined, he poured himself a whisky and sat down again to continue our conversation, in deep armchairs either side of a roaring country fire. After a while he realized I had nothing. 'I do beg your pardon', he said, 'I formed a rash inference from a single premiss, that you would be unlikely to drink if you did not smoke. An error, I confess.'

The Russell interview went down well on the whole, and it might have had an influence upon Neil Kinnock's decision to join the Campaign for Nuclear Disarmament, a commitment which in years to come would cause him some anguish. Thus are the tiny footnotes of history penned. It was hardly the journalistic scoop that I had hoped for, and when such a prize did beckon, I failed even to recognize it.

We must jump ahead a couple of years for this great clump of *naïveté*, and to Algeria. During my compulsory year of study in France, which I spent in Montpellier, I made the acquaintance of an Algerian student called Brahim Djotni with whom I used frequently to share meals at the Cité Universitaire canteen (the cost of a three-course dinner with bread and cheap wine was 100 old francs, i.e. 10p). He was politically well-informed, and would one day become Mayor of his home city Annaba, and our conversation daily turned upon events in Algeria, where France was waging a fierce and merciless war against insurgents. In 1960 the French still considered Algeria, across the Mediterranean on a different continent, as an integral part of France itself, not a colony but a province, and when the local Arab population rose in revolt against foreign rule, they were astonished at the impertinence. Resolving to put down the rebellion at once, Arab resistance kept them at war for many years, breeding bitter hatred on both sides. The commonest form of attack was to hurl a bomb into a queue at the bus-stop, or into a crowded bar, and run. I naturally heard a great deal of French resentment among students in Montpellier, but also from Brahim I learnt much about Algerian aspirations, and I was very keen to go and see for myself. The danger in such an undertaking did cross my mind, but did not obliterate the idea, and when Brahim told me I could stay with his family in the *casbah* of central Algiers, I knew I would have to go.

There are only two kinds of people in the world who know how to make a guest feel truly welcome, who will urge themselves to every endeavour to please him, who will reorganize their day to accommodate him. One is the American people, and the other is the Arabs. I could not have been treated with greater honour, invited to eat with the menfolk, learning how to belch (if you did not make a loud noise, it was thought you were displeased, so the polite thing to do was to burp), and taking part in a wedding which lasted two whole days ululating through the tight streets of the *casbah*, being showered with rose petals, and presenting oneself to the bride who sat demurely, eyes closed, with two attendants. She was not allowed to open her eyes until she was led into the marriage chamber and could finally discover whom she had married.

The one thing I was forbidden was to invite the daughter of the house to come and have a cup of coffee, an insult to her father and brothers which could have banished me from the house forever. Anyway, the point was that I found myself, a European, at the centre of Arab life, unmolested, perfectly safe, greeted with smiles and warmth

everywhere. Had I been French I should have been slaugh-
ered.

During my stay in Algiers there erupted the famous *coup
des quatre généraux,* when four military toughs – Challe,
Zeller, Jouhaud and Salan – grew tired of waiting for the
French government to have the guts to rid the world of
Algerian Arabs once and for all, and declared that they
would thenceforth be in charge, that they would wage the
war in their own manner and to their own liking. It was
a rebellion against order, and threatened to spill over into
mainland France itself, where it was rumoured that the
generals were planning an invasion to take over the reins
of government in Paris. Protective tanks encircled the capital
and preparations were made for civil war. (It seemed to some
as though the French were always at play, that they were too
immature for real war.)

The four generals did not last long, but the point for me was
this: Algiers for a short time was completely shut off from the
world. Journalists from half a dozen countries were desperate
to get in, and quite a few people were anxious also to get out,
but the military authorities would permit no travel at all. It is
easy for anyone to see that I was in a unique position. I was
there, I could describe what was happening, I was protected
by my friends in the *casbah*, I could gain access to people
normally kept hidden. With no London newspaper able to
send anyone to compete with me, I suppose I could have
written world scoops for *The Times*, had I been good enough,
and might have made my name. But it never occurred to me
to aim high. Yes, I did write four centre-page articles on the
experience, but I sent them to the *South Wales Echo,* which
could scarcely believe its luck, and I received £5 for each.

Broadsheet published two other interviews, one with Aneurin
Bevan, only months before his sudden death, and one with a
luscious British film star called Belinda Lee; she committed
suicide in her late twenties, for no obvious reason, and is now
obliterated from film memory as well. Other delights besides
journalism tempted me away from study. There was a chess

group which met regularly, evenings of dancing classes, in which one learnt how to guide a partner, how to hold her, how to inject fancy steps like 'the whisk' and 'the weave' into a plain waltz, how to anticipate the terribly tricky off-beat in the fox-trot. Dancing was a pleasure when there was a point to it and when one could make the acquaintance of a partner. There was a debating society, at which I never shone, and which recalls to my mind one of the silliest things I ever said. Ready to earn plaudits for the profoundity of my remark, I told the audience that nothing in life was a problem unless you made it so by excessive deliberation. It must have been my inane delivery which was at fault, for I attracted giggling derision, and was so ashamed that I blush now as I write this and revert to the self I was on that day.

The Dramatic Society consumed more spare time than any other activity. I had dabbled in stage work at Wilson's, playing Alceste in Molière's *Misanthrope* and Donal O'Donnelly in O'Casey's *Shadow of a Gunman*, but each was relentlessly amateur, and I was sure the boys only endured to the end because they had to. University College, Cardiff, however, had a solid reputation, and tickets for their productions were on public sale. Only two years earlier they had bred a true classical actress in Siân Phillips, so we had a great deal to live up to. After some shortish pieces by Ionesco including *La Cantatrice Chauve* (The Bald Prima Donna) performed in French, our big piece for the year was Sheridan's *School for Scandal*, in which the cast included Vincent Kane as Sir Peter Teazle and Keith Ward as Crabtree. With a voice so full of authority he could have played God and been thought typecast, Vincent went on to spend the whole of his career as a BBC presenter and political commentator. Keith Ward's future was less predictable. A brilliant mimic and stand-up comedian, with a mind so mercurial that he would be half-way through one story when another would occur to him and be slotted in forthwith, and so many adverbial clauses in his discourse that it was extremely difficult to keep up with him, he would find something hysterical in every circumstance and amongst the most serious reflections. His ideas were allusive, profound, demanding, stimulating and packed with surprise. Another of his interests was music, and he had the intention of studying to be an orchestral conductor once his philosophical studies were completed. In the end he followed none of these paths, and is now Regius Professor of Comparative Theology at Christ Church, Oxford, as well as an ordained clergyman, still challenging with unlikely conceits, and still laughing at himself.

It was Keith's idea that to publicise the play we should hire an eighteenth-century horse-drawn open carriage and parade through Cardiff in our costume. I think it did little but cheer us up, and of the performances we gave I have no vivid recollection. I played Joseph Surface, not too well and not too badly, but with sufficient indication of talent to make it clear I was not destined to be an actor.

Thus the first two years passed with the requisite amount of work and no more, yet I was determined eventually to heed Gilbert's advice and work hard in the final year. He would have been angry had I emerged from such an opportunity with a degree as poor as his had been. Before that, we in the French Department had an obligatory year to spend in France, where we should be placed as *Assistants d'Anglais*, taking three or four classes of English conversation per week in secondary schools. I applied for a post at Montpellier, a city unknown to me even by reputation, but which appeared on the map to be drenched in Mediterranean sun. It was a fateful choice. Forty years later, I am still spending five months in the year there. I write these words in a village less than ten miles away.

It was a long journey by train, changing stations in Paris (itself a maturing experience for one essentially still untried), and building an exhilarating anticipation as the smells and the colours and the sounds gradually assailed my senses. It must sound pretentious in an age of easy travel, but I assure you that when one is used to the smell of boiled cabbage and beans on toast and to the drab greyness of London or even Welsh air, my migration through the whole of France, from top to bottom, was an unparalleled adventure, like painfully shedding a skin and emerging from the débris freshly born with a new one. People ate freely in their seats, munching long *baguettes* stuffed with pungent sausage or impossibly reeking cheese, garlic oozing from their pores and impregnating their clothes, so that the entire train soon seemed like a massive fast-track salami. The powerful blast of a *gauloise* cigarette made even more potent through being inhaled through harsh red wine drove me into the corridor, which was still more crowded and smelly. But none of this did I mind. Quite the contrary; these, I felt, were the simple innocent portents of liberation. The future was opaque, but it was wide open. The rich, raw smells of France would enable me to breathe at last.

As we passed through the vineyards of Burgundy one felt in touch with antiquity, that those hills had been growing those vines since the time of Christ, and that nothing was more reassuring than the doing of things the way they had always been done. The onward roll of tradition and habit, so un-revolutionary, so cosy and heartening, held the gorgeous paradox of heralding change and renewal for me. No doubt the cockney traditions of London which had surrounded my infancy, and the Welsh traditions into which I had lately been thrown, were just as strong and just as exciting as those I was about to adopt, but I had not looked at them. They had been there, untouched and unobserved, part of the decor and the script, part of the definition of myself which I had accepted without challenge. That momentous train journey down the Rhône–Saône corridor into the southern light suggested to me, however idiotic it may sound, that I was about to become French.

It was the light especially which thrilled, and still does. The Mediterranean climate is hot, dry and invigorating, but it is not so much the heat which gives it such life as the astonishing clarity in the air. Even on a cool day in winter you have to shield your eyes against the glare of the limpid blue sky. The sun seems to be there, immediately above you, like a central ceiling light, bathing everything with life and enhancement and joyous illumination, whereas in England it had been like a dim single-watt bulb on a skirting-board, casting shadows and discouragement. As I descended the steep steps from the train at Montpellier station and walked out into that startling light, I knew I should never have difficulty getting up in the morning. The sky calls you out and embraces you.

The first few weeks were, however, lonely. I had been allocated (Heaven knows by whom) a small room in the rue Gustave, on the first floor, within sight of the majestic eighteenth-century elevated aqueduct known as *les Arceaux*. About six feet wide and ten feet long, the room held only a bed, a small table and chair, and makeshift wardrobe. I unpacked quickly, anxious to walk the streets and feel my new environment, but there was little pleasure to come 'home' to, so I soon developed the habit of staying out most of the time. All my reading was done on the terraces of bars, nursing a cup of coffee for three hours, and all my eating at the university canteen next door. The two bars frequented by students were both on the central square, which is not square but oval, and is therefore known locally as the *Place de l'Oeuf*, though its real name is the *Place de la Comédie*. On the north side was a bar called *Y a Bon* (It's Good Here), and across on the south side was the rival bar known as *Y a Mieux* (It's Better Here). *Y a Bon* is still thriving, but its rival gave way years ago to a chemist's shop. There it was that I read all of Sartre, Camus and Proust, slogged over the implications of Existentialism (then the rage among intellectuals), and wrote my first articles for the *South Wales Echo*. I was in a sort of mini-heaven, and saw myself as an expatriate, destined one day to write books in French which would be accepted as coming from the pen of a Frenchman.

Foolish fantasy! In fact I was teaching English conversation to groups of little boys who would rather be doing something else. The workload was not strenuous, at least. My duties were limited to two hours a week each at two *cours complémentaires* (which we used to translate as 'secondary modern'), where I had the freedom to shape the lesson how I wished, to choose whatever subject that took my fancy, to question pupils or lecture them, to amuse or bore them according to my mood. I found I enjoyed having attention paid to me by crowds of adolescents, and as I was not very much older then they were, and the rise of British popular music coincided with my arrival (the Beatles had just been discovered), I appeared to them somewhat exotic, which was a novel sensation.

Still, I was friendless. One man opened the door to French domestic bourgeois life, and that door in turn (without design on his part) knocked open other doors towards new people. He was Monsieur Cueilhes, nominally the teacher of geography at both schools, but whose passion for English language, literature and countryside led him to abandon his collection of rocks and maps to become the *de facto* English teacher. He was responsible for me, charged with introducing me to my classes and keeping order when they threatened to erupt (though he later left me to cope by myself). A kindly, avuncular man, sweet-natured and studiously polite, he enjoyed trying out his English with me, which was at once charming and funny, because his grasp of pronunciation and phrasing did not match his enthusiasm or his command of grammatical rules. Anyone who based his learning of the language on M. Cueilhes' instruction would in time speak with impressive fluency but be rather unintelligible.

He took to inviting me to lunch or dinner at his flat in the rue Levat, where we could chatter away in English over a massive meal prepared by his wife, who pretended not to understand a word. They were a textbook French couple, devoted to one another and guided by the proper roles of each in life. He, I am sure, had never once boiled an egg. His breakfast was laid out for him by his wife, who then had to get rid of everything and go to work (she also taught at a neighbouring girls' school), return in time to cook a real lunch, dispose of that, hurl back to work, and concoct a three-course dinner in the evening. I imagined her hours were as demanding as his, but he did not share the burden, because it was not the husband's place so to do. I have no idea how she managed to produce such delicious food in so short a time. It was at their flat that I was introduced to *bouchées à la reine*, which quickly became such a favourite that I cheekily requested it in advance. They were merely the beginning, and since there was always a lavish plate of cheese to follow the main course in anticipation of a delicious home-made dessert, it was virtually a banquet every time. Mme Cueilhes was timid, smiling, self-effacing and obliging, a slim, pretty woman whose life had been shaped by marriage and work, and who seemed perfectly content with the box into which she had been placed; she almost fashioned it for herself and walked willingly into it. M. Cueilhes, tall and solid, broad-shouldered but not fat, with thin permanently pursed lips (like most French people), a saucy twinkle, a ready laugh, not much hair on the head and incipient thickening of the neck, he was a man rigid with discipline and control. One felt with both of them, but especially with him, that if control were relaxed, if rules were flouted, then existence would unravel before their eyes. It was fear that kept him on the rails, and although he had once, one could see, been a handsome young man (he was now about forty-five), he was entirely without sexual allure. His wife had once been a catch, and having been caught, obediently switched off her allure as well. Neither of them was tactile in the slightest degree; one shook hands, and that was that.

I trust these words do not appear grudging, for this couple became my closest adult friends in Montpellier and many times rescued me from despondency. Their kindness was wholesome and warm, the substitute, perhaps, for that urgent spontaneity which colours the conduct of genuinely free people. And their attachment to me was patent.

On about my third visit I was surprised to find another person at the table. A girl of about thirteen sat there, silent, nervous, even a little scared. This was their daughter, who until that day had been considered a child and was now, all at once, to be introduced to adult conversation and behaviour. She was every inch their creation, the living evidence of their belief that regulations engender happiness. Marie-Anne Cueilhes was an imprisoned soul, restricted by love (for there was never any question that her parents loved her dearly), destined to fulfil ambitions which had been set for her, unable to fly, to sing, to soar, or to express any doubts without hurting those who planned for her. It was almost painful to see her spirit sapped by this obedience born of affection, for it would be unthinkable for her to bang the piano, as it were, although inwardly I felt sure she was wreaking havoc all by herself. And there was a fierce intelligence about her eyes which made one aware that she knew what was happening, even as she would do nothing to avert it.

Marie-Anne became a teacher herself, as her parents intended she should, and studied furiously to please them, gaining not only the highest doctorate in France but growing to fluency in several languages (she is the only person I have ever met who is bilingual in French and English without having been brought up in both languages). She married without love, as an obvious escape, and divorced. She travelled widely, pounced on experience, and eventually settled happily with a Breton, Michel, who gave her a son. She figures in these pages not simply because she was an occasional companion at dinner, nor because she afforded me the opportunity to observe how character may be formed and unformed by fraudulent domestic harmony, but because she is today my closest friend in France, a woman of extraordinary tolerance and benevolence, sharp and jolly, supremely un-vain. It was she who found with me the house in which I now write. Yet the scars are still there. She is still the frightened little girl at the dinner-table.

This house, in a village called Castries, comes much later in the story. I bought it when I was fifty-eight, sadly too late to anticipate as many years in it as the house (and I) deserve. Montpellier in 1960 was like a neglected picture in the attic. Its main avenues and squares were fine enough, and the city wore its elegance with some pride, but it had hidden what it thought was a squalid past behind the draperies. The extensive mediaeval and seventeenth-century quarter lurked just inches beyond the main road, but was scarcely ever explored. The stonework was black with grime and age, the shutters shut, bird-droppings plastered the window-sills, weeds grew between the paving-stones, sunlight barely penetrated. It had all been abandoned and forgotten, except by the miserably poor and the stray dogs. Yet it was packed with jewels. Now, those streets are lively with enterprise and fun, the stonework brisk and clean, the architecture rich with harmony and history, a perfectly gorgeous, fresh place in which to live and stroll. When I was there in 1960 I did not even bother to look at it properly, yet I could have borrowed £500 from a bank and bought a sumptuous property on three floors with twenty rooms and the smell of untouched antiquity. Nobody then wanted such musty stone-dusted lodgings (now worth a million pounds). Not the first, and certainly not the last instance of missed opportunity. I have never really grabbed chances in life, which means I now look back with cheerful, not bitter, regret, amused at my own incorrigible lack of initiative.

Once or twice, however, I was slightly pushy during those months. Intrigued by the incongruities of content and style in the novels of François Mauriac, I wrote to him in Paris and was summoned to a meeting with the old man. Another long train journey, another adventure, another tingle in the hairs on the back of my neck as I negotiated the streets of Paris as if I had been born for cosmopolitan life and the drab pungent prison of Herring Street had been a peculiar misdirection of fate. Mauriac was courteous and helpful, disappointingly commonplace for a great man of letters, whose mandarin prose had made him seem colossal to me. His deceptive ease with words was the most forbidding and irritating aspect of his work, for he appeared to write as if he were sending a letter to his wife, without much effort, without fashioning phrases, with no detectable desire to build monuments or blaze trumpets, yet with results as brilliant as diamonds, as true as earth. One despaired that prose should attain such simple perfection simply, it seemed, by putting pen to paper, and that, in an odd way, the writing was even better than Mauriac himself could have realized. I resented his facility. Meeting him both confirmed and undermined this feeling, for he was, in truth, an ordinary man doing ordinary things, his suit and tie as correct as his prose, his kindliness as simple as his sentences, so that it was easy to imagine his writing a masterpiece after breakfast. At the same time, however, the mystery of artistic creation remained intact. Who could ever know what torments he endured when dissecting the cruelties of the characters he described, so apparently out of tune with his own equable personality? For their secrets must, in the end, be buried in his breast, not in theirs. Sartre famously berated Mauriac for interfering with his characters, for controlling their destinies like a puppet-master whereas he, Sartre, set his people free to realize themselves uncontaminated by his influence. Poppycock, of course, but a very popular intellectual fashion of the time. Every writer must, finally, write about himself in disguise, and those nasty people Mauriac created issued from some troubled introspection. But Mauriac was a gentleman. He would never tell. Art was a private affair.

The other advance I made was mild and personal, yet with repercussions which last to the present day. I have already said that I found myself in Algeria at the time of the insurrection by the *pieds noirs* against de Gaulle and singularly failed to spot the uniqueness of my position or to take professional advantage of it. My reason for being there in the first place was complex.

In the front row of one of my classes sat a bothersome little boy called Jean-Philippe Bertrand. About twelve or thirteen, with a cheeky appearance, deep-set, soulful eyes suggesting difficult thoughts, generous lips and an endearing giggle, he was always showing off; playing to the gallery, attracting attention to himself. I was too stupid to notice that it was my attention in fact that he was after, and the day eventually arrived when he secured it. He had saved from a previous lesson some colourful pieces of sticky paper, which he proceeded to adhere to his face while I was trying to say something useful. Suddenly I was moved to make an exhibition of him, to shame the child into some kind of calm. I hauled him in front of the class for everyone to see and to mock, holding his hands behind his back to prevent his removing his ludicrous adornment. I then announced that the Headmaster should not be deprived of his treat and told the class to wait while I took Jean-Philippe to be carpeted. The poor boy was by now pleading with me, close to tears, frantically trying to wipe his face whenever I released a hand to open a door. It was an interesting situation, which I now understand better than I did then, for we were linking ourselves to each other by this shared ordeal, we were each a part of the same experience, which could not have occurred without the participation of both. I appeared to be humiliating him, and he appeared to be apprehensive, but in fact he had captured me. The penny did not drop until two years later.

The interview with the Headmaster was not long. Jean-Philippe was chastised and apologetic. But the Headmaster's secretary was Jean-Philippe's mother, and she, having chided him some more and apologized to me more fulsomely, proposed that I should come to the house for lunch one day. Thus began a lifelong connection.

Mme Bertrand was a young widow bringing up three sons in a first-floor flat on the rue Bonaparte. Her aged father-in-law also lived with them, and to make ends meet she let one of her bedrooms to an occasional tenant whom she cheerfully discouraged from turning up, by using his room and bed for her middle son, Jean-Philippe. She had a limp, presumably from some congenital defect which I never enquired about, and was clearly of peasant stock, with the broadest meridional accent, nasal and loud, every vowel enunciated (quite unlike the clipped spat-out style of Parisian speech) and vocabulary peppered with rich slang. She was a splendid woman, direct and honest, an immediate friend. To this day she still expects me to call her *Maman,* as I quickly became an additional son, a companion for her own three and, to some extent, a restraint on their behaviour. She found it tiresome to cope with them and they, missing a father's presence, responded, each in his own manner, with bold individualism. The eldest, Yves, was then fourteen and the youngest, Xavier, was ten. I was to impinge, however slightly, upon the lives of all three in time.

It transpired that M. Bertrand had been killed in the Algerian war about four years earlier, in his early thirties. His widow was now about thirty-five years old and still mourning. The government had not told her how or when he died, only that he was killed in action, and that was that. This great void, the bald lack of information, caused her continued distress, for she would still have liked to share in her husband's pain, at least by knowing in what it had consisted. She could not go to Algeria to find out, and in any case the authorities would not reveal anything to her; that much had already been made clear. I said that I would stand a better chance of discovering the truth; at any rate I would try, and I determined to go to Algeria at the first available break from school.

The long story must be curtailed. I did contrive to pass through several blockages, on the grounds that I was a British investigating journalist gathering material for the *South Wales Echo* (to those hardened old hands I must have looked like a choirboy), and that this was a story of human interest, quite devoid of political content. I eventually met the soldier who had been with M. Bertrand when he died. They were both in a jeep and ran over a landmine; the mine had exploded on his side of the vehicle, killing him instantly, while his companion escaped with the usual cuts and bruises. Bertrand had not suffered. He had not known what was about to occur, nor was he ever conscious that it was happening. He had often spoken about his wife and sons with pride.

With this simple but important news I returned to Montpellier, and thereafter had a third home on the rue Bonaparte (my second being the Cueilhes' flat, and my first the dingy room in which I only slept). I ate there once a week, and bought a *mobilette* – a noisy motorized scooter – to make the journey more fun (and, I suppose, subconsciously to make myself younger and closer to the boys). All three would lean over the railings on their first-floor balcony to wave me goodbye as I sped up the road. It was the happiest feeling.

Ten months later the entire Bertrand family were on the platform as I mounted the train back to Britain. Yves and Xavier were minimally engaged by the event. Jean-Philippe was in tears. He tried manfully to fight them back, but they would not be contained, and he eventually gave in and clung to his mother. 'Promise me you will come back', he said. Alas, how easy it is to speak, to launch words upon the air. I gave him the promise he sought, and no doubt at that moment hoped (at least) that I would be able to keep it. For Jean-Philippe, however, it was more than just a promise; it gave him his centre, his heart.

Yves was not a very bright young man, but very handsome in the Alain Delon, utterly French manner, dark, sensual and clean, almost clinically beautiful. His girlfriend, two years older than him, had pounced very early and was clearly not going to let him escape. She need not have worried, for Yves was lethargic to a degree and could not have been bothered to play the field. He was contented enough to nestle in Monique's clutches, in effect to pass from one mother to another. They were married when he was seventeen. There was one passion he would not forego, however, even for her. Like hundreds of young men in Mediterranean France he lived for horses, the wild white variety known as the Camarguais. They are ridden for the most part without saddle, and are used to round up the huge black bulls which are bred to be murdered in the bullring. (I went once with all three boys to watch a bull fight in the Roman arena at Nîmes, prepared to experience the poetry and skill which had been vaunted, and was so depressed by the mindless viciousness of the slaughter that I found myself shouting *Vive le taureau* and was very nearly lynched by the mob. Eight bulls were despatched that afternoon, not one of them standing any chance to escape with his life, for they were each weakened by *picadors* and *banderillos* long before the *matador* made his vainglorious entrance, their neck muscles severed so that they could not raise their heads and that their backs were bared ready for the killer's final thrust into the heart. They were panting and exhausted, blood dripping from their wounds, by the time they had to face their tormentor, and yet they contrived in their sleek smooth darkness to be more noble, more austere than the inexpressibly silly man in pink tights and laced finery who waved his braveness to the crowd. The way in which those thousands of people rose to their feet as one, cheering and hooting, salivating with orgasmic glee, every time a bull was killed, made me feel that I was surrounded by blood-lust, by something primitive and ugly which I did not want to touch or to know. (I say all this in parenthesis, yet it testified to my utter detestation of cruelty, whether to human or to animal, which was more an emotion in me than a rational conclusion, though it could be that as well. And I always looked at it again whenever I was so glibly accused of being 'obsessed' with murder and indifferent to the pain of victims.) Anyway, Yves spent most of his waking hours, when not at work, on horseback, directing the bulls into their fields, or herding them for the fun of it, feeling at one with the earth and the sun which had nurtured him. His mother deplored his fixation, declaring that it was dangerous and would one day be the death of him. Monique did not even try to deter him, but their marriage failed some years later, after the birth of their two sons, because, she said, 'I always came second to the horses'.

In 1996, when he was just fifty, the horse he mounted was frightened by a bull, reared and threw him. The bull then hurled Yves on his horns twice into the air, with enormous force and speed, and he landed the second time on his head.

He now lies in a permanent semi-coma in a hospital at Marseilles, awake but powerless. He cannot speak, move, eat, urinate, or communicate, but his eyes tell you that he knows the condition he is in and that he is desperate to say something. He can manage a grunt, and one clawed hand can lift in a parody of greeting. He does not want you to leave, and the pathos in those eyes is heart-rending. Every time I see him I think of his mother's admonition when he was a boy, and it is no comfort to recognize that she was right.

Xavier was much put upon by his two older brothers, teased and humiliated ritually, without malice but without thought also. They had no idea of the damage they were causing. Too young to have a clear memory of his father, Xavier was very much the odd-man-out, effeminate and sweet, quiet and subservient. He wanted to please, to do the right thing, to meet expectations and cause no trouble. He was determined to show that he was every inch as vivid as his brothers, but it was an effort, for he was naturally timid and had little imagination. Still less was he endowed with a healthy introspection, which might have come in handy.

A few years after my departure Mme Bertrand telephoned me in London, distraught. Xavier had tried to commit suicide, and had only been saved in the nick of time (he was then fifteen). She was beside herself, and did not know what to say to him or how to relieve him of an unknown distress. Would I please go out to Montpellier? She felt sure I could talk to him, and perhaps I could find out what was the matter.

Of course I went. Xavier was still in the clinic. He could not be persuaded to leave, although medically he was ready to, and would not respond to any enquiries from doctors, family, or psychiatrists. He told me he had been waiting for me to arrive before he would budge. I took him away from Montpellier, to a small town where he was not known, and we spent two days there talking. He had formed an attachment to a girl which was, to him, a pleasant and harmless friendship, but which appeared to everyone else to be the prelude to marriage. Everybody had made clear to him what was expected, and as he had spent his entire life fulfilling expectations, he gradually felt himself sinking into a trap. He did not at first know why he was so scared, but he did know that he could not feel the kind of attraction for the girl that a boy should, and wondered whether his inadequacy would be discovered and how he would explain it. He could not even explain it to himself. He only knew that he was bound to let everyone down, and that the only way to avoid catastrophe was to remove himself, to obliterate the problem once and for all. Xavier did not say all this quite so plainly; indeed, he could barely say anything at all for some hours, but it was manifest he was far from rid of his anxiety, and that it was deeper and more acute than these careful words suggest. I helped him find ways to say what he needed to say, and I remember the shattering look of relief he gave me when I said I would talk to his mother for him.

I told Mme Bertrand simply that she could either have a happy son or a dead one – there were no compromises or gradations. I felt sure he would try to take his life again if he was pressured, and recommended that he be left in peace to form his own friendships in his own way with people unknown to the family. I also said that homosexuality was neither a sin nor a disease, and that the best she could do was to feign an indifference to the subject.

Xavier is now a contentedly busy gay man, respectably earning his living in a bank, his nature open and frank to everyone. He has travelled a long road since that bleak day with the sleeping pills. I sometimes wonder whether, had he lived a generation earlier, before sane tolerance replaced the ignorance which infected the world, he would have survived. And how many young men of that generation did not, for reasons still unacknowledged by their families.

Another call from Mme Bertrand concerned Jean-Philippe. This was about a year before Xavier's trouble, when Jean-Philippe was sixteen. He was in trouble with the police for having broken into a number of cars. He had not been interested in theft as such, but had keenly wanted to drive, and the only way he could manage it was to take other people's cars and drive them. There were a number of offences, making the case serious enough to threaten a custodial sentence; he had already spent a night in police cells. The only hope was for me to stand in for his father, by proxy, and take responsibility for him.

This time I appeared before a magistrate and gave a solemn undertaking that I would answer for Jean-Philippe's behaviour in future, even at a distance, and signed a paper to that effect (the French have never lost their passion for filling in bits of paper). It was not lost on the boy that he could not risk getting me into a mess, although I do not think anybody actually ever said that. As for me, I felt some pride in being *quasi*-parental (not for the last time, as it would transpire), and realized, rather belatedly, that I was very fond of Jean-Philippe and wanted to be necessary to him. He said to me, with such painful directness that it woke me up, 'Why did you take so long to come back?' I suddenly remembered my promise, and felt waves of love and remorse sweep over me.

By this time Jean-Philippe was sleeping in what was laughably called the lodger's room (*la chambre de Monsieur Lépine*), though the lodger never dared show up and claim his furniture. There being no spare room, during the two weeks that I stayed, I shared the bed with him. It was a small double, so there was plenty of room. On the third night, I felt his movement towards me. Not one word was said that night or any other – it was an utterly silent coupling, for speech would have forced recognition of the truth of what was happening. I suppose by being dumb he could pretend to himself that it was an illusion, or that he was really asleep, and I felt I had to respect this cosy protective discretion. So we panted and parted, nightly.

I went to Montpellier for a week or two three times a year for the next two years, specifically to see Jean-Philippe. There was never any question of his being gay, for he was robustly a man and would have recoiled from any attempt to seduce him, but he felt the urge to express a kind of love.

He married twice and has a daughter and a son. He now lives with his second wife near Nice.

It was this stuttering, half-expressed, half-concealed relationship that finally made me face the fact of my own nature. I must clearly abandon the pretence that I was going to burst into the bright sky of woman-love one day very soon, and must henceforth be honest with myself. I had been able, with Roy, to comfort myself with the notion that an attachment to him was a measure of retarded childhood, not to be taken seriously. I had been shown by Gilbert Harding that a predilection could be disguised as didactic care, far removed from desire, and my intervention to assist Xavier Bertrand had kept me aloof and avuncular. But it was obvious, to me at least, that I knew what I was talking about when I advised Xavier because I was actually describing myself. And it was equally clear that I was embarked upon a journey which would make me welcome every opening which allowed me to provide the same kind of influence upon others that Gilbert had generously bestowed upon me. The fitful relationship with Jean-Philippe brought these strands together.

Montpellier marked me, and deposited a silt of contentment which I would relish on nostalgic reflection for many years, albeit with diminishing *élan* as I matured. For it was a contentment of sprightly youth, almost unwhiskered, with no gravity or importance attached and no purpose envisaged. I was still, though twenty years old, a green and greedy adolescent, which is doubtless why I enjoyed the flattery of M. and Mme Cueilhes, the gawping of my classes, and especially the friendship of the Bertrand boys; they allowed me to delay my growing-up, to pretend I was one of them. I recall an incident which demonstrated this foolishness with embarrassing clarity. One of my classes had played up badly and left me fed up with them all. I lost my temper and stormed out of the classroom half-way through, spitting out the words, '*Vous m'emmerdez tous. J'en ai marre, et je rentre en Angleterre demain*' (You all piss me off. I've had enough, and I'm going back to England in the morning). Quite a tantrum, really, and unforgivably weak.

That evening, as I sat glumly in my room at the rue Gustave after nightfall, I heard the tinkling of bicycle bells in the street below. Peering out of the window, I was astonished to see about twenty boys on a bunch of bikes huddled together, all faces glancing up at me. They were a delegation from the class I had abandoned. I opened the window and asked them what they wanted. 'Please, *monsieur*', one or two of them said, 'We didn't mean it. Don't go back to England, we'll be good from now on. Promise.' An endearing story, but at the same time faintly shameful. I was still so childish as to attract, and welcome, the loyalty of children. Perhaps it is a failing endemic among schoolmasters, and accounts for both the strength of the best and the shortcomings of the worst; I certainly knew that I would have enjoyed a career teaching the young, and that I must at all costs avoid such a fate if I was to achieve any kind of maturity.

My degree was a good one – First Class Honours with high mention. Gilbert would indeed have been proud. I am sure my parents were, as my father tried hard to suppress a glowing smile when he diverted his attention from the television to hear my news, and shook my hand for the first time in his life. My mother exclaimed, 'I don't know where you get it from!', which was congratulation of a sort. (As I have said, I believe I got 'it' from her.) Only two of us had the distinction of a First, the other being Margaret Davies then, as now, living a horizonless existence in the valleys. I think Margaret had a spark of genius, which she has deliberately wasted. My success was due to crafty, ingenious swotting; I suspected there might be a question on Proust, for example, and deliberately acquainted myself with the last volume of his sprawling novel, whereas our assigned task had been to study the first four volumes only. With this ruse I gave myself the appearance of diligence and scope. I have often used the same guile since then.

There was little unemployment in those days, and offers of jobs came unsought through the letter-box. One involved helping to set up a television service in Sierra Leone, which intrigued me until I heard the temperature there was 120 degrees in the shade. Another was to start at the bottom in Fleet Street, which ought to have been perfect, but I recoiled from the anonymity of a reporter (a mistake, I now think). Heywood-Thomas even proposed that I should do post-graduate work at Oxford (he mentioned Lincoln College) and eventually return to Cardiff as part of his team. But academic life did not, at that stage, sufficiently entice.

One appointment I did accept, for a few hours at least. I went to London to be interviewed by Lintas Ltd., the advertising arm of Unilever, and was immediately offered a place as trainee account executive, with the promise of early promotion and huge riches beyond the foothills. No sooner had I signed the contract than I trembled at the prospect; surely I was not a businessman in any sense, and surely I would demand more of myself than the successful sale of a washing-powder. (Another pompous mistake. Cecil Woodham-Smith told me years later that the best training she ever had for her final career as an historian and biographer of Florence Nightingale and Queen Victoria were her years writing advertising copy: 'it taught me the invaluable lesson of concision, to pare everything down to half a dozen words'.) So I went to see Gerry Graber.

During two university vacations I had worked for Gerry taking groups of American tourists round England and Europe as a 'courier' – not the guide but the man with the hotel reservations and train tickets. He struck me as a successful man who had avoided being trapped by work – he did enough to earn a living. He ran his company – Worldways Ltd – virtually alone, with the help only of a part-time secretary, and he managed to lead what appeared to me a charmed life with it. He was thirty years old, married with two sons, a posh car and a big house in Hampstead. Yet he never turned up for work at his two-room office in Oxford Circus before ten o'clock, and was often back home straight after lunch. The expression 'laid back' was not then current, but it described Gerry to perfection.

'There's no doubt that the jobs you have been offered will make you a rich man in time', he said. 'They are internationally-respected companies, with huge opportunities for ladder-climbing within them. Mind you, you will have to work your arse off. These are competitive places, and only the energetic and the resourceful make it to the top, in addition to which you will have to hone your ingratiating techniques. I'm not sure it's you, somehow. Why not join me here? I could do with some help, but the company is small and I could pay less than half what Unilever will offer, even for a beginner. There's no ladder to anywhere. On the other hand, you will not have to fight with colleagues about who sits next to the window or who has the bigger desk, you will not have to jostle for importance, and nobody is going to notice what time you get here or what time you leave. As long as the job is done and I don't have to pick up the pieces, I would ask no more.'

It seemed ideal. Free time and independence, with an income of £18 a week as well. Still, I was not quite ready to settle as an adult. I asked if I could start in a year's time, as I wanted first to travel across the United States of America. Gerry agreed.

Chapter 6

Say Something British

When I went to America I was a vapid creature, without profundity of any sort and without direction. My tastes were superficial, my goals no further than tomorrow. Sydney Smith recommended one should take short views on life – 'no further than dinner or tea' – if one wished to avoid unhappiness. By that reckoning, I must have been happy indeed. I bought the cheapest flight possible to New York, on Icelandic Airlines which went over the North Pole and took sixteen hours to get there, and moreover made a terrible racket shaking the entire machine with its four propellered engines, had a few dollars and one address in my pocket, and set out to find new experience of whatever kind for however many months it might take me.

The address belonged to Harvey Donegan, an impossibly languid southern gentleman who made an art of slouching even when standing up, his body an inverted S, his head nodding like a toy dog on the back seat of a car, his vowels stretched to breaking-point and his nasal cavities never at ease. I had met him on one of my European travels and accepted the card he pressed upon me. Thus it was to him that I repaired when I arrived in New York, wide-eyed with wonder.

Harvey's tiny apartment was in the heart of Greenwich Village, at a rent fixed years before, which would have sufficed to buy a week's supply of breakfast cereal. Not before or since have I encountered such living accommodation. The bed, the lavatory, the kitchen, the sitting area, the eating area, all fitted into what would have made a large wardrobe at the end of a corridor so narrow that one could only walk along it sideways. This Lilliputian space was then crammed with as many objects as one might reasonably have designed for a three-storey house. There were so many pictures they could not all be hung, but leant two or three deep against the walls, including huge canvases and eventually a vast poster by David Hockney. Little bits and pieces, like a Nazi ashtray, a bust of Mark Twain, a tiny Tiffany lampshade, an art nouveau mirror, or one of Monet's brushes, littered the place in their hundreds, were to be found under clothes which lay across the breakfast-table or in the pockets of others which hung from hooks on the walls. There was no room to move, so that having negotiated a spot to stand or perch one dare not relinquish it for fear it would fill up again. It was like living in a junk shop, except that a great deal of that artfully collected débris was surely exceedingly rare and valuable.

Harvey was talented and benign. He had written several novels, none of which had even been considered by a publisher, and was now writing plays destined for a similar fate. He went to the theatre once a week, always in the cheapest seat, but never missing a show, however difficult to get into. He kept up a long correspondence with Gore Vidal, launched when they were both as unknown as he still was, and had friends all over New York, mainly because he was so obliging and mild. It was to two of Harvey's friends that I was sent as temporary lodger.

They were Jim Branciforti and Bob Covais, both then about twenty-four years old and both like characters out of a Neil Simon comedy. They had met a few years earlier and were now as inseparable as if they had been attached at the hip. They even shared the same mind, for a sentence uttered by one was foil for the anticipated response of the other, and since virtually everything they said was hilarious, they were the perfect non-professional comic routine. I spent all of my time with them laughing until my body hurt, and eating out at neighbourhood restaurants, for they believed that whatever they earned (in different branches of the travel business) was meant to be spent; Jim and Bob were estimable children of the Consumer Society. On the other hand, they were also stand-ard victims of the Propaganda Society, convinced that they were doing me good by limiting my breakfast plate to twenty-five different coloured pills, each representing the required nutrients and vitamins for a Healthy Life (when I wanted egg and bacon I had to slip out unnoticed to a corner bar).

They moved from one apartment to another every three of four months, never satisfied that they had the best view at the best price, and took their furniture with them each time. As the years went by I would learn to recognize exactly the same low table bearing exactly the same ornaments in precisely the same order and position as I had seen them in thirty different locations. Jim and Bob were a capsule, self-contained, self-sufficient, self-regenerating. They were not so complacent as to appear tedious, making other people feel *de trop*. On the contrary, they had firm friendships and entertained with lavish Italian meals and non-stop repartee. (One guest, a pathologist, arrived one hour late for dinner; as Bob opened the door to her he said, 'What happened? Did somebody *live*?') They were quite plainly a working example of a couple who had each found his mate and would never be tempted to look anywhere else for a replacement. The connections went further than that, for Bob's sister married Jim's brother, making them one another's brother-in-law and uncle to each other's nephews and nieces.

Forty years later, they were still moving house and still roaring at one another's spontaneous jokes when Jim con-tracted cancer and died after a lingering illness, his laughter unsuppressed but less lively. Bob waited a year, and on the exact anniversary of his friend's death he committed suicide with painstaking preparation and a message which declared that he simply would not continue living without him. Never was there a more eloquent example of bonding.

Jim and Bob accompanied me to the freeway out of New York and left me standing by the road. I had said that I would try my luck hitch-hiking, heading north and west, and see how far I got. I might return in six months, or I might come limping home, defeated, that evening.

Before leaving Britain I had worked out that, to be successful as a hitch-hiker one must not *look* like a hitch-hiker. The uniform, blue jeans and a back-pack, tended to cancel personality and alarm drivers, for they could not know what they were getting underneath that uniform. I determined to so arouse their curiosity that they could not resist me. I packed my only good suit, supplemented with white shirt, black tie, a bowler hat which I bought in London and a pencil-thin black rolled umbrella which I intended never to unfurl. In those days it was still routine to watch hundreds of bowler-hatted gentlemen at eight in the morning walking across London Bridge on their way to work in the City, so that my appearance, together with a suitcase which I could clearly not carry (this was to be all hitching and no hiking), made me look as if I had been lifted from Threadneedle Street and dumped from a helicopter. At one point about four months later, I stood at an isolated crossroads in the middle of the Nevada desert, no building in sight save for a petrol-station, alone on the planet, and when a car eventually did loom on the horizon it slowed, drifted, meandered, and stopped at a safe distance while the driver got out to take some air; he actually thought I was a mirage. For the most part, my clothes did the trick; I rarely waited for longer than ten minutes, and sometimes cars would screech to a halt, two or three at a time, enabling me to choose whether I wanted to be driven by a Cadillac, a Buick or a Lincoln.

People would sometimes stop just to be helpful. 'Gee, we're

not going anywheres, but we'd sure like you to come over to our place for some breakfast and coffee, to set you up before you go on your way.' Or complete strangers would offer me a bedroom, three meals a day, the opportunity to work and earn some money, and some jolly excursions thrown in, for a few days (I was never told how many – that was for me to choose). The Americans' domestic welcome to a nomad, the almost bounden duty they feel to accommodate and share, is akin to the open house of the Arab and the touching care of the Hindu (though I doubt whether any of those who were so good to me would accept the comparison, their ignorance of the rest of the world being unfathomable).

On one occasion I was given a lift by a GI on his way to Fulton, Missouri, where his girlfriend was in college. (It was at Fulton, I noticed with childish excitement, that Winston Churchill made his historic 'Iron Curtain' speech after the Second World War.) We arrived after dark, when it was impossible for me to continue, even in a bowler hat, so I was hauled into the college with the soldier, climbing up sheets which were thrown for us from a second-floor window. There I was given a bed which somebody relinquished for my sake, but before lights-out a half dozen of us sat chatting happily. A girl passing in the corridor popped in for a few minutes, time enough to say, 'Did I hear you were going as far as San Francisco? Oh, please call my parents when you are there. They'd be *so* pleased to hear from somebody who has seen me two thousand miles from home. Tell them I'm OK, would you?' I took a note of her home number, and she left, as quickly as she had come. It was not until three months later that I found myself in San Francisco, and not until I was about to leave that enchanting city, tired of sleeping on park benches and in sauna baths, that I remembered the telephone number that I had promised to use. I went into a drugstore on my way out of town and dialled the number.

'Why, you must be Brian', shrieked a lady's voice at the other end of the line. 'We've been *waiting* for you. Where

are you? How long are you going to *stay*? We have a room
all ready for you and are looking forward to having you as
our house-guest. Now tell me where you are, and I shall
come and pick you up *right away*.' Minutes later a huge car
pulled up outside the drugstore and a uniformed chauffeur
opened the door for me to sit next to my hostess, the mother
of the young lady with whom I had exchanged a few sentences
at midnight in Fulton, Missouri. We drove up the colourful
steep streets of San Francisco to the hill at the very top of the
city, she talking all the while, myself overwhelmed with the
kindness of it all, and as we went through some heavy gates
we were saluted. Thereafter every pedestrian was a soldier
in uniform, and every one of them saluted us. We finally
stopped at the largest most perfectly situated house on the
hill, overlooking the Golden Gate bridge on one side and the
deep calm blue of the Pacific Ocean on the other, where I
discovered my hosts were the Commander of the Presidio,
and his wife. There I spent a gloriously happy week, with my
own batman and my own constant and overflowing welcome
at the officers' club.

My return for such lavish goodness was ordinary to me,
but presumably rather fun for them. I had to talk a great
deal and to make sure I did so with the plummiest accent
I could muster. I was an entertainer in fact, and quite right
too. There were times when my ability to talk was something
of a salvation, as when I was given a ride by two gunmen
on the run from the police in Pennsylvania. It was obviously
not until I was in the car with no avenue of escape that I
discovered this and found the guns on the back seat next
to me (I had not until then ever seen a gun with my own
eyes, and have still not handled one). The men were quite
at ease, until they invited me to take a pot-shot at a bird and
considered my reluctance suspiciously wet, whereupon I had
to keep their attention off my unsuitability as a companion
by telling them stories one after another. I did not find out
why they had even bothered to stop for me when they were
being hunted by armed police, but they got rid of me soon

enough when they were getting close to Harrisburg, where the number of their car was known and they would be in danger; they were sorry but they would have to leave me to get another ride into town; they hoped I wasn't 'sore' at them. I assured them I felt nothing but the deepest gratitude and wished them well.

A fortuitous encounter, for the car which then rescued me was driven by a teacher at Penn State University, where I was forthwith invited to give some lectures on French writers and accommodated for a week by the professor and his wife, who taught me to play the first movement of Beethoven's 'Moonlight' Sonata by storing a memory of where each of my fingers was for each note and chord.

I came closer to crime when I spent a night in a police cell. It was at a small town in Illinois where, once again, I found I was stranded after dark, with no money to pay for real accommodation. It dawned on me that one place where there was certain to be a bed was in prison, so I walked into the police station, explained my predicament, and asked if I could be put up in one of the cells. The officer, as corpulent and gun-laden as if he had been cast in a movie, was tickled pink by the notion, and, noticing that I looked like a baby stockbroker in my suit and hat, thought he was the victim of an elaborate joke and behaved as one annoyed at having his authority mocked. When I convinced him I was in earnest, his mood changed to perplexity. He scratched his head, again as if instructed by the script, and said, 'Gee, don't you know you have to commit a crime to stay in here?' I said I would willingly oblige in order to qualify for admission, if he would just give me an easy crime which attracted only a short custodial penalty. 'What about insulting an officer?' I suggested, 'would that do?' 'I guess I would be within rights to keep you in for a night, sure', he said. 'Well, then', I countered, 'consider yourself insulted.' At that he roared with laughter, shook my hand heartily, and ushered me in.

He did not bother with exhaustive paperwork, just enough

to file a report, and then we talked late into the night. He locked me into the cell, however, in accordance with procedure. It was jolly comfortable, and a huge relief (I had by that time spent three nights in fields). The following morning he made me a copious American breakfast, and sent me on my way westward, waving good cheer. I wished I had been able to keep in touch with him, but it was pretty obvious that I should be made to disappear and leave no trace of an irregular favour. I like to imagine he told the story repeatedly for years afterwards.

My only other encounter with police was in the State of New York, where I was waiting on the side of the motorway when a squad car passed. It stopped, reversed, and two very heavy, unsmiling, gum-chewing cops got out and questioned me. It was clear they did not share the good humour of my jail-keeper in Illinois. They told me that hitch-hiking was illegal in the State and that I must desist forthwith or I should be arrested. Of course I accepted their knowledge of the law, protested my ignorance of it, and promised to comply. 'But what happens next?' I asked. I explained that, law-abiding though I intended to be, I was nevertheless also immobile. There were no train stations or bus depots anywhere nearby, and I was alone on a big, wide, open interstate freeway. If the policemen did not do something for me, then I should abide by the law and die of starvation on that very spot. I had to get somewhere somehow. Could they, please, be so kind as to give me a ride to the nearest town? Logic overwhelmed them. So they ended up assisting me in the crime for which they had threatened to arrest me.

New York was not the only state which forbade hitch-hiking, and with good reason. There had been a number of murders committed by men who had pretended to be merely looking for a ride, and more than one driver had warned me that the risk went both ways and that I should be careful. One man in Maryland stopped for me, and told me he was only going ten miles up the road. 'Every little helps', I said, and jumped in. We talked so much that I did not notice for half an hour that the ten miles had long since been passed. 'That was just to cover myself', he explained, 'so that I could get rid of you if I wanted. A few years ago my wife picked up a young man about your age, and he killed her. I vowed I would never let a hitch-hiker into my car or any of my family's, until you showed up. Still I wanted to make sure of you. You seem pretty straight to me, so you're in for as long a ride as you like. I've got at least a thousand miles to cover.' I stayed with him for several hours, and he so trusted me that he asked me to take over the driving while he had a rest, and promptly fell asleep in the passenger seat. A number of times over the months I gave good return by sharing the driving, but that was one occasion I cherished.

I was moved for quite other reasons in New Orleans, where I stayed for a few days at the house of a teacher in the history department of Tulane University, yet another acquaintance acquired in a driving seat. After the first two days he made a startling request. 'There's something the faculty members have long wanted to do here, which you might be able to help us achieve', he said. 'We have a number of black students, as I expect you've noticed, but they are still segregated, and are not allowed into the student canteen. Only whites eat there, the niggers have to fend for themselves. We all know it's wrong, and the system will have to change one day, but we can't do it ourselves without its looking political – the faculty against the student body, if you see what I mean; they won't want us to dictate to them, to tell them they have got to eat with black people. They run the canteen for themselves. So we don't interfere. But you could. You drop out of the sky and nobody knows who the hell you are. You can't have any agenda, any smart-ass political move to make. It's a godsend. We on the faculty would be very grateful to you if you would go into the canteen with a black student and see what happens.'

It might have been a very risky undertaking. The Deep South of the United States in 1961 was still backward in civil rights, black people routinely humiliated by segregation laws on a daily basis. They used different buses and different lavatories as well as different restaurants, and tensions were dangerously high whenever these antiquated social regulations were infringed, as they were increasingly by the emerging 'sixties' generation. A black student, brave enough to be a guinea-pig, was duly selected, and we walked side by side (*not* one in front of the other) into the cafeteria. It was vast and noisy, and we had to walk the length of one wall to get to the counter, where we each took a tray and proceeded along to the hot-food section. Thankfully there was no queue, or the enforced waiting might have ratcheted tensions up higher, giving time for indignation to swell into anger. As it was, the clatter of knives on plates and buzz of a hundred conversations suddenly ceased, and a hush fell upon the entire room. The lady behind the hot-food counter, herself black and bosomy, with the look of a frightened cat declared, 'I can't serve him, mister.' I had already worked out that discussion, argument, reason, would be counterproductive, and knew that I should simply have to ignore any hindrance. I asked my black friend to choose first, and I would follow, because he knew southern food so much better than I did, and I needed his advice. 'We'll have two portions of that' I said, pointing to something made of corn (I was too nervous to pay much heed to what it really was). Slowly, the lady spooned food on to two plates, her eyes barely leaving mine, thinking no doubt that I must be mad but it was not her fault if I got lynched; slowly, too, the sound of talk and cutlery resumed. I wondered if it was hostile talk, but the cutlery seemed to suggest not. We were stared at as we took our seats at a table, for perhaps five seconds, then life went back to normal. The revolution was over, so placid it would not even merit a footnote in history.

I went through forty-three states before I turned up again on Jim and Bob's doorstep in New York to claim my plate of pills as reward, and I saw some magnificent natural wonders. The Grand Canyon in Arizona in early morning is paralysingly beautiful, and moreover totally unexpected. One knows what one is looking for – it is not unexpected in that sense – but one does not anticipate its sudden appearance. I had assumed, with no certain evidence, that such a gash on the earth's face must be amongst mountainous scenery. I drove instead over flat land (I had borrowed a car from one of my 'lifts' in Tucson), deserted and mysterious, dotted with joshua trees, their arms sticking up rigid, and tickled by tumbleweed brushing over it, a land quiet, peopleless and eerie, as one might imagine the surface of the moon. All at once I was on the edge of a precipice, staring down into the vast space of the canyon, so deep that you could not see the bottom of it and could not hear the raging torrent of water which sped through it. I exaggerate, but it was almost as if I had to brake suddenly to stop going over, so stark and sudden was its appearance. I got out of the car and looked with passion, my mouth agape in unconscious parody, at the mighty walls opposite, probably a mile or two away, distances being difficult to measure with the eye, the whole history of the world's skin told in horizontal lines of geological deposit, some thicker than others, all of different colours and hues, made possible by the simultaneous erosion of a valley by water and the swelling of the crust it was eroding, ever so slowly over millions of years. I was a speck in space and time, an ant of little moment, diffused and evaporated into the air of aeons below and around me, reduced to the paltry significance of one specimen of one species of the thousands which crawled, galloped and flew their tiny shadows across this gigantic monument.

I have carried the American experience with me for the rest of my life, marvelling at the ebullient optimism of the people, depressed by their political naivety, warmed by their kindness and hospitality, horrified by their waste, delighted by their humour (they lack irony, not humour) and amazed at their ignorance. I was asked by a man in Florida to prove that I was British. How, I enquired, could I do that? He suggested I should speak in my own language, for him to hear what it sounded like. 'Say Something British', he cried.

They have not changed much since. Nor has my gratitude, regard and exasperation.

On returning to London I had first to find somewhere to live. Herring Street and the Old Kent Road now appeared shoddy and contemptible to me, and there was no circumstance which would entice me to live south of the river. (I was so young, and so wrong. A flat in Camberwell would have been a delight, but I then felt my ankles would have been stuck in mud, and that freedom and fun resided in the West End.) While I was looking, I commuted up and down from Wales, and occasionally stayed overnight at my old digs in Dulwich, relying meanwhile on Gerry Graber's tolerant acceptance of my postponing employment until I was settled somewhere. I saw some pretty awful rooms in Bloomsbury and Russell Square and grew despondent very quickly, until one bright lady who was trying to flog her flat to me saw that I wouldn't like it anyway, and said, 'Why not come and see the flat I'm moving into. It's in a brand-new block, and there are still some flats going. Look sharp, and you might get one.'

So I accompanied Tina (her preferred version of Christine) to Mecklenburgh Square, a handsome Georgian terrace tucked between Gray's Inn Road and Coram's Fields, spacious and airy, with a key-accessible park of lawn, shrubs and flowers in the centre. This was elegance indeed! Byron Court was thoroughly modern, with a lift and carpeted corridors, but it was disguised in that it maintained the façade of the terrace and one need not know it was there at all. Tina had taken a two-bedroom flat on the park side, which she would share with another girl, an old friend. I could not afford such luxury, so applied for a one-bedroom unit at the back, with noise from Gray's Inn Road thrown in. The kitchen was small and open-plan, in the fashion of the day, separated from the sitting-room by a counter and venetian blind. When the blind was up, the counter became a bar and a dining-table, with stools ranged in front. One *almost* had the feeling one would be living in the style of a minor Hollywood celebrity, and I fancied I could make this modest modern oblong into a hub of society. I would later learn a vivid Spanish expression for this kind of vanity, which translates as wishing to fart higher than one's arse.

The rent was £12 per week, an astronomical sum which would swallow two-thirds of my starting wage with Gerry (£18 per week and no expenses), but which befitted my ambitions. I certainly wanted to feel slightly grand, and I used most of my savings to buy a handsome sofa from Heal's (I still have it, restuffed and re-covered many times) and some floor to ceiling curtains; no swags and tails – as yet. Getting to work at Oxford Circus and to the Shaftesbury Avenue for the theatre, where I determined I should find all the entertainment I required, were both easy. Thrown in with all that was the unexpected bonus of a new friendship; Tina intended that I should be part of her new experience of life at Byron Court.

We were constantly knocking on one another's door to borrow something or other or to open a bottle of wine and chat for a very long time, and she frequently invited me to share a meal. Somewhat older than me, I would have guessed thirty-seven, she was openly sensual, in her expansive way of talking and throwing her arms about, in her pointed pleasure at dragging on a cigarette, as much as in her dress and manner. There was something desperate about her which I could not locate, an impatient graspingness, a fear of losing life if she did not devour it immediately. This was never more apparent than when she was a sexual predator.

Tina initiated our relationship. It was based entirely on lust at first, and grew not into love but into panic. She was in my flat one evening when she announced that she would not cross the corridor to go to her own place, but would stay where she was. With that she walked into the bedroom and made herself comfortable in my bed. (This appears to be part of the standard repertoire of female seduction, I mean taking charge of a situation and shaping it to her own design. A neighbour in Brook Green did the same thing many years later, after dinner with her husband and myself, calmly telling the husband that she would be staying with me that night, and getting into my bed as if we had jointly planned the event.)

Tina was frighteningly avid. I had only to place my hand on her stomach and her body writhed as if she had been on horseback, moving this way and that, groaning, greedy for touch and possession. I wanted to ask her to keep cool, to control herself a little, but knew this would not be a very romantic suggestion to make and allowed myself to be swept along by the passion. But only in semblance. It was like being in bed with Vesuvius, and I wanted escape for my own safety. Though I enjoyed being squeezed and drained, I did not relish the feeling of having been pulled behind Ben-Hur's chariot as well. Where was the tenderness?

Tina sensed my want of fire, which catastrophically mir-rored her want of self-love and was the excuse, though not the reason, for an act of desperation. She needed me to swamp her with desire, in order to make up for her void. One evening she came to me very late, well after midnight, looking and sounding drowsy, lethargic, adrift. She lay on the bed and told me that she had taken an overdose of sleeping-pills and would I please let her slip slowly away, holding my hand. I did not berate her, nor did I question myself. From the sitting-room I telephoned for an ambulance, and accompanied her to a hospital, thankfully very close at hand, where her stomach was pumped and she was saved from herself. It was not, I soon learned, the first time she had done it, and I would be surprised if it turned out to be the last. I had much difficulty in explaining my role in the drama, but my anxieties were self-driven. The doctors did not enquire or intrude; it was my own alarm which spoke, my own need to exonerate myself. I had been inadequate, not cruel; hopeless, not wicked. I wanted them all to know I was not as bad as the circumstance made me appear. I was, in fact, appallingly selfish, and looked at myself with considerably more distaste when Tina thanked me.

We saw less of each other after that incident, and never

sought intimacy again. She herself was not of paramount importance in my evolution, but the effect of her exhausting demands upon my circumspection with women was lasting. She taught me to walk gingerly among humankind, to look beyond the eyes and behind the words. Gilbert Harding had shown me that appearance was an illusion and that each human being was contradictory in essence. Tina showed how dangerous was the neglect of this truth.

There are so many different ways to remember. Evelyn Waugh chose to pretend that he was not remembering at all, disguising his bitter-sweet recollections as a novel. He disclaimed the truth of *Brideshead Revisited* virtually on the title-page, insisting that he was not the 'I' of the first-person narrative, nor were his characters precise portrayals of actual people. The events, the format, the conversations, were all fictional in so far as fiction is ever entirely invented, but there can be no doubt that Waugh captures in this uniquely beautiful book a large chunk of his past. One does not need to be a literary historian to feel both the warmth and the sadness of his recall of place and time, or to recognize the sparkling veracity of Sebastian, Julia and Anthony Blanche, this last alive forever in three or four pages of shimmering dancing monologue. Even the narrator, Charles Ryder, is wholly Waugh in his cool tart detachment, the clever outsider aching to be yanked in and embraced. More than all this, the words themselves are redolent of the gentle pain of recollection, the quickening heartbeat, the sudden wetness of brow, the *quasi*-fear of stepping into the past. There is brinkmanship in the language, the author daring himself to risk hurt and damage to self, the prose smells and palpitates with life relived, not things manufactured, and the reader simply *knows* that through this novel Waugh is plangently appealing for sympathy – not that we should feel sorry for him, but that we should understand his luscious misery, his indulgent distress.

This is what a first-person novel should be – a long endless tunnel into the psyche, through which the reader is pulled towards a pleasurable, sensuous experience of his own memory. The gorgeous language of *Brideshead Revisited* is more than the architecture which seduces, it is the flesh and blood of Waugh himself, that which is best and greatest and most endearing in him (the everyday Waugh being, by all accounts, an acerbic and brittle bully). It is the masterpiece which, I suspect, he did not realize he was writing, being greater than he intended. Cyril Connolly (the 'Palinurus' of *The Unquiet Grave*) maintains that a book is not worth writing unless it be a masterpiece, a self-discipline that would certainly rid our sagging shelves of vast tons of junk. But Connolly, like Waugh, relished his cynicism and, also like Waugh, longed to be rescued from it. Waugh had the Catholic Church as palliative (the same Church which saves his *Brideshead* characters from themselves), whereas Connolly was denied this questionable comfort and wallowed in his own unforgiving spleen.

Only recently have I discovered my own reserves of rancour. Writing the occasional page of advice *à la* Chesterfield *For Sam* (a red leather-bound handwritten volume to be passed on to my great-nephew after my death), I am astonished how much of it is couched in terms of prohibition. Like the Ten Commandments, it is all negative, and is clearly fed by a lifetime of disappointment and distress. Yet the source of all this spleen is a mystery to me. It must lie lurking in stale bedsheets or undeclared ambitions. We shall see. Perhaps.

Is there mystery or interest in those first days of office routine at Oxford Circus? I hardly think so. I already knew I was lucky not to have to turn up at a precise hour, sit at a designated desk in a room with scores of other people, wait to be preferred for an honourable task or summoned for promotion. I was free of the baggage of competitive ambition, and that, probably, in the long term prevented my doing anything really worthwhile or seeking any searching challenge. (A year in compulsory National Service might have helped too, but I missed that by one month – those born in April 1939 were called up, those born in May escaped. At the time I had been jubilant, hating the very notions of uniform and harshness and learning how to kill; I think differently now.) Gerry spent the morning at the office, hoping I would turn up for lunch. I would arrive about twelve, learn from him what had happened that day and what I would need to do that afternoon, then we would retire to the German restaurant round the corner (Gerry's family were among those who had fled the Nazis) and do *The Times* crossword over lunch. He would then go home to wife and children and I would get through my own work in a couple of hours and finish about four. We shared a secretary who made tea, typed letters, ran errands and made excuses for us. It was a charmed life, if somewhat lacking in excitement.

Several times a year I would travel with groups of our tourists in Britain or in Europe (Gerry hated travel, and I welcomed it). They were always American, which meant that I could act as guide by reading a guidebook the night before and spouting it out to them on the bus microphone as if I had known it all my life. They were not demanding. (Indeed, they are still not. Very recently I was a passenger on an American-dominated cruise supposed to be for the intelligent discerning customer, where the highly-paid Egyptian guide gave information which was written on a notice beside every museum exhibit we saw.) Occasionally I made mistakes, but there was never an occasion when anybody noticed.

Twice a year I took a garden tour of England, designed for ladies who were dead keen on flowers and had lavish borders of their own. I knew how to get them around and book them into hotels, but I knew nothing whatever of flowers. Foolishly, I thought that the worst answer to any enquiry was 'I don't know' so when I was asked to identify a tall flower with bells hanging all the way down the stem, I said it was a giant bluebell, a species peculiar to this country. (I learnt later it was something called a delphinium.) Driving through Warwickshire there was a profusion of yellow shrub on either side. A voice shouted to me, 'Hey, what's that growing at the side of the road?' 'It's called a *rodum sidum*', I said somewhat irritably, then turned to see people writing the name down.

In Europe I fared little better. We once left Genoa to make for dinner and overnight in Nice, only to discover, two hours after departure, that we were supposed to have seen Christopher Columbus' house. It said so on the itinerary, which was a document sacred to the punter, so it had to be included. Somebody yelled that they had been sold short. I turned up the radio in an attempt to smother this discordant note, but it spread and grew into a rebellion. I explained that if we were to return to Genoa, that would add four hours to our schedule, we should arrive in Nice after midnight and miss our dinner, which was prepared and waiting for us. It did not matter. Columbus had discovered America (or so they thought, as did most people), and he was more important than *salade Niçoise* and *daube de taureau*. So I instructed the Italian driver to go back to Genoa.

As we entered the city, I asked him, '*Sa dov'è nato Cristofero Colombo?*' '*Io?* No', was the disconcerting but not unexpected response, accompanied by a Tuscan pout of amusement. I suggested we drive into the old part of town, where we stopped in a fairly narrow street and I pointed to a house which I identified as Columbus' birthplace. Twenty-eight ladies with blue hair and spectacles dangling from chains descended from the charabanc and took twenty-eight photographs of the house. I noticed the curtains twitch as the bewildered inhabitants wondered why on earth they were being treated thus, but thankfully nobody came out to remonstrate and we loaded again quickly and sped off. Later I found out that nobody knows exactly where Columbus was born, and that no trace of any house associated with him in Genoa survives.

There were disasters of which I was not the cause but very much the victim. Two of them, very similar in effect, must stand for the lot. I was with a group of twenty-two in Vienna for three days, going on thereafter to Venice. I had by then established a routine whereby I would confirm whatever tickets I held for the next leg of the journey on my first day in a city, and therefore called in at the Alitalia offices with twenty-two tickets for a direct flight to Venice. In those days all tickets were written out by hand by the issuing agent, who in this case was a small travel office in a small town in Wyoming. One little square on the ticket was reserved for the letters OK if the seat was confirmed, or WL if it was merely requested (WL for waitlisted). My tickets were all OK, or so I thought. The officials at Alitalia soon disabused me.

The distant little girl in Wyoming had failed to show that the seats were all waitlisted, and had been for months. There had been no follow-up since the original request, and no change in circumstances had occurred in the meantime. We had no reservations at all.

Oh well, I said, here we are now, and we have to get to Venice, so let's do something about it on the spot. Do what? I was asked. The flight was entirely full (a small aircraft for European flights, with about ninety seats) and there was no other that day. What about another airline? No other airline flew that route. What if we flew via Milan or Rome and connected? Sorry, they said, we do have flights to Milan and Rome but they are full as well. Frankly, it would not matter if you flew via Moscow or Singapore, you would still not get anywhere. All flights to any destination were chock-a-block. It is difficult to credit today, but in 1963 air-travel was still a luxury purchase and there was not such a vast choice of routes. Within half an hour it was made clear to me that all flights to any destination were full not only on the day designated, but for three days before and for three days afterwards. It seemed we were marooned.

I was reaching a state of panic when I realized that we should also be on the streets, for the hotel in Vienna could not accommodate us beyond the dates booked. Moreover we should have hotel rooms in Venice lying empty which still had to be paid for. I went to the railstation. There was indeed an overnight train to Venice, but it was first-class, available on advance reservation only, and anyway it was full. A moment's reflection loosened a situation which threatened to be throttled by anxiety: there were ninety seats on that aeroplane – I needed twenty-two of them – the solution was obvious – I would have to persuade twenty-two people that they did not want or did not need to fly to Venice after all.

The people at Alitalia, seeing my distress and fearing no doubt that I would have a nervous breakdown on their floor, broke all their rules and allowed me to see the list of passengers. A little further pressure and they revealed the addresses that I required. Some of them, at least, were local, within Vienna itself. I then spent about four hours, accompanied by an Alitalia official to give me authority, knocking on doors and asking bemused travellers to sacrifice their seats for me. Most were sympathetic but unable to help. Then, one by one, they began to realize that they could postpone their journey by a week, that they did not feel well, that they intended to cancel anyway, and with a variety of other excuses I managed to pick up some eighteen seats. The official worked feverishly on refunds and re-issues as I collected my precious tickets. We were still not quite there, but word came through that a few more had missed connections or failed to show up at an earlier part of the journey. Finally, we had twenty-one seats. I, the twenty-second, was obliged to sit with the pilot, on which occasion I observed that he cannot see the ground as he lands; the windows of the cockpit all look upwards and show only the sky.

The other near-catastrophe concerned an hotel in Innsbruck. We arrived with about twenty university students one evening in June, just before dinner, hungry and tired after a long day crossing the Alps. The receptionist had no idea who we were. I pointed out that we had reservations, but she could not find them. The hotel manager was summoned. He, too, was perplexed, until he examined the diary to discover that we were certainly booked in, though for July, not for June. Somebody somewhere had made a ghastly slip of the pen. Responsibility for the error was not important at that moment, however. The manager set to the task of finding alternative accommodation – in several hotels if need be, I said – while I shepherded the troops in for a meal, they all unaware of the drama which was unfolding at reception. Once again it was a hopeless situation, for we could not find any accommodation anywhere, unless we travelled fifty miles into the mountains. I was almost ready to do precisely that, when I told the manager that there must be twenty empty beds in Innsbruck, and it behove us both to find them. If they were not in hotels, they must be elsewhere. We walked up and down the residential streets behind the hotel, asking house-owners if they had a spare room and would they mind putting up an American student for one night. Fortunately most people who could help thought it a bit of an adventure and were most obliging; as for the students, they were happier than they would have been in a twin-without-bath, but I doubt if I would have found such ready compliance with a group of middle-aged blue-rinses.

I expect the hotel manager came to some financial arrange-ment with the twenty families we invaded; that was not my concern. My only worry arose the following morning, when I realized I had not made an accurate note of all the addresses, and had to roam the streets of Innsbruck looking for stray American students on the pavement. We scooped them all up eventually. In the near forty years that have passed, I have never once made a journey without checking every detail two or three times in advance, telephoning ahead, obsessively making lists. It is one obsession which requires no apology.

Back in London my life was assuming new shapes in several directions. I spent three evenings a week at the theatre (top price £2), where I developed a sort of intoxication with the stage and an inchoate appreciation of the actor's art. I could not have written a sensible review of anything I saw, but the enthusiasm I felt was deeply enriching in ways I could not explain at the time. I assumed it was an echo of my childish attraction to fame, but it seemed too effective to be explained so glibly, and it was not until very recently that I attempted to celebrate my love of the theatre in *Thunder in the Air,* which purports to trace the legacy of English actors from Burbage to the present day, but which also slyly rejoices in my own addiction. As with everything else I have written, it is the enthusiasm which informs the text more than the facts.

The 1960s were a glorious period for the English stage. Some productions make my skin tingle even now as I recall them. I can see myself standing outside the theatre after a performance, shaking with the unfamiliar emotion of catharsis, when the actors had made me experience their pain and their anguish. Gwen Frangçon-Davies and Anthony Quayle in *Long Day's Journey Into Night* at the Piccadilly Theatre shocked me to the bone; Uta Hagen and Arthur Hill in *Who's Afraid of Virginia Woolf?* frightened me into such paralysis that I could not go straight home afterwards but walked the streets, thinking, for a couple of hours. Rosemary Harris as Ophelia, Judi Dench as Sally Bowles, the wonderful repertory group at the Old Vic in the early days of the National Theatre (Laurence Olivier, Maggie Smith, Derek Jacobi, Frank Finlay, Joan Plowright, Robert Stephens, and so on), the Royal Shakespeare Company's history plays all in one day, with sequential performances in morning, afternoon and evening, when one saw the incomparable Peggy Ashcroft age from a naive eighteen to a bitter angry eighty in a day, and be utterly convincing all through – I can still hear the clatter and bang of sword against shield in the swirling fog of the stage as Richard III (Ian Holm) desperately fought for his life in weighty unwieldy armour; all this and much more is as vivid to me now as it was then and continues to enrich in recollection.

Mrs Simcox, a walk-on part with one word of dialogue, was played by an unknown actress called Penelope Keith, whom I subsequently met back-stage. Hugely theatrical, grandiloquent in gesture, extravagant in voice as well as laughter, she was effervescent company in every circumstance. Her clarity of diction would make her the envy of many a less bubbly actress. Penny would fly to the rescue to take over domestic duties or listen to a bout of *angst*, for she had the biggest heart. We became friends for life, and I am godfather to one of her sons.

I also saw my first opera, but only just. Maria Callas was due in London to sing six performances of *Tosca* with Tito Gobbi as Scarpia, and it was announced that these were certain to be her final performances at Covent Garden. At first I made no attempt to get a ticket, for Callas was already a legendary, figure and the performances were sure to be sold out. In time, however, I reasoned that if Callas was singing in London and I was living in London there could be no proper excuse for missing the occasion – it was not as if I was resident in Tierra del Fuego and I should never succeed in explaining my want of initiative to my grandchildren. Tickets were changing hands on the black market for £100, a lunatic sum of money in those days. I bought a ticket for *Cavalleria Rusticana* scheduled for July 16 (I think), having noticed that there was a performance of *Tosca* on June 16 (that old confusion between June and July would this time be to my advantage). I arrived at the theatre at 7:25 p.m. for a curtain at 7:30 and promptly ran three times round the block so that when I came to hand in my ticket at 7:29 p.m. I was panting with anxiety and relief. The ticket collector was as pleased as I was that I had made it in time and did not notice as I held my thumb over the month (the tickets were the same colour – I had made certain of that), and in I went.

Of course I had no seat, but it did not matter. I stood at the back trembling with wonder at the magic of that glorious woman, an actress of deepest quality who happened to sing. She *was* Tosca, and I swear there was an involuntary collective movement in the theatre when she saw the knife lying on the table in Act II as the audience willed her to take care of the danger she was courting; we were *afraid* of what was going on in her mind and had buried our knowledge that she was Callas. She sang part of *Vissi d'Arte* into her armpit, leaning on the back of a chair, and sang two lines of something else upstage into the heavy drapes, with her back to the audience. These were not gimmicks; this was life.

My other lucky ticket was for Peter Shaffer's *Black Comedy* at the Old Vic, in a double bill with Strindberg's *Miss Julie*, I turned up at 7:00 p.m. hoping for a return, and hung on forlornly at the end of a queue of twelve people. When a solitary ticket was produced, it seemed that the twelve were six couples, so I was the first eligible to buy it. I sat in the centre of the front row of the Dress Circle, arguably the best seat in the house, with two empty seats next to me until just before the curtain went up, when the Queen walked in with Lord Mountbatten and took the seats. I swear I heard her say to him, 'I see we managed to sell our ticket'.

I know. Nobody ever believes the story. I may have made a mistake about Mountbatten, who was, after all, known to be a brute philistine. Perhaps it was somebody else. But the Queen was a frequent theatre-goer in a private capacity. I saw her in the centre of the stalls at the Aldwych Theatre, accompanied by the Prime Minister Harold Wilson, who had clearly taken her out for a treat, and on another occasion at the end of a row at Covent Garden with her sister Margaret. So the story is not as impossible as it must seem in the telling thirty-five years later.

It was the era of young, fresh, sharp, iconoclastic satire of a kind not seen for generations, brave in its sarcastic attack upon revered figures. We suddenly realized we had been far too polite and supine, and that the theatre could and should be subversive. It took four undergraduates to start the revolution with *Beyond the Fringe*, first at the Edinburgh Festival, then in London, finally in New York (Peter Cook, Dudley Moore, Alan Bennett, Jonathan Miller), and the ironically-named Establishment Club in Soho carried the movement forward with satire sometimes so acerbic as to be embarrassing. It was said that Prime Minister Harold Macmillan was so mortified by Peter Cook's deadly impersonation of his moral vacuity that it helped demoralize his government. It was exciting to think that the theatre could once again find the power to influence events.

There was much, much else during that fertile decade, and I was lucky that my youth coincided with it. The exhilarating freedom of the musical *Hair* seemed to shout for all of us that the past belonged to dusty old Macmillan, and the future to us; when the audience was invited on to the stage at the close of the show it was not a mere gimmick, it was a joyous seizure of control, a firecracking moment of birth. Above all, the theatre asserted itself against the tepid threat of television. It now seems absurd that, ten years earlier, the theatres of the West End had black-balled any actor who dared to appear on television, refusing him or her work on the stage. Such was the fear that TV would kill off the theatre for good. It was not to be so, for TV cannot match the keen immediacy of live theatre, its sense of danger and surprise. The playwright who boldly relished this intimate emotional contact between the stage and the audience was Peter Shaffer. The intellectual critics preferred Wesker and Pinter, but Shaffer knew as well as either of them what the theatre was for. I shall never forget the first night of *Equus,* when we had no idea what to expect from a play named after the Latin for horse and were transfixed by the sight of an adolescent boy derailed by religious fervour and sexual guilt, while four actors around him bowed and neighed and clip-clopped perfectly convincingly as stylized horses. Shaffer was especially good at final scenes. That of *Equus* had Alec McCowan as the psychiatrist addressing the audience to muse about the dilemma of his vocation, ending with a comma rather than a full-stop and leaving us all so full of thought that we would have preferred to leave the theatre in silence (a whole minute passed before anybody started the applause, breaking a spell).

A similar spell was cast by the final scene of Shaffer's *Royal Hunt of the Sun,* which paraded (that *is* the right verb) the astonishing performance of Robert Stephens as the Inca king Atahuallpa. Stephens had so altered his voice, his gait, his demeanour, even his height, that he appeared unearthly, truly like a living god to evoke awe in his people. As a god, he was immortal. The Incas had no fear of the impudent little Spanish invader because their king and protector could not die. When he was slain in the final scene, the Inca elders, wearing expressionless masks, looked on in pained silence as they waited for him to resurrect himself. The silence was almost unendurable. We felt their anguish and their bewilderment. Tears of pity and impotence welled in my eyes, and when the masks finally turned towards us – the audience – staring, looking, challenging us in our knowledge, pleading for explanation, we invested them with the expressions we felt in our hearts. There was no last speech. That was it. We shuffled out of the theatre shamed and subdued. I don't think I have ever experienced anything so devastating at the end of a play.

All this exposure to the creative spirit made me itch to do something myself, something beyond booking hotels and completing *The Times* crossword. I was beyond the age of fantasy and knew well that I could not write a play or a novel; invention was too risky an enterprise. But I felt I might be good at explaining, at presenting a subject in a readable and accessible way. I also deplored the fact that there were no useful little books on French literature in English. Whereas in Paris one could find half a dozen different studies on Sartre, of use to first-year university students who don't quite know where to begin, in London there was nothing at all. So I set about producing a little volume on the theatre of Molière, cribbed from my own university notes and filled out with extra reading. It had no originality, but it had clarity.

In the course of this work I had met the Assistant Keeper of the Public Record Office, Kenneth Timings, a colleague and contemporary of Noel Blakiston (who had known Cyril Connolly), a man of excellent education and exquisite manners, erudite, diffident, Trollopian, nineteenth-century and delightful. We became friends. He offered to show my *Molière* to a young agent he knew called Gillon Aitken.

I can still recognize the vapid young man who charmed his way across America, empty of purpose, and who took a cosy, undemanding job which would leave him free to have fun. But none of him stays with me today. It was the theatre, more than anything else, which impelled me towards some sort of creative endeavour as a means of developing the self which had been buried beneath the bombed sites of the Old Kent Road, but which Gilbert Harding had slyly detected and encouraged. I owed it to him to make an effort, to be dissatisfied and to reach up. The person I now think myself to be began to emerge when I was in my late twenties – thrusting, vigorous, unwilling to make do or put up with second-best. With my first serious attempt to write, laziness was banished once and for all.

CHAPTER 7

High on Theatre

Last night I rescued a butterfly. From the corner of my eye I caught its frantic flapping against the small windowpane of the garage as I was getting out of the car. The window is recessed, its sill piled with the junk of years (paper-bags, nuts and bolts, empty boxes), its corners hung with the gossamer thread of spiders' webs. Two daddy-long-legs poised upside down, apparently in mid-air but attached to strands so thin they might have been dissolving smoke, waited for the butterfly to tire. It was not caught in the web, but fluttered despairingly at the window-pane for freedom beyond, while the web blocked its retreat. I retired to the sitting-room and started a book, but my mind kept returning to the insect's plight. Should I leave it and let nature prevail? Does it know fear? It cannot ponder its end as I can, but surely it can feel the end threatens. Perhaps it does not matter, to the butterfly or to the daddy-long-legs, whether this particular little drama takes place or not, whether this especial butterfly survives or not. Yet it mattered to me. The butterfly became a thought in my head, it had a separate existence within me, and for the sake of my own salvation I could not abandon it.

I swept most of the web away with a brush (for I cannot bear to touch it, to have it stick to me) and the spiders scuttled. The butterfly did not rest. Its efforts redoubled, it flew against the pane resisting every attempt by me to encourage it in the opposite direction. It was stupid and obdurate and, I felt sure, frightened. Eventually I cupped my hands over it and took it into the courtyard in triumph. When I opened my hands, it did not fly away as I expected, but stood there on my forefinger, feeling the air and holding its wings folded tight against the light breeze which might dislodge it. Why did it not immediately embrace liberty? Who knows! I shook my hand and watched it fly prettily into a shrub, perhaps there to be consumed by another creature within seconds. At least I could not grieve over a death which I did not witness. My act of mercy troubled me, for I believed that I wanted the butterfly's life to be saved for another day, and yet I was also aware that I wanted to feel good about myself. I worried lest goodness be always an illusion, a veil to disguise moral self-regard. It was the problem which pervaded all Iris Murdoch's novels and which, I later realized, attracted me to them in the first place. Was altruism possible? Was it even desirable? Would not selfish ambition be more natural, more honest, more energetic, more organic?

I have spent my life trying not to do harm, trying to be amenable and helpful and compatible, and I have written, apparently with conviction, about people capable of wretched evil deeds, people who have taken life and gloated. I am weak and ineffective; Nilsen, Dahmer and West are predators. Why do I understand them? I have written about the spiders, not the butterflies.

Moreover, I am made almost ill by the contemplation of suffering. The television advertisement put out by the Royal Society for the Prevention of Cruelty to Children, which depicts an infant boy standing in his cot and waiting hopelessly for someone to come to him, his big, bold eyes eloquent with disappointment, grief, sadness and solitude, has haunted me ever since I saw it. No TV slot has ever had such an impact, at least where I am concerned. It produces far more than quiet pity; it speaks of the endless incorrigible cruelty of a human nature capable of visiting such woe upon a child. There is no question that my sympathies lie with the innocent; and yet my interest is engaged by the wicked. It seems to have been thus, subterraneously, for a long time.

The man who prodded me into a literary career by showing my manuscript to Gillon Aitken, Kenneth Timings, was a gentle and good man, sweet-natured but incurably sad. An only son, he had doted on his mother, whose death as he was launching into adulthood and a career had felled him at a stroke. He had staggered on, but never really forward, with the sustaining affection of a substitute older female figure, the historian Cecil Woodham-Smith, whom he visited regularly for dinner at her large Mount Street flat. He was also lucky in that he loved his work. The Public Record Office in Chancery Lane held no secrets for him; he knew every shelf and had fingered practically every document. The dust in its corners was breath to him, the echoes of its long corridors were his pulse. He was happiest showing scholars around, treating the vast Victorian building as his playground, and I do not think he ever minded having to spend a night there alone, when it was his turn in the rotation among keepers to sleep in for security, in a little cell with a naked bulb and a narrow bed.

Kenneth's own flat in Hyde Park Square was his office in miniature, with deep leather armchairs, a dainty sofa, a polished round table for meals, watercolours covering every available wall-space, a Landseer print of the young Queen Victoria with her beloved Albert (which I now have), Victorian ornaments and collections of plaster impressions, and above all books. They were in revolving bookcases, in waist-high shelves in the sitting-room, in cupboards in the bedroom, and from floor to ceiling all the way along the narrow corridor to kitchen and bathroom. Kenneth's clothes smelled of books, his hands were fashioned to hold them, his eyes lit up as he took one from its place and opened it. There it was that I first saw a complete set of Trollope, in the pocket-size Oxford World Classics (a series never yet equalled in publishing history), and was introduced to books I had never heard of which became instant friends; Sturgis' *Belchamber* springs to mind.

He must have been a little over forty when we met, but he always seemed old. No vanity, no care for appearance, no pride in attire upset his mild and inoffensive eccentricity. His suits, even when they had colour, were always grey, his hair always thin and uncombed, his spectacles always slightly grubby, his teeth slightly yellow. He might have stepped out of Dickens, and indeed I felt sure that he would have preferred to have lived in the nineteenth century, or perhaps in Imperial Rome. But he was possessed of that polite charm which in this world belongs only to the English gentleman – thoughtful, considerate, generous, kind and especially classless. His behaviour did not vary whether he was with a duke or a bus conductor.

His relationship with Cecil Woodham-Smith was obviously crucial to him, and she, aware and canny, treated him with amused affection. After a while I went once a week to dine at Mount Street, a ritual preceded by gin and tonic and the latest literary gossip from Cecil, her bird-like sharp face and searching eyes an amalgam of Edith Sitwell and Emerald Cunard as she told her stories, usually with a deliberate touch of madness to watch reactions ('Do you *know* the Atlantic?' was one wildly irrelevant question put to me). Kenneth was constantly in laughter in her company, and visibly happy. The standard English food, cooked by a servant and left on the sideboard for us to serve ourselves, suited him perfectly. No fuss or fashion. There might occasionally be another guest, Roger Machell the publisher (who had been born in St James's Palace and was descended from Theodora, Queen Victoria's half-sister, though he preferred people not to know), Arthur Marshall, who for once took the centre and made Cecil laugh, Alan Bennett, who took notes of the conversation to use one day in his plays.

To complete the trio of Kenneth's solace, after the PRO and Cecil, was the Garrick Club, a centre of conviviality and congenial chat as well as a thing of beauty in itself. The thousands of theatrical portraits which crowded its walls, the width, sweep and turn of its magnificent staircase, up which Dickens, Trollope, Thackeray, Irving and God knows who else had climbed, the perfect musical proportions of its Coffee Room, so harmonious, warm and comforting as to induce contentment in the most worried brow, all combined to make the Garrick a home. It was here that Kenneth felt less lonely.

When two of these props collapsed, the fragility of Kenneth's emotional stability lay bare. The Public Record Office was due to move to modern graceless buildings in Kew, too far away for him and far too twentieth century, and he knew that his career must come to an end. He would take early retirement. He simply could not abide the thought of abandoning Chancery Lane, of chucking away a mainstay of life. And Cecil Woodham-Smith died. The two events recalled the loss of his mother and were like a rehearsal of his own end. Being intelligent as well as sweet he had long anticipated these matters, and prepared himself in advance. I had noticed on the occasions when he had taken me to dine at the Garrick that he tended to speak louder than other people, shouting across the table, and that, when he entertained at his own flat, he had been drinking before his guests arrived, as if to gain courage. Now his drinking went off the map.

Kenneth took to becoming drunk all day long and not turning up for work. When his friends remonstrated and investigated, they found dozens of bottles under his bed and in his wardrobe, for the most part empty and shoved out of sight lest they remind him of sin. He was taken to hospital and thence to a convalescent home in Surrey, where he remained for two months. After that he returned to Hyde Park Square, never touched another drop of alcohol, and pulled the shutters down on life. He resigned from the Garrick, as if pleasure belonged only to the past.

His last years were pitiful. I tried to keep in touch, but he generally deflected any suggestion of a visit by saying he was too busy. When I did manage to prise an opening, I found the flat smelled of old skin and unmade beds, of unwashed crockery and stale breath. He was living on tins of soup and abjectly staring at television all day long. He detected reproach in my glance, and never asked me back. An out-of-work actor did his shopping, such as it was, and little else. He went on in this vacant manner for almost ten more years, and when he died his socks had to be peeled from him, taking skin with them. He had not bothered to undress for months.

A clever and good man dribbled to an ignominious close. There were four people at his cremation. Prescient, he had always known there would be, for he had no children or relations, and had stopped living on purpose, starting his own funeral ten years in advance. I cursed the doctors who had made him stop drinking, for he would surely have looked upon life with a wry smile if he had been allowed the disguise of alcohol, instead of which he saw it through bitter tears. Better to die five years earlier, drunk, than to sink into such lethargic degradation.

Apart from some of his prints and his grandfather clock, I have from Kenneth a scrumptious recipe for a dessert called Apple Caroline, written by hand in his grandmother's recipe book and invented by her in the nineteenth century. I still sometimes make this tart, to universal pleasure, and feel that something of his genial company is served up with it.

To go back. In his happier days, Kenneth and I found that we shared an addiction to the theatre and went often together. He had an especial liking for a form of theatre which was untried by me and to which he introduced me – the ballet. The sumptuous Royal Opera House at Covent Garden became one of my regular haunts, its Crush Bar with the fastest barmen on earth my own little club. I saw Frederick Ashton's later ballets and all Kenneth Macmillan's as they were created, watched the historically incomparable partnership of Margot Fonteyn and Rudolf Nureyev dozens of times, and felt the indescribable tingle of experiencing perfection of shape, drama and technique which only ballet can produce. *Symphonic Variations* is the twentieth century's most subtle and simple masterpiece, and *Romeo and Juliet* ballet's most thrilling spectacle. On such evenings one did not want to go to bed at all. More pointedly, Kenneth knew one of the dancers, the son of an old friend of his from Beverley, Yorkshire, called Graham Usher. And it was through Graham that I came to move among dancers as friends of my own. From that ordinary circumstance, going backstage one evening, a whole facet of life has since emerged, the repercussions of which are with me to this day.

They were all exquisite creatures, the girls wonderfully delicate and strong at the same time, who held themselves nobly and walked wobbly, the men virile or effete or both, but always arresting to look at, with proportions devised by an Old Master. Workers of huge dedication, regularly sweating it out twelve hours a day, they also liked to drink, smoke, and giggle. There was not an intellectual among them, and I swallowed their company like a draft of cool tonic.

Georgina Parkinson, dark and sultry with eyes that could hold you still (her husband Roy Round caught those eyes in a perfect photograph of her which included the rest of her face as an afterthought), yet with a belly-laugh and a theatrical exaggeration of manner and speech which were entirely captivating because not mannered or adopted, was the best-ever cast in Nijinska's *Les Biches* in which Monica Mason from South Africa – solemn, well-behaved, correct – also gave one of her two best performances, the other being *Rite of Spring*. I watched David Wall, aged seventeen, learn the part of Siegfried in *Swan Lake* in a rehearsal room in Stratford, taught by Erling Sunde, and wondered at his talent. (So did he, for he did not know who were his natural parents.) A shock of ginger hair, a face as fine-featured as a sculpture, a winning eager laugh, he seemed more at home in a pub than backstage at a theatre, yet he was the youngest partner

Margot Fonteyn ever had and he grew much later into a character actor of unsurpassed insight, creating the role of Rudolf in *Mayerling* with such authority that nobody has ever done it as well.

An idea of the fun which surrounded these people – so distant and unknowable on stage, so faultless and divine – might be derived from an evening spent with them playing games at Sybil Burton's. Donald Macleary, tall and majestic with jet-black hair *à la* Valentino, the regular partner of Svetlana Beriosova and the purest *danseur noble* of his generation, suggested a game of 'Categories'. We had a piece of paper each, with categories along the top and initials down the left-hand side, and were required to fill in the squares where these lines crossed with a person, fictional or factual, to match the category and the initial. Mischievously, Donald proposed E.T. to match one of the categories for film star, and we all struggled not to write in Elizabeth Taylor, as Richard Burton had recently deserted Sybil for her, and Sybil was overtly and copiously distraught by it all. Of course, the only person who wrote the dreaded name was Sybil herself, who won the round.

I have written elsewhere* of the intoxicating partnership of Margot Fonteyn and Rudolf Nureyev, she English and reserved, disciplined and apparently pious, as well as virtually middle-aged and ready for retirement; he wild and torrential, blatantly sexual, greedy and dangerous. There was never anything like it for theatrical magic, and I do not find it in the least ridiculous to recall that they were often given curtain-calls which went on for twenty minutes and brought them before the conquered audience twenty times. I once watched Nureyev rehearse in Chelsea, and in a break he asked me for my telephone number. That evening I was in bed by eleven when he rang to say, 'You have not eaten, I believe'. I had, of course, but I willingly dressed again to join him for supper at a popular scrubbed-table eating-place

* in *The Swinging Sixties* (1985) and *Thunder in the Air* (2000)

in the King's Road. I tried not to stare, but his face invited study, for it was craggy and sensuous, drawn by an artist to be admired and absorbed, deep and thoughtful yet obviously bursting with energy. I invited him back to my flat for a drink. 'Keep it clean', he warned as we entered the lift. I mention this only because it is a remark which does not fit his reputation in that area. We discussed Beethoven and Wagner. I have said that the ballet world was not stuffed with intellectuals, but Nureyev was an exception. His greed for knowledge – of languages, literature, philosophy, architecture, mythology, music – matched his known appetite for sex. He was wonderful company when he was stimulated, an arrogant bore when he was not. We met a few times, but did not become friends.

My closest friend of those early days was the *prima ballerina* of John Field's Royal Ballet touring company, Doreen Wells. A woman of exquisite line and beauty, as fragile as bone china and as graceful as a doe at peace, Dor exuded Englishness, that understated, almost apologetic talent for not showing off, a natural reticence which rendered holding back as thrilling as thrusting out. On stage she moved with glorious ease, as if God made her for the dance, her fingers and nose as shapely and perfectly placed as her feet and her back, and off stage she dressed like a princess. She listened more readily than she talked, but it did not matter, for she was a porcelain presence, a companion to make any man preen.

Dor came from a surprising background. Born in Walthamstow, she was the only daughter in a family of cockney men, a circumstance which drew us together. Her four brothers (I met with two of them, Jack and Fred) were all in the building trade. Her parents were likewise untutored, and her mother, diminutive at less than five feet, with false teeth that occasionally lost their place and clattered in her jaw, spoke the broadest cockney imaginable. Doreen was a surprise after four sons, all considerably older than she, and they clubbed together to make her special. They all had various musical talents, largely unfulfilled, and Mr Wells had been adept in his youth at the soft-shoe shuffle; when I knew him he still played the spoons. So they channelled their ambitions into Dor. She took elocution lessons to wipe away the accent (which was all the more amusing when she very occasionally sent herself up, once telling me that she was due to perform in *Swan Like*), and dancing lessons to give her poise. Nobody imagined that she would rise to become a *prima ballerina*, and her brothers never lost their palpable bewilderment at finding themselves actually in a theatre. The one thing they could not provide for was confidence, however, and her lifelong search for the correct pair of shoes, often changing them three or four times during a single performance, was the overt sign of her fear that something might one day let her down.

This meant that her performances, though objectively gorgeous and delightful, nearly always lacked that spark of danger, that tension of the untested. Twice did I see her give performances to raise the roof. The first was when she had to rush down from Manchester to stand in for an injured Svetlana Beriosova in *Sleeping Beauty* with the staunch Donald Macleary as partner. She stayed with me at the time, and I cooked a full breakfast for her at tea-time, before she went to the theatre. She danced with abandon, holding her balances in the Rose Adagio with greater assurance than she had ever known and fairly throwing herself at Macleary in the *Grand pas de deux* of the last act, because it was not really her on stage, but a mirror-image of her. She must have felt that she was not, for once, being judged for herself. The second was her farewell performance at the Opera House as Juliet, the very last time she would ever have to put on those dreadful shoes which never fitted, the last time she would have to worry and fret, the last time she would have to hope that she would simply enjoy herself. All her caution evaporated, and she gave a performance which brought tears to the eyes, at once passionate and serene, explosive and controlled. All her talents were concentrated on that evening, and she gave the best Juliet I ever saw, even including the dramatic star for whom Macmillan created the role – Lynn Seymour. It was a lesson in the frailty of the moment, that a truly creative performance in the theatre issues from a confluence of the right circumstances which may occur but once in a lifetime.

Another such occasion arose when Margot Fonteyn's husband, Tito, was shot in Panama just before she was due to dance the opening night of *Raymonda* at the Spoleto Festival. At once she left the theatre to fly to his side. Doreen was told she would have to take over and dance the lead with Rudolf Nureyev partnering. With only twenty minutes before the curtain, and no leisure for anxiety, she changed costume and danced the entire evening with panache.

A pair of Dor's shoes lies at the bottom of my wardrobe today.

Dor and I got along so well that we were sometimes thought of as a couple. She once said to me in a taxi, 'You know, Brian, we sometimes end up marrying old friends rather than lovers', but I was very glad that the thought was never put to the test. I could not have touched her. She was the pedestal itself. Of course I was wrong, and the hesitation was within me, not attached to her.

Meanwhile I received word that Gillon Aitken had managed to place my little book on Molière, only 120 pages long and with not a word of originality in them, with Heinemann Educational Books on condition that I should write another, on Jean-Paul Sartre, and accept the role of General Editor of a new series of which these were to be the first two titles. The series was to be called Student Guides to European Literature, and I would eventually contribute five volumes and commission the rest. Although it never took off as required reading, it sold modestly and continuously, and moves a few dozen copies a year even now. I felt competent, and looked forward to being in print with a kind of childish glee, but I knew well enough that this was not real work, and wondered if I would ever produce something solid. On the whole I thought not; it was simply not within me.

At about the same time I spied an advertisement in the

personal ads of *The Times*. Strange to think that I had never bothered to glance at them before (they covered the front page, the real 'front page' of world news being in the centre of the newspaper); nor did I ever consult them again after that day. And yet from that wholly random choice arose a lifelong connection.

The advertisement sought a teacher to give private lessons in French language and literature, and offered a box number for reply. This promised a neat little bonus to my £18 a week (£6 a week after rent), which was beginning to be stretched painfully by the cost of theatre tickets, so I wrote with some enthusiasm. The letter which came in response was on headed notepaper from an address in Hampstead – Old Grove House – and it was mysteriously signed with the name of a city in Ireland – Londonderry – just that. It proposed an initial meeting to see if we were suited and to discuss terms, and specified that the lessons were intended to prepare for A level examinations. So entirely ignorant was I of a subject which in later years would become one of my own areas of study that I know I wrote back to 'Dear Mr Londonderry'.

It was Kenneth Timings who alerted me to the fact that I found myself in correspondence with a Marquess, in time, I believe, for me to be able to excuse myself with his lordship when he turned up at my little flat in Byron Court. I told him that I did not know how to address him, to which he replied that 'You' would do fine. (Odd to reflect that some eleven years later he had to ask me what title his second son should bear. He wanted to call him Lord Seaham, the courtesy title attached to his earldom of Vane, as his elder son was already known as Lord Castlereagh, the second title of the Marquessate of Londonderry. I had to point out that the courtesy title could only be borne once, by the eldest son, so that Lord Castlereagh was already Lord Seaham, and that the little boy could only be Lord Christian Name Surname, i.e. Lord Reginald Vane-Tempest-Stewart. By that time I knew more about Names and Addresses than he did.) I was surprised to learn that the lessons were to be taken by himself. Londonderry was then twenty-eight years old, married with two little daughters (the sons came later *en deuxième noces*), he had inherited the lands and titles at the age of seventeen, lived in a huge pile in County Durham and an impressive house in London, but was wracked by a sense of non-achievement. All that he possessed had come to him by right of birth, not through desert, and though he had been educated well enough at Eton (he claimed not to have enjoyed it), he had never been to university because he had not needed to. Now he felt that he wanted to accomplish something through his own efforts; ironically, he wanted to *be* somebody. Thus he was subordinating everything for the time being to the tight discipline of correspondence courses, not for A levels but for a university degree. Would I help him?

Of course I would. It was going to be fun. But why not, I suggested, do the thing properly by going up to Oxford? The suggestion was only half-hearted, but his reasons for rejecting it were interesting. It was not because he was too old, or had family and estate responsibilities to attend to, but because he could not abide to be *seen* to be trying. He did not want witnesses. I subsequently learnt that he knew a great deal about Liszt and played the piano with more than a competence, but he never allowed anyone to hear him play. His birth and upbringing had not prepared him for disappointment, the rough-and-tumble of competition, or the risk of display.

Alastair Londonderry was a young man of striking physique and presence. Very tall, with long, generously waved shiny black hair, a heavy brow and handsome dark mien, he was obviously a catch for the ladies and could not have experienced any serious setbacks in that area. He had a firm hand and steady voice, as well as that natural confidence which comes through centuries of position. Yet the confidence was paper-thin. He appeared as nervous as I was at our first meeting, diffident and shy, almost stuttering despite the firm voice. It was as if the Marquess was the role, and Alastair the actor striving to fill it.

In due course I gave lessons also to his two daughters, Sophia and Cosima, which they treated as a huge joke; they lacked the earnestness and obstinacy of their father, who always *tried* to see a challenge through to the end, no matter how many doubts assailed him along the way. I also met his gorgeous Marchioness Nicolette, an aristocratic much-photographed icon of the sixties, with cascades of blond hair and a noble chin hiding a slightly crooked mouth, a tendency to giggle, and a frank indifference to intellectual pretensions (though not to true intellectual worth, which she admired even if she did not understand it); she would mock the self-important, to their impotent chagrin. She and Alastair had met and married very young, too young even to know themselves (she had just turned seventeen), and were bewildered by the gradual slackening of their regard for one another. Only after their divorce in the 1970s, and Alastair's subsequent re-marriage, did they finally realize what close friends they had always been, and he loved her more when she was not his wife than he had done when she was. I also came to love Nico, for she was bewitching in a quiet, girlish way – she whispered every sentence, as if she had been told it was improper for ladies ever to raise their voices, but more likely because she was afraid what she had to say was of no great moment; and she teased. Nico took to turning up at my silly little office in Oxford Circus and we would rush off to have coffee at a bar in Carnaby Street. Or I would take her for a ride in my ridiculous first car, a black shaky box called an Austin 7, pre-war and held together by glue (I had seen it for sale in somebody's front garden and paid £5 for it), giggling the way down Bond Street. She was, above all, fun, and it was she who first invited me to Wynyard, the Londonderry estate in the north of England. I have a photograph of her here on my wall in France, as she was in 1966, hair over her shoulder and down to her waist, head seductively thrown back, the beginnings of that crooked smile just touching her lips. Her suicide in 1993 was a dreadful shock, but that belongs to another age.

Lord Londonderry was proud of Nico, as he was of many people whose qualities he recognized and cherished. It was he who launched that gentle giant of British music John Ogdon, paying for his first public piano recital at the Wigmore Hall and loudly celebrating his meteoric rise (for once the hyperbole is justified) to international renown. He was proud of his family and the past, of their impact upon national affairs. But he was not proud of himself. Though he wrote a majestic imperious prose, correct to every comma, sardonic, biting and occasionally full of bile, and though he spoke with grand oratorical flourish, he never took his seat in the House of Lords (I saw his peg in the cloakroom there once, bearing his English title Earl Vane; I don't think he ever saw it himself, for he never set foot in the place). He said he was afraid he might stutter. In reality he had a mighty contempt for the affairs of men, saw political and social posturing as Lilliputian, and did not want to add to the pantomime. He was a misanthrope, beset with an ineradicable melancholia which came with his father's genes and had tormented generations of Stewarts (the mystery of his predecessor Lord Castlereagh's death in 1822 was no mystery at all when one knew the family – he died through grief for himself). When he felt the onset of an attack of melancholia, Alastair knew himself well enough to protect those around him from the sight of disintegration – he locked himself in his study and would not emerge, neither for meals nor repose, for two or three days at a time. He became my closest and most loyal friend over the years, but I soon learnt not to disturb him at such moments. There was no help I could offer.

Alastair took refuge in dark humour and dumb animals. He found much delight in horror films, the more grisly the better, and put on special showings of the more recondite stuff from unknown Hollywood studios, which used to terrify Sophia and Cosima and thoroughly satisfy his nephews Rupert and Robin, while he chuckled. And he doted on his two dogs, sad misshapen creatures that they were, bulldogs who could scarcely breathe as the result of intensive breeding, but would

snort and grunt their way across the floor. Alastair roared at
their discomfiture, but I think it made him feel more akin to
them. He also read widely about the animal inheritance, introducing me to Robert Ardrey's then influential books *African
Genesis* and *The Territorial Imperative*, and he supported
the seminal revolutionary work, still yet unapplauded, of
his friend John Aspinall. He also introduced me to the more
esoteric bits of Wagner, but twenty years too early, sad to say.
Der Ring des Nibelungen was then to me so much intolerable
noise. (Poor Sophia was taken to sit through the whole lot
at Bayreuth when she was twelve years old – Alastair was
no judge of childhood.)

I advance slightly to the divorce, if only for the record.
Nico had a son, acknowledged as the heir until she blurted
out that his father was Georgie Fame the jazz singer. Blood
tests were then taken, revealing that Cosima had been fathered
by Robin Douglas-Home. She was thirteen years old when
the discovery was made, leaving her deeply scarred. Nico,
following her divorce from Alastair, married Georgie Fame
and gave birth to a second son. She wrote to me, explaining
that the divorce had been her fault, that she had been silly,
but that Fame excited the kind of love which occurs only
once in a lifetime. Alastair retreated into impregnable gloom
at Wynyard, causing some anxiety to his sisters Annabel and
Jayne and making himself a stranger to his daughters. I was
writing another of my French books at the time, and stayed
with him at Wynyard where I had the use of the old library
next to the dining-room and saw him only at meal-times.

One of my besetting faults is that I am quick to exploit
a favour and exact a second, and I am lucky that those
I have so treated have not reproached me as they ought.
Once Wynyard was open to me, I began to spend more and
more time there when I was free from working with Gerry
(which was more or less whenever I wanted), or when I had
a chapter to write. I would go for weekends or for three
weeks at a time, at first invited, but subsequently at my
own suggestion. There were times when I was alone there,

Alastair being called to London for some duty or other, and I sat at the head of the table, my meals prepared for me by servants in the vast kitchen. Alastair was too well-bred to draw attention to my impertinence, or perhaps he was amused by it, but I shudder now picturing myself as I was then, a tactless upstart impervious to embarrassment. Years later I did the same at Chatsworth. I had been staying for several days and it was my tenth or eleventh visit. I felt I knew the place. An old school-friend was staying at the Cavendish Hotel on the estate, so I excused myself for the evening and went to dine with him at the hotel. Afterwards I said, 'Let's go up to the House and I'll show you what it's like'. It was after eleven when I took *my* guest into the *Duke's* private drawing-room, where he was lounging alone on a sofa, feet up, in the sure knowledge that he was by himself in his own house. It was a monstrously rude (and crude) thing to do, but Andrew Devonshire simply rose to his feet and made my friend as welcome as only he knew how. People like me are fortunate that the aristocrats of England have kindness and tolerance bred into them; I ought to have been turfed out on the spot.

It was not long before I discovered for myself what Nico had meant when she spoke about Fame. One of my new acquaintances in the theatre world was a very amusing actor called Peter John, destined to remain forever below the title but gifted with the nineteenth-century music-hall technique of the stand-up comic. He called one evening to announce that a young man he had met in repertory in Crewe had arrived in London to seek an agent and establish himself as an actor. He knew nobody, and Peter was trying to introduce him around to get him started. Could they come to my flat for a coffee?

Thus my first sight of Trevor Jones was framed in the doorway at Byron Court, white-blond hair, twenty-one, freckled, friendly, eager. He was the last of a large family in Crewe, with two brothers and two sisters scattered in a variety of sibling social arrangements from dire enmity to non-speaking tolerance. None of the family had anything remotely to do with the theatre, and there was no plausible reason why Trevor should aspire to be the exception. He went to work in an office, but did not fit, was restless and unhappy. He then presented himself at the stage door of the thriving repertory theatre in Crewe and told the director, Ted Craig, that he wanted to be an actor. Craig offered him a job as ASM (Assistant Stage Manager, essentially an errand-boy but traditionally the way to start in the business, for it affords endless opportunity to watch and learn and guarantees that either the graft of theatrical life will not take, or that it will intoxicate forever). Subsequently he was given a number of small parts. He was completely untrained, but he was endlessly keen and he had great natural charm.

Trevor was therefore a novice in every sense. He had only ever lived with his parents, he had never been to London, he had never had an Equity card or been on the books of an agent. His life was about to begin, and I was there to help him launch it.

Despite initial hesitation, Trevor was persuaded by me that we should set up home together. I could do nothing to influence his career, but at least I could offer domestic security. I bought a house in Brook Green with the impulsive *élan* of a man whose future was suddenly revealed before him. We needed a home and a dog to go with it. The dog was easy enough. We found him at a kennel just out of London, a frisky beagle pup whom we called Nicky. The house, which came first, was more problematic. It was cheap enough at £4,500, with four bedrooms, but it had been empty for some time and we had to cross the road and take a run in order to jump over the hole in the hall floor. Rats were living there, and a tramp or two had recently taken refuge within its walls for there were faeces on the stairs. The garden was so overgrown with weeds that one could not open the back door. Yet the house was exactly as it had been built in 1890, and to my lasting shame and regret I ripped out some of the best features, for it was the fashion in the sixties to modernize rather than preserve. Out went the wonderful old Belfast sink and the wooden plate rack above it. Out went the Victorian cast-iron bath with its dainty legs. Out went one of the great marble fireplaces, to make room for furniture. Out went the magnificent Spanish mahogany doors which separated the front reception room from the back reception room (I weep now to admit they were burnt in the back garden). We set about decorating the fusty old rooms one at a time, gradually, enjoying the illusion of playing at houses and families. For, as so often occurs when two men live together, the whole inebriating enterprise was based upon a fundamental pretence – genuinely and innocently embraced, but a pretence nonetheless.

It was, however, just as intense as the real thing, which meant that its ending, which was inevitable though unimaginable in advance, had to be brutal and thoroughly undermining. I was not allowed to pretend for long. It was too good and too enhancing an experience. If only the depth of our loves were proportionate to their plausibility, we should be protected and safe. But the converse is more often true. That which is foolhardy and cannot endure compensates with an emotion so overwhelming that transience becomes unthinkable and is thereby banished from the possibilities. That which has a basis for survival excites but lukewarm enthusiasm and doggedly refuses to take flight. Fantasy is more potent, more pervasive, than reality.

Every subsequent domestic involvement of mine has been difficult to the point of agony, and though I maintain against all criticism that I have never consciously sought difficulty, there must be a magnetic force which draws me to danger and drama, which ensures I shall be hurt and left wounded. Selina Hastings told James Lees-Milne that I was a masochist (I only know because he, mischievous as ever, having promised confidence promptly told his diary, which was published posthumously). She cannot have meant that I enjoyed pain, because we were never intimate and she would have no means of knowing, and in any case that would have been seriously wrong. But she was right if she meant that I relentlessly move towards situations that are going to cause me distress, and far from escaping them, once the danger is obvious, I sink deeper into them, either because I feel in my soul that I deserve frustration and unhappiness and must therefore welcome them, or because I know in my head that I have a duty to face harsh circumstances and must not run away. These are opposing motives. I still do not know which one is nearer the truth. But there must surely be some corollary with my embrace of difficult murder cases which forces me to contemplate the most wicked and upsetting acts, to comprehend the most disturbed and destructive personalities. Other people might find the subject disgusting, and avoid it accordingly. I will not rest until I have explained it to myself, and though I have repeatedly denied it in public, explanation brings with it a hint of exoneration (*tout comprendre c'est tout pardonner*). Why on earth should I want to speak up for Nilsen and Dahmer? Because nobody else is inclined to do so, and I cannot accept that there is nothing to explain; that is the cogent answer. But the incoherent answer, the one that issues from the soul and drives me into involvement against wise judgement and sane feeling, is as yet mysterious to me. Am I the butterfly who blunders blindly into the web and invites the spider to entrap it?

Trevor's was the only human connection that was without difficulty of any sort. It was easy, and it was fun. He was loyal, attentive, amusing, creative, a tireless home-builder and affectionate companion. He never gave cause for alarm or concern, and I counted myself lucky among men. We lived in that house together for barely eighteen months, yet the tone and warmth of that partnership is so enduring that it might have been eighteen years.

Trevor was very excited to land a part in the revival of Sandy Wilson's joyous musical *The Boy Friend* at the Comedy Theatre in London's West End. For a young man from Crewe, bereft of qualifications from any drama school, this was heady stuff. It was also, though I could not see it at the time, the delayed beginning of his independent life, to which the months with me had been only a preamble, a rehearsal without script.

I revelled in his success and would often meet him at the stage door after a performance to journey home together. We celebrated with special meals and gifts for the house, proclaiming the present and cementing the future. I anticipated status for him and associated pride for myself through him. Until one evening I came home to find Trevor had already returned from the theatre and was sitting forlorn and anxious in the front room. More peculiar, he was listening to the new LP he and the cast had recorded of their production. I pointed out that I thought it odd he should want to hear it all again when he had just been throwing it out at a live audience; didn't he want a rest from work? At which he avoided my glance and his lip began to tremble.

Trevor's affections had been diverted by his success and he found himself, to his own shock and dismay, infatuated with the man who played the lead in the show; it was his voice he was listening to on the LP. His distress was pitiful to behold, for he was palpably at sea with no idea how to reach shore again, nor even certain that he wanted to. The sensation of being helpless, out of control, was at once liberating and terrifying, for the last thing he wanted was to sow misery, yet he was bound to by virtue of his predicament. He could not do what was right. He could not *do* anything at all. The situation was rendered all the more senseless because his attentions were observed but not reciprocated. Had they been scorned, it might have been easier; but they were, with some mischief, merely encouraged and left hanging.

My own initial response was wonderfully adult. After all, I was not assailed by this monster and could still see clearly. My own sanity must be spread wide, it must make do for us both. I must remain calm, resist chiding, attach no blame, and wait patiently for life to resume a normal pattern. It would not take long. Above all, I must not myself disintegrate, for the spectacle of a man in ruins would exacerbate Trevor's self-contempt and drive him further from me. I remember his looking up at me as he sat in the high-back winged chair, confessing as it were, and asking. 'Why are you being so good about it?' Why, indeed.

I was good about it only for a couple of hours. It took that short a time for reason to be felled, and for a fetid field of poisonous weeds to grow in its place. These were the weeds of self-pity, of fear, of doubt, of worthlessness, of hope extinguished and future cancelled. I was walking down the staircase when the realization hit me – that I was being chucked away as expendable – and I stumbled with the ghastly impact of it, ricocheted against the wall, collapsed in a heap on the stair, and sobbed.

It would be otiose to indulge the anguish of those ensuing months, and would risk embarrassing the reader as well. Other people's distress causes discomfited marvel, always out of proportion to its cause, one thinks, because the cause can only be seen from the outside, not felt, and as such, it can only be described, not experienced. Words of description from the inside betray an intensity and a scope which are risible in their outlandish effect. There is a sense in which the only audience which might understand the language of the spurned lover is the lover himself; he is doomed to consult endlessly with himself and hear the same answers repeated over and over again as questions. There can be no resolution, only circular restatements of wretchedness. It is a ludicrously futile business.

Kenneth Timings understood the solace of literature at such a time, and gave me Cyril Connolly's collection of bitter essays entitled *The Unquiet Grave* (published under the pseudonym Palinurus). There I found my own reflection and felt warmed by it, as if cuddled by a friend. 'If, instead of Time's notorious and incompetent remedy', he wrote, 'there was an operation by which we could be cured of loving, how many of us would not rush to have it?' My sentiments entirely, and so powerful were they that for several months thereafter I had twice-weekly sessions with a psychiatrist in Harley Street, where I lay on a couch and stared at the ceiling, telling of the disappearance of self, trying to recapture it precisely by finding that cure. I wanted the therapist to operate upon me, to rip out that toxic part which could suffer so enduringly.

And yet at the same time I knew that if I succeeded I would die a second time, a final death against which the present woe, apparently so overwhelming, would be a mere trickle of pain. For, as soon as I realized that the partnership with Trevor was terminated (and indeed, I made the situation for him so impossible that he moved out within weeks to stay with a girlfriend, returned for another attempt, and finally decamped before the year was up), I clung to the grief which was all that remained, for if that went too, there would be nothing. The reminder of absence and loss was a torment, but at least it was the absence of something and the loss of something, and if the torment evaporated, so too would the memory and its source. I should be invalidating myself, wiping out an event in life which I wished on the contrary to cherish. So I wallowed instead.

Proust's narrator experiences similar disquiet as he realizes that Gilberte's feelings for him have diminished (in *A L'Ombre des Jeunes Filles en Fleurs*, Vol I), and shudders when he thinks that the day will come when it will not matter, for that will be:

> 'an even more cruel grief; not to feel it as a grief at all – to remain indifferent; for if that should occur, our old self would have changed, it would then be not merely the charm of our family, our mistress, our friends that have ceased to environ us, but our affection for them; it would have been so completely eradicated from our heart, in which today it is so conspicuous an element, that we should be able to enjoy that life apart from them the very thought of which today makes us recoil in horror; so that it would be in a real sense the death of the self, a death followed, it is true, by resurrection but in a different self the life, the love of which are beyond the reach of those elements of the existing self that are doomed to die.'

There is a compensation, which only 'Time's notorious remedy' can reveal. While it is true that the self who shared a brief time of commitment with Trevor was interred after his departure, the self who appreciated his qualities is intact today. I still maintain that he is one of the kindest, most gentle people that I have ever known.

Alastair Londonderry's sisters and friends were concerned about his determined isolation from the world, shut away at Wynyard for weeks rolling into months, resisting every attempt to entice him to London and some social life. He was nursing the hurt caused by the revelation of Nico's deceit. As I have said, I shared some of this time with him, working on my little study of Sartre and meeting him for lunch and dinner. We fell into the habit of taking a walk together before dinner, down to the lake and along the walk into the wooded shores of the river, discoursing, philosophizing, coming to grips with life's dilemmas (or so we thought). When I found out that the Royal Ballet were due to perform in Newcastle-upon-Tyne, not so far away on the motorway, I suggested we have an evening out there to break the routine. I intended a dose of the medicine my mother used to recommend, to 'get him out of himself'. Alastair declined without hesitation. He would not be moved.

I then made a rash gesture on my own initiative. I borrowed one of the estate's cars and drove to Newcastle to see the performance; I seem to recall it was *The Two Pigeons*. The ballerina that night was my old friend Doreen Wells (we are talking of 1971, and I had known her since 1965. Alastair I had known since 1966, and yet they had only met once, in company with Nico after a performance at Covent Garden, when it was Nico who had noticed how pretty she was, and wrote to me to say so; Alastair had been unimpressed). I asked Dor what she was doing the following day. It appeared she had class in the morning and rehearsal in the afternoon, but was free that evening, so I took it upon myself to invite her to Wynyard for dinner. I suspect my cheek would have exasperated anyone else.

Instead, when I announced what I had done, he said, 'Well,

you'll have to entertain her. I'm not seeing anyone, so I'll leave you both to dine together and I'll disappear upstairs.' My plans to drive morosity from him by a surprise event were to be still-born.

It turned out otherwise, because Doreen was ever a scatter-brain. Mistaking the time of arrival that I had suggested, or misjudging the length of the journey, her taxi came up the mile-long drive one hour ahead of schedule, at six in the evening, while we were out taking our walk. Alastair was thus thwarted in his intention of making himself scarce, for when we came up the lawn to enter through the grand French windows into the living-room, there seated, making friends with the slobbering grunting dogs, demure, elegant and utterly unconscious of being early, was Doreen. The effect upon Alastair was electric. He darted into the kitchen to alert the cooks to prepare something interesting (we normally had soup and warmed-up leftovers from lunch), darted back to see that Dor was comfortable, offered her champagne, rushed upstairs to shave and change, enjoining me to look after her meanwhile. It was clear he was captivated, bewitched. She certainly did look uncommonly pretty that day, but she could anyway never look drab however much she tried.

Alastair was a man renewed. Loquacious and energetic, he treated his guest to a display of his innate good manners and acquired knowledge of the world, telling her more than she knew (or could absorb, I imagine) about music, ballet and opera, and escorting her to the front door and into her taxi. We stayed up afterwards, he pensive and perplexed. He was obviously taken aback at his own behaviour, and asked me, would I mind if he invited her to accompany him to the opera? (It is a nice point in social relations that we do not wish it to appear that we are kidnapping our friends' friends for ourselves, and indeed there are many who go to such lengths to avoid this kind of pilfering that they keep their acquaintances in compartments and can carry on separate social engagements with each for twenty years or more without allowing any of them to meet.) Of course I did not mind. I was delighted.

There followed months of carefree outings and holidays, most often at Alastair's Tuscan retreat, an isolated farmhouse with chapel and outbuildings in a perfect spot not far from Radda-in-Chianti. The house was called Vercenni, and it was without question the happiest abode I have ever set foot in, calm and restful, rooted in the earth, ancient and shrewd, ochre and orange by day, haunted in the early evening by fireflies blinking their semaphoric signals. The smell of olives, the rustle of high branches and the smashing blast of hot sun as you went out after breakfast were the very same sensations enjoyed by the ancient Etruscans whose language lingered in the strange accents of Florence.

I would go alone, while the others were all coupled. Alastair and Doreen, Georgina Parkinson of the Royal Ballet, wife of the photographer Roy Round (with, on one occasion, their noisy infant son Tobias, now a respected musical impresario), and frequently Alastair's friend Simon Elliott, with his future wife Annabel. Annabel's grandmother was Sonia Cubitt, whom I would later consult for my book on hostesses, since she was the daughter of Edward VII's mistress Mrs Keppel, and Annabel's sister was Camilla, later Mrs Parker Bowles, known the world over for her friendship with the Prince of Wales. We were all young, sybaritic, drunk with the feeling that life was to be grabbed and enjoyed. I was gloriously happy at Vercenni.

After one such holiday, back at Wynyard Alastair took me by surprise in the kitchen (where we liked to wash up after dinner, the servants having gone home). He asked whether I thought he should marry Doreen. It seemed the last question upon which to seek advice, but I should have expected it, for Alastair was prone to sound people out on matters of so personal a nature that their opinion could not, or should not, have counted for anything. Privately I felt quite sure the match would be hard to make work. He was too intellectual for her, she too frivolous for him.

He was attracted by her working-class origins and admired the fact that she had made good in spite of them – she had been given little and achieved much, whereas, at that time, he struggled to rid himself of the notion that he had been given much and achieved little. For her part, Dor was attracted by title and status, as anyone would be, but I wondered where she would discover the strength to withstand those frequent changes of mood consequent upon a shared life.

They were duly married in the chapel at Wynyard and embarked upon a decade of gradual, insidious disenchantment. At first all was splendid illusion, disguised by the real happiness of the birth of their son, which took place upstairs at the small Chelsea house Doreen had owned before, enlarged by Alastair when he bought the house next door (he had long since abandoned Old Grove House in Hampstead). I was downstairs and heard some of the labour, then visited Doreen with her son minutes after the birth. There is no sight on earth more heart-warming. She was drained, exhausted and happy. The boy was christened Frederick and bore the title, by courtesy, of Viscount Castlereagh. I was one of the godparents.

Another son, Reginald, followed three years later, but the marriage was already by then under strain. Alastair's nervousness undermined Dor's confidence (this was before her triumphant farewell performance in *Romeo and Juliet*, mentioned earlier), and she transferred her anxiety more and more to her shoes, fussing over them seconds before she was due to go on stage. Theatrical nerves inevitably transfer to the spouse. On one terrible occasion in Paris she stumbled and fell in mid-solo, and Alastair wrote a cruel letter to her, accusing her of humiliating him, which thankfully he showed to me and I confiscated. Doreen took refuge in pseudo-scientific cures and remedies involving the waving of hands and the direction of energies in which she subsequently herself became proficient. Eventually she would hurl herself with great courage into the discipline of musical comedy, starring in *On Your Toes* in the West End.

If I mention all this, which is strictly only tangential to my life, it is because I was still held by the sour writings of Cyril Connolly, and seemed to find confirmation of his savage bitterness all around me. 'Is it possible to love any human being without being torn limb from limb?' he asked. His answer was obviously not: 'There is no pain in life equal to that which two lovers can inflict upon one another . . . the avoidance of this pain is the beginning of wisdom, for it is strong enough to contaminate the whole of our lives.' This little book had a profound influence upon my outlook, to the extent that passages from it tumbled round my head for years afterwards. Both experience and observation served to support it, or rather I used it to give me succour when experience and observation tended to depress me. I needed to know I was right to be disenchanted. I determined that I should never allow life to be so contaminated, and that henceforth I should always live alone.

CHAPTER 8

Discovering Dukes

Having decided by the age of thirty that I would prefer thenceforth to live alone, I embarked upon a period of promiscuous conquest which was by no means incompatible with the ambition for solitude. On the contrary, it was the flip side of the coin – being alone meant that one could be with everyone, in the dark, as often as one wished. I was swept along by the revolution in sexual mores which nobody born after about 1955 can possibly comprehend. England emerged from dark ages of repression, when sex had been shameful and furtive, never to be mentioned in conversation, never to be alluded to in print, never to be allowed between strangers, into the wide skies of free association, of orgies and casual encounters engaged purely for fun. It was out of the frying-pan into the fire, of course, because liberation brought with it attendant dangers quite as nasty as those of the repressive habit. But I was a young man in the midst of it, and was not about to question its philosophy. For those who had been adolescent in the fifties, it was time to breathe at last.

At the same time, sexual release gave me the confidence to pursue my potential in other directions. It was like being

uncorked. I no longer wrote my short books on French literature with an apologetic air ('they're not much really, nothing
at all, I haven't the talent to write anything substantial'),
but with the conviction that I could do them, such as they
were, better than anyone else. So when Alastair Londonderry
invited me to write a short history of his ancestral family
at Wynyard, to be published privately and distributed to
eventual visitors, I jumped at the chance. I went through
archives never before consulted, got my fingers dusty, filled
my nostrils with the scent of old documents, and thoroughly
enjoyed myself. The book, spoilt by a stupidly lyrical opening
paragraph (I was in love with Wynyard, and to this day have
a picture of the house behind its lake permanently on my
desk), was an adequate summary. The story was later filled
out in a proper book by H. Montgomery Hyde, who had
been secretary to Alastair's grandfather, the 7th Marquess of
Londonderry and Minister for Air in the thirties, and who had
the best archivist's nose of his day. When Kenneth Timings
alerted me to the imminent release of papers from the Public
Record Office concerning the Cleveland Street scandal of the
1880s, and suggested I might make a book out of them, I
arrived at Chancery Lane to find Montgomery Hyde already
up to his neck in ribboned packs of letters, and I gave up on
the spot. It would have taken me many weeks to sift through
the contents of cardboard boxes, but Hyde did it all in three
or four days, because his fingers knew which bundles to open
and which to leave untouched.

Then something else turned up. I met the flamboyant young
publisher Anthony Blond at dinner and he, into his third
bottle of wine, commissioned me to compile a collection of
dreams that infect the sleep of Her Majesty Queen Elizabeth
II's subjects. The idea was that everyone in Britain dreams
about her at some time or another, so let's see what the
dreams are like.

It was hardly an onerous task, nor did it promise to produce
a book of lasting worth. But it was fun. I wrote to everyone I
knew and advertised in the newspapers for people I did not

know, seeking the royal dream experiences of the British from Judi Dench and Alec Guinness to the local greengrocer. Some of the stories they told were bizarre, and all of them amusing by reason of their mad implausibility (the very quality which distinguishes a dream from a waking thought). The Queen was depicted driving a lorry up the M1, running a post-office, travelling with her family to the State Opening of Parliament on the Piccadilly Line, in full regalia and crown, because it was quicker than fighting one's way through traffic. Nearly all of them involved a cup of tea. I especially liked the one sent in by a housewife from Leeds who had met the Queen on a bus and invited her to tea ('I expect you don't get much chance of an ordinary good cuppa, do you, love?') and, when the Queen arrived and knocked on the door of her terraced cottage, she sheepishly confessed, 'I hope you don't mind, I've brought my mother along too'. The Queen Mother was hiding round the corner in gumboots, awaiting permission to be included.

A good number of the entries involved scenes of embarrassment, which made it clear that the Queen was only in the dream as the ultimate symbol of authority before whom it would be disastrous to make a *faux pas* of any kind. The dreams were naturally enough all about the dreamer's state of mind (how could they truly be about anything else?), in which the Queen had a useful walk-on part. My own recurring royal dream (which, come to think of it, had introduced the subject at that dinner-party with Anthony Blond) concerned my turning up for dinner at Buckingham Palace and noticing, as I sat down, that I had forgotten to put on any clothes at all. As I fumbled to protect myself with a horribly small napkin, the Queen and her exceedingly well-bred family made no allusion whatever to my nakedness, but chatted on as if nothing were amiss (in real life, I am told, all of them would have been more likely to have giggled uncontrollably).

I also spent a couple of weeks in the glorious domed echo-ringing studious womb-like reading-room of the British Museum, researching every piece of nonsense that had ever been written about the interpretation of royalty in dreams over the centuries, for a final wrap-up chapter which quoted Artemidorus, Cicero and Montaigne. I doubt if many people read those pages, and Blond himself wondered why I had bothered. Dottily illustrated by Michael Ffolkes, printed on peach paper and clothed in a pink dust-jacket, *Dreams about H.M. The Queen* was destined for frivolity from the start, yet it drew a sober review from *The Times* and sold modestly well. I heard from a friend of a lady-in-waiting that the Queen had three copies scattered round the house, and was wont to corner people with the ingenuous remark, 'Have you seen this frightfully funny book about *me*?'

Next, Blond came up with an even better idea, at which I initially scoffed. Nobody, he said, had ever written a history of all the dukedoms in one volume. Would I do it, and he would publish it? I said that I could not possibly attempt such a thing, for I was utterly unqualified, knowing nothing whatever about the subject. He should find an historian. Anthony paused and said, 'Think about it'. Very wise, for the following day I realized, as in a flash, that my unfamiliarity with the subject was the very best reason for undertaking an exploration into it. It seemed to me that I should approach history with open eyes and ears, free of preconceptions and axes to grind, eager to find out for myself. More important, the fact that I would be discovering as I went along must inevitably influence the words I used and the tone I adopted, the enthusiasm would tumble into the prose and might possibly make the book a better read. From that day I have never wavered from this principle, which is why my subsequent career has been that of a grasshopper, forever delving into new subjects which were strange to me. I hope it has worked. It has certainly made the business of writing more enjoyable. I suppose it must be true that an expert on ducal history could have produced a more reliable book (although for a quarter of a century now mine has been a source of material for researchers, journalists and obituarists), but there was always the danger that a man who had become an expert might also have become a bore, and that his tiredness would be reflected in his prose. At least mine would be fresh.

So I accepted the commission, and launched myself into two years of laborious compilation of facts and agreeable dissection of character spread over five centuries of history into twenty-six families (I did not include the royal dukes, as their lines tended to peter out and they were but upstarts against the ancient aristocracy). Virtually by accident, I found that I had a talent for tracing lines of descent and for understanding the use of titles and the circumstances of special remainder. It seemed easy to grasp that Lady Bloggs was the wife of a marquess, an earl, a viscount, a baron, or a baronet, whereas Lady Ethel Bloggs was the daughter of a duke, a marquess, an earl or a viscount; that Ethel, Lady Bloggs, was the widow or the divorced (and not since remarried) wife of said marquess, earl, etc., and that the Dowager Lady Bloggs was the widow of former Lord Bloggs whose son had since inherited the title. All of which was very useful when unravelling the half-dozen Duchesses of Westminster who appeared in the press, and yet the press almost wilfully refused to understand any of it. They repeatedly referred to 'Lady Diana Mosley' when there had never been such a person (the widow of Sir Oswald was the Hon. Lady Mosley, Hon. by virtue of her rank as daughter of a baron, Lady by virtue of her marriage to a baronet; to be Lady Diana she would have had to be the daughter of a nobleman higher in rank than a baron). It was all a matter of accuracy, and it was astonishing to me how few people could get their minds around it. Even Buckingham Palace got it wrong with the announcement that H.R.H. Princess Anne would be known after her marriage as 'the Princess Anne, Mrs Mark Phillips', when she could not conceivably ever be Mrs Anything. She was princess as the daughter of the monarch, and she was Lady as the daughter of a duke, thus she could only accurately be styled 'the Princess Anne, Lady Anne Phillips'.

The Americans were even more at sea, and with much more justification. The Duke and Duchess of Devonshire had been

Marquess and Marchioness of Hartington from 1944 to 1950, as the 10th Duke (Andrew's father) was still alive. When they found themselves once at Chicago airport waiting for a connection, Lord Hartington received a telephone message, which in those days could only be communicated through a tannoy loud-speaker. The twangy voice loudly announced, 'Would Claud Hartington come to the telephone, please?' His wife has called him Claud ever since.

There was also the curious problem of precedence, which depended to some extent upon which order of peerage your dukedom belonged to. There were not just dukes. There were dukes of England, dukes of Scotland, dukes of Ireland, dukes of Great Britain, and dukes of the United Kingdom. Some of them were dukes twice over (Hamilton and Brandon, Buccleuch and Queensberry, Argyll and Argyll – yes, that is accurate), and one overloaded figure was duke four times, Duke of Richmond, of Lennox, of Gordon and of Aubigny in France, and descended from a bastard son of Charles II ('bright sons of sublime prostitution'). The Duke of Somerset, who bears only one subsidiary title (Lord Seymour), takes precedence by a long chalk over the Duke of Atholl, who has nearly twenty titles and lives on a remote farm in South Africa. The matter of precedence greatly exercised duchesses when their husbands mischievously declared themselves aloof, and even in the twentieth century two such ladies were spotted squeezing through a doorway side by side rather than one allow the other to take precedence.

I worked in muniment rooms and attics, in outhouses and local museums, sorting through papers which had sometimes never been touched before. The Duke of Atholl invited me to stay at Blair Castle and gave me free use of the family papers, ranged in scores of black tin boxes on the floor. There I discovered the pitiful story of the lunatic 5th Duke, who lived in a padded cell in St John's Wood, London, in the early nineteenth century and was completely forgotten by history. It was at Blair Castle that I encountered my first personal evidence of ducal eccentricity. Iain, the 10th Duke and last to live in the castle, was a tall, stooped man, with large Wellington nose, narrow vertical mouth, horse's teeth and a tendency to dribble. He was kind and gentlemanly, but living alone was comforted by routines, one of which was to dress for dinner whether there was anyone present or not. At our first dinner he sat at one end of a long, highly-polished mahogany table laden with eighteenth-century silver, myself at the other, both in black tie. Conversation was a trifle strained. I had given up smoking a few days earlier, but now felt an urgent need for a smoke. I asked if perhaps there might be a cigarette available. 'Don't have such a thing in the castle', replied the Duke. Could I perhaps ask Snape, the butler? 'Do what you like', said the Duke, and rang. Snape came in and was motioned towards me. I made my request. 'I'll see what I can do, sir', said Snape, disappearing into the kitchen. When he returned, he bore on his high left palm a beautiful large silver salver, and in the centre of it was rolling one solitary Woodbine.

The Duke of Leinster was a shy man, bearing the burden of a sad and bizarre family history. The Fitzgeralds are one of the most illustrious families in Ireland, with a proud ancestry stretching over nine centuries. There are monkeys on their coat of arms in recognition of the rescue of a sole heir by a pet ape in the thirteenth century, but the monkeys might signify less worthy events in the twentieth. The Duke's father, 7th Duke of Leinster, was the third son of the 6th Duke. As such, he did not expect to inherit any titles, and only a mild sum of money. A dashing young man fond of limelight and adventure, he conceived many a foolhardy scheme in order to cash in on his name, taking on wagers set for him by the newspapers. Still he did not make enough to live in the manner he craved, he ran up debts at the casinos, and had quickly to hoist himself out of them. He found salvation in one final gamble. A rich businessman called Harry Mallaby-Deeley (owner of the Fifty Shilling Tailors which used to be on every high street) agreed to settle Fitzgerald's £60,000 debt in return for a piece of paper declaring that he legally and wilfully surrendered to Mallaby-Deeley all of his rights of inheritance on the Leinster estate. Since he stood to inherit nothing, it seemed to him like a very nice deal indeed, and he signed. Unfortunately his two elder brothers then died, one fighting in the First World War, the other in a hospital for the mentally deranged in Edinburgh, and young Fitzgerald suddenly found himself Duke of Leinster, without the right to live in any of his grand houses, use any of his silver, hang any of his pictures. Everything now belonged to the businessman, and the Duke had only his titles to console him. He spent the rest of his long life hunting the world for an heiress to marry, was once reduced to running a tea-shop in Rye, and took as his last duchess the housekeeper who looked after the block of flats in which he lived (his first wife and mother of the present line of dukes was May Etheridge, a musical comedy actress). The contract had been clever enough to include a clause stipulating that the Duke should take no measures to shorten his life, which would artificially curtail the number of years the businessman could enjoy the fruits of his arrangement. It was astonishing to me that the 8th Duke displayed not a flicker of resentment for having been so deprived of his inheritance. He always knew he would have to work to earn his living, and would live in accommodation provided from the Mallaby-Deeley coffers. He ran a training-school for pilots at Oxford. The Premier Duke, Marquess and Earl of Ireland was gracious, unsophisticated, grateful for a treat, modest and appreciative. I did not continue to see him after the book was published, because it was clear that he did not like a fuss to be made.

The Duke of Portland had also seen his inheritance stripped from him, and he most certainly did want a fuss to be made. His kinsman the 7th Duke had disentailed all property from the titles, enabling Welbeck Abbey and the millions in the bank to go to his daughters instead of his heirs. Oddly enough, he bore the nickname 'Chopper' long before this act of chopping the dukedom from the property, which effectively meant that the 8th and 9th dukes had to fend for themselves and were never even allowed to set foot at Welbeck. The 9th Duke was the one I knew. As Bill Cavendish-Bentinck he had been in charge of co-ordinating intelligence services during the war and was subsequently His Majesty's Ambassador in Warsaw. An urbane and genial man, he lived in a detached house in Carlyle Square, Chelsea, and enjoyed the life of gentlemen's clubs. He actively encouraged me with the book, making formerly secret papers available to me, and was most keen that I should expose the wickedness of Chopper's theft. Bill was the last Duke of Portland, although there is an earldom of Portland which has passed to an actor whom I did not meet.

It almost felt as if I had 'discovered' the Duke of Somerset, living quietly in Wiltshire without anyone being apparently aware of his existence. Though the dukedom is well known to history since the 1st Duke was Lord Protector in the reign of the infant Edward VI, and his sister, Jane Seymour, had been one of Henry VIII's wives, and despite also the title being second only to the dukedom of Norfolk in antiquity and seniority, a surprising number of otherwise learned people did not realize the dukedom survived into the twentieth century. Percy Somerset lived in the house at Maiden Bradley which Henry VIII had given to his ancestor, rarely went to London, never took his seat in the House of Lords, was not fodder for newspapers. He lived like a country squire, with wife Jane, two sons and an assortment of dogs, ate hearty British food (meat and two veg), amused his guests and bothered no one. He was the most genial host, and his house the most warm and friendly of any ducal establishment. Percy readily confessed that he could not quite understand all the intricacies of the Seymour descent, involving special remainders, disputed titles, bastard births and what not, and was frankly pleased when I managed to unravel it (a task which absorbed me for weeks among the records of the House of Lords). His son John is the present Duke.

I did not contrive to visit and stay with all twenty-six dukes, either because they lived abroad, or because they did not want to see me, or because I did not want to see them (Marlborough being one of the latter kind). Two became firm friends. Freddie Richmond and his wife Elizabeth were frequent visitors to my house in Caithness Road, and so easeful and uncomplicated was our relationship that I mostly asked them to dinner alone rather than include them in a party; we simply enjoyed one another's company. Freddie had what is known as 'the common touch' – there is no improvement on the cliché – and could have passed for a cab-driver instead of a duke. My father, on being introduced to Alastair Londonderry, had told me afterwards, 'Blimey, yer wouldn't look at 'im twice if yer passed 'im on the street, would ya?' He would have had the same judgement on Richmond, a man of true modesty and inherent decency. He had in fact been a racing-driver in his youth and had worked on the shop-floor in a car factory as 'Mr Settrington', none of his mates having any idea who he really was. He needed no special manner to learn, no heavy disguise to assume, for he was hearty and chatty to all comers. There is that contrived modesty which boasts of being ordinary, when a man assures you repeatedly that he is not worth the attention which is lavished upon him and wishes he could deflect it, all the time alerting you to the fact that the attention is there, in case you might not have noticed, and making you feel that he really is some special kind of individual graciously prepared to mix with the lads for a change. Freddie Richmond was not remotely like that. He could not have acted a part, for pretence was utterly foreign to his thought. He did not go out of his way to avoid mentioning that he was a duke; if the subject came up, it was addressed, and he cheerfully admired the character of his ancestor Charles II, whom he would talk about gaily. But it was just one subject among many, not one to drag in without warrant. He was very much aware of the lottery which awarded him a mighty birthright, and would chuckle about it disarmingly. His father's generation had been much more stuffy, and he would chuckle about them too. When he had announced his intention to marry

Elizabeth, the daughter of a local vicar, there was uproar in the family, for he ought to have chosen a duke's daughter like everyone else. That made him roar with laughter, as it did Elizabeth. I don't think I ever saw Freddie without a smile on his face and the hint of a chortle in his voice. And he had withal a sympathetic ear. I did not hesitate to discuss problems with them both, and when I came to look after a troubled teenager – Gary – I knew that their benevolent spirit and beneficent interest would work quiet influence upon him and so I asked them over. Without strain or design, they were simply a wonderful example to set before him.

I held that it was impertinent to write about people during their lifetime without their approval of the content. It is a principle which I maintain to this day, in defiance of criticism which shouts about censorship. The answer to these critics is simple agreement: that your subjects have a perfect right to censor what you say if they find it to be wrong, misinformed, misguided, or even merely awkward. The time for elaborated candour is after their death, which is why historical gossip feels so free and fresh, when contemporary snooping inevitably contains a snigger. My chapter on the dukedom of Devonshire came right up to date with the present Duchess and involved some account of her own remarkable family, the Mitfords. She was the youngest of six sisters (brother Tom having been killed in the war), each in her own way a figure of outsize glamour and vivacity, yet each an individual. Nancy the novelist, acerbic and brittle, with sharp hilarious wit which was, however, intolerant of the mentally slow, and who suffered a horrible lingering disease before death released her (she sent to one of her twenty-odd doctors a postcard of a cemetery with the message, 'no wonder these places are full up with people like you about'). Unity the idealist, beautiful and wilful, intellectually obstinate, who flirted with Hitler and shot herself when war broke out between her two beloved countries (she, too, lingered, dying nine years later in a semi-paralysed condition). Diana the fascist adventuress, with the most perfect beauty of face in the twentieth century, bookish, polyglot, gifted with style in manner, dress and the pristine prose she wrote, who deserted her husband for Sir Oswald Mosley, whom she then married, and spent the war in prison as a danger to the security of the land. For years after the war she attended annual fascist reunions and was revered by the surviving Blackshirts as their own icon. Jessica the communist, who had fought in the Spanish Civil War, had eloped with a nephew of Churchill, later married an American Jew, lived in California and wrote scorching sarcastic books on the American way of life (she and Diana had been the closest of friends in their adolescence, and were since separated by a political gulf so wide that they only met once in fifty years, at Nancy's funeral). Pamela, known to all the others as 'Woman' because she was grown-up before her time, solid and sensible, who kept rare chickens in Wiltshire and was happily ignored by the press. Debo was the last, so much younger than the others that she was able to observe their high-spirited cavortings, ponder, and keep her own counsel. Later she would be the guardian of her sisters' reputations. She had married Lord Andrew Cavendish, who survived his elder brother and became Duke in 1950.

To show the paragraphs that concerned her, I invited the Duchess to lunch at Mark's Club (I was not a member, but Mark Birley was then married to Annabel, Alastair's sister, and was well disposed towards me). It was, I thought, sufficiently posh a place, and just round the corner from the Devonshire's London base in Chesterfield Street. She walked in to be greeted by old friends, elegant and classy but pragmatic at the same time, a sparkling brooch perfectly placed on her lapel, rows of pearls, greying hair immaculate, and the rough straw bag which she carried everywhere and into which she threw everything she would need that day and a quantity of other stuff she might need (who knows?) one day. Her cornflower blue eyes were bewitching and her straight friendliness enchanting.

In years to come I would learn to know this extraordinary woman well enough to spot the special qualities which had enabled her to chart her path with care, determined to avoid the heady but dangerous excitements which had variously interfered with her sisters' well-being. It had been she, after all, aged barely twenty, who had gone to Switzerland to recover the wounded damaged body of her sister Unity and escort it, with special permission, back to England. She had tremendous discretion. Whereas one always knew what Jessica thought, because she told you without your asking, and could easily learn what Diana thought, because she did not dissemble or divert any enquiry, Debo was cautious to a degree. I have not once heard her express a political view in near thirty years. I can make guesses, based on short evidence of predilection, namely that she was quick to point out that Jessica's book on their childhood *Hons and Rebels* was packed with lies, which suggested she did not trust her communist sister very far. On the other hand, she kept in touch with Jessica until the end of her life, once saying to her little nephew, who had been warned by his mother that aunt Debo sold slaves, 'Tell your mother that if we had slaves, we certainly shouldn't sell them'. She was devoted most to Diana, but then so was everyone who ever knew her, myself included, for Diana was far greater than her fascist connection, far softer than her skewed reputation – in fact she was the Mitford with the biggest heart of all, a woman of such compassion that she tried to lessen the unhappiness of others by absorbing some of it into herself. Debo herself remained doggedly enigmatic, astute but circumspect.

She was also far cleverer than she let on. Indeed, it was a *leit-motif* of hers to exclaim in the presence of writers, 'Oh, it must be wonderful to be so clever!', which was very flattering until one realized that she wrote better than any of them and saw the world more clearly, with no fog or double-vision to intervene. She loved Chatsworth with a passion and a curiosity which never diminished, always finding out something new about it, always working on some new scheme to brighten and enliven it. To everybody on the estate it was known as The House. Debo privately called it

The Dump, which was no more than an affectionate tease. She gave her life and energy to it and, together with the Duke, did more to make Chatsworth breathe and thrive than any of their predecessors since early in the nineteenth century.

Debo was also the funniest of her sisters. I never knew Nancy, but fancy her wit might have been cruel, and that she would have intimidated me. Pam was funny without knowing why, Decca so committed to The Truth that she only poked fun at Its Enemies, and Diana was wary of being frivolous lest she be misunderstood. Debo had a wonderful sense of mischief. When Major Spowers came up from Christie's to compile the first inventory of Chatsworth books for 150 years, on the first day he was immediately nicknamed 'Bookworm', and this was reduced by day two to 'Worm'. Debo never called him anything else from then on. The Czechoslovak Ambassador and his wife came to lunch (during the Communist era, of course). He spoke perfect English, but it did not extend to a familiarity with Mitford nicknames. When the Duchess called out, 'Worm, you really should have some more of these delicious potatoes', I saw the Ambassador's face glaze with disquiet, as he deduced that this was how, in capitalist countries, aristocrats were expected to treat their guests.

On another occasion she sat her sister Diana next to George Thomas, Speaker of the House of Commons and a well-known firebrand anti-fascist, then watched gleefully as they virtually fell in love and would not stop talking to each other. She told me that she had once surprised a man sitting in a chair beneath a naked light bulb in one of the empty rooms on the top-floor. 'I said, "Oh I'm terribly sorry," and closed the door again. I've no idea who he was. He might still be there, for all I know.' And she delighted in telling stories about her grand-mother-in-law, who walked the long corridors in to dinner tapping the furniture with her walking-stick. 'Woodworm, you know', she explained. 'Give them concussion!'

It did not take long to work out why Chatsworth was such

a happy place, despite its vastness and imposing grandeur. Debo set the house to work, started new small businesses within it, and treated the private quarters as a cosy little cottage. As a result, that is what they became.

Andrew Devonshire was quite simply the most noble of the noblemen I encountered. His behaviour was impeccable whether he was entertaining his friend the Prince of Wales or chatting to the gardener's wife. One never had the impression that he divided people into categories, except in so far as he made it clear he regarded himself as the luckiest man alive to live in such a beautiful house with such privileges attached to his position, and the rest of the world was less fortunate and more deserving. Consequently, he went out of his way to earn his perks, accepting virtually every new duty required of him, never refusing a favour asked if it were within his ability to oblige. All this when his eyesight was so poor that he needed a huge magnifying-glass to read letters, and recognized people in a room by their voices, their tread, the size of the shape they made before him. He ought really to have taken life more easily, but he thought it was incumbent upon him not to. I once saw him leave his own table and guests in order to rush off to Buxton, where he had months earlier promised to attend a local boy scouts' meeting. He never broke a promise.

When you drove up to the gates which opened the drive to the West Front of Chatsworth, a doorkeeper rang a secret bell to alert the Duke of your arrival. Magically, then, he was there on the steps to greet you as you emerged from your car. He asked me if I would like a drink before dinner. That would be very nice, I said. Vodka and tonic. Fine. He showed me to my bedroom and then disappeared. I expected a servant to come with a tray as I was unpacking. Not a bit of it. Andrew walked down the stairs, along an immense corridor, round a corner, along another corridor, found the drinks table outside the door to the drawing-room, poured a drink which he could hardly see, then walked all the way back and up the stairs to deliver the drink to me personally.

I was his guest, not his servants', that was the point. Years later, I told Debo and registered my continued astonishment. She was in turn amazed that I should be surprised.

One mystery has never been dispelled, and I hope never will be. It must have been the first time that I stayed a weekend, for I did not yet know the ropes. I drove up to Chatsworth and took with me two fairly silly pornographic magazines that I wanted to get rid of, the kind of matter you find on top shelves in high street newspaper shops. I thought I would stop at a service-station on the way and throw them into a dustbin. But everywhere I stopped were crowds of people, and I did not dare. Well, I would chuck them on the way back! On arrival I was greeted and entertained before being shown to my room. There, to my horror, I found that a manservant had unpacked my luggage, and hung my clothes. On the bedside table he had carefully placed my two magazines. God knows what was said in the kitchen that evening.

The enjoyment I derived from writing *The Dukes* was disproportionate to the job in hand. Obviously, it was important to find myself engaged on a *real* book, to be published in hard covers about a large subject and one which required a good deal of original research, and when these things hit me in solitary contemplation a satisfied smirk would spread across my face. This was to be, perhaps, the beginning of a career. But two other circumstances made this book a crucial step in life. The first is difficult to explain, yet central to my view of myself. That which made my heart stop when I talked to varied dukes was the baggage of ancestry which they carried. I do not mean that there were important historical figures in their past – that was a fact without being an emotional pull – but that there was a traceable past at all. To them, it was all a matter of course. When Andrew Devonshire spoke about 'us', he meant not just his immediate family but the ten Dukes of Devonshire that had preceded him. His domestic horizon was five centuries long, and he seemed as familiar with Bess of Hardwick, who had built Chatsworth, as with his own mother. To me, who could ally myself with certainty only to one generation, this was all a source of exquisite wonder. In a sense, I did not know myself, I could not point to a bunch of characteristics accumulated over the centuries and talk about 'us' in that way. I was dropped in the world, unclothed and undocumented. And this ability to hold a personal past in one's hand was something I frankly envied.

When the Duke of Northumberland took me to a high point in the grounds of Alnwick Castle and pointed to a distant hill and valley where Hotspur had fought his ancient battle, I shivered with excitement. That finger on that hand was of the same flesh and blood as Hotspur's himself. It seemed so simple, but to me it was an inaccessible joy. There was a sense in which I lived the lives of old families, writing this book, by proxy. That may seem both stupid and impudent, but I feel sure such was the case. I have had frequently to withstand an accusation of snobbery, which has caused me no pain at all because the people who imputed it never understood what the word meant or what was in my heart. But when Jim Lees-Milne wrote that I wanted to mix with society people in high life, he was not wrong – he was merely incomplete. He did not say why. Idiotically, I was purloining the IDEA of a past.

Even more now, I feel adrift as I mysteriously felt before delving into the history of dukedoms (and later of Corelli, Benson, Aspinall and so on), almost undefined. There is no real past that I can grasp, and perhaps not much of a future either. I do not think of death except of as something to postpone as long as possible. I assume one feels nothing afterwards – how can one, when the subject, I, is no longer there to do any feeling? – but am beguiled by the conscious mind's urgent need always to contemplate an unconscious state, which is both logically and imaginatively impossible. What was possible was to contemplate the past – the real past that I was studying and the imaginary past that I invented for myself. I did not for one moment fancy, in the manner of a romantic novelist, that I was descended from an illustrious mediaeval baron; what I imagined were figures like me, dressed differently, speaking with a different accent, engaged upon different tasks, but recognizable as myself four hundred years ago. I once found myself studying the character and gait of a Cavendish of the eighteenth century, when I looked up from the desk I used at Chatsworth and spotted Andrew Devonshire walking past the window; it was the same man as the one I had been reading about. The shock of that realization was palpable, and very pleasant.

The other circumstance which made *The Dukes* a milestone was my meeting with Camilla Osborne.

It was sheer accident that brought us together. We were separately invited to a drinks party at the mews house near Berkeley Square of the pianist Moura Lympany, and we both found ourselves meandering through strangers. We eventually meandered into one another and propped up a wall together. We were soon chatting so intensely that the rest of the company ceased to exist, and I knew that I had made a friend for life. She was younger than me, in her mid-twenties, with big round eyes deep with emotion and sentiment, a high forehead suggesting reading and rumination, thin lips spreading to reveal lovely teeth, and a charming confidential giggle, which she made no attempt to suppress but enhanced by conspiratorial glances and fluttering fingers. Camilla was deliciously feminine, soft, so light and fluid that one wanted to pick her up, and I soon found she had a wonderful habit, which I like to think she reserved only for me: when walking side by side, instead of placing her hand through my elbow, she would run it under my armpit and up in front, bent back over my shoulder. It sounds clumsy, but it is delicately intimate.

She naturally asked me what I was doing, and when I said I was writing a history of dukedoms, her huge eyes grew and glowed, and she could scarcely credit that I had no idea who she was (not because she attached any importance to herself whatever, but because the coincidence was too striking). As the only daughter of the late Duke of Leeds she was the last in the line of Osbornes that descended from the great Danby, and had she been born male, she would have been Duke herself. The dukedom had petered out with a distant kinsman who succeeded her father and had no offspring. All the genes culminated in her, so that she was not only beautiful and sweet, but an heiress as well, in the best sense, the repository of disappeared character and ephemeral personalities. She was her own history.

Though I used the name Osborne, she was in fact Lady Camilla Harris, divorced from the father of her daughter Emily. I said she could not allow the name Osborne to be concealed in this way, and urged her to return to it. She was so excited by my book that she asked if she could help with it, which was a delightful excuse for us to see each other often – at dinner, at the theatre, for long talks into the night, for being together. Every time she looked at me with those great eyes, which went into my soul, I melted and flushed with the knowledge that I was loved. We stayed in one another's houses, went for trips together (including one hilarious outing with the middle-aged ladies of the Byron Society, when we shamelessly mocked their subconscious frustrations like naughty schoolchildren), and we worked as well. Camilla did all the proof-reading with me (and allowed me the use of a picture of her father as a boy, looking just like her; I felt sure that was a gesture intended to be not merely professional), correcting for hours on end. We finally had the terrible task of compiling an index, which we did in one eighteen-hour day, journeying by train to the printers at Tiptree and being shut in a room with masses of bits of paper, mugs of coffee and dry sandwiches. It could not have been done without affection, for it was in essence a dire, grim strain.

When Camilla and I spent a holiday in Moscow, along with travelling companions Anton Dolin and Jane Buchanan-Michaelson, I knew that I should have to make a decision. The holiday was entertaining enough, to be sure. We laughed at Jane's rigid routine, spending all morning having her hair done and never once going out to see Red Square – she might as well have stayed in Chelsea; and at Dolin's outrageous flirtations, which the Russians endured because he was so famous in that country. Through him we were able to sit in class and watch the immortal Plisetskaya put her body through its movement – a rare privilege, we were told, and through Jane we were invited to the private home of Bolshoi dancer Maris Liepa, whom she knew well (his son, then ten years old, sat quietly at the table, hardly speaking – he is now a big star of the ballet himself). Despite all this, we were aware that we were being followed wherever we went. Police would stop us at traffic lights, three or four times in one journey, to check papers, and Dolin responded by shouting his fame at them. At a restaurant we once waited two and a half hours for the first course, as permission was sought to serve us.

But behind all the fun of new adventure there hovered the bitter-sweet nature of our relationship. I resist the use of the word 'should' in any human circumstance, as imposing a dimension of authority upon fine and difficult choices, but I have been tempted ever since to say that I 'should' have asked Camilla to marry me. She would have accepted. She wanted me to ask. We discussed it frankly. Yet I had not rid myself of fear, and knew very well that I ran the risk of making her unhappy, even miserable. I could not take that risk, for I loved her too much to upset her future. This, of course, is the logic of reason, of weighing the problem and assessing its consequences, and this alone must show that marriage would have been a mistake – it is accepted by all that one marries because one cannot bear the thought of life without the loved one. But it had not always been so. Before the selfish era in which we live, marriages had often been built upon regard, respect, fondness and affinity as much as upon passion, and had been none the worse for that. I was happy with Camilla in the way that Montaigne was happy with La Boëtie, because she was she and I was I. Hardly a week passes, even today, when I do not think about her and wish I had had the courage to make her my wife. Life without risks is but counting the clock.

I had by this time different circles of friends which eddied around one another without colliding. There were those who evolved from my answering that advertisement in *The Times* placed by a man called Londonderry, which included his sisters Annabel and Jayne, his friends John and Brenda Ogdon, John Aspinall, Earl Wild, Simon and Annabel Elliot; those who came from the ballet world – Anthony Dowell, Merle Park, Antoinette Sibley, Wayne Sleep, Freddie Ashton and of course Doreen; those literary folk whom I had met with Kenneth Timings – Cecil Woodham-Smith, Alan Bennett, Arthur Marshall, Hester Chapman, Angus Wilson; those gathered from work on the dukedoms, already mentioned; those who were patients of my doctor, Patrick Woodcock, who looked after everyone in the public eye. It was through Patrick that I met David Hockney, a lifelong friend with very sharp views on life and the irrepressible honesty to express them wherever he might be, and, only once, Noël Coward, at whose knees I literally knelt, for he was too frail and too deaf to talk much otherwise.

Patrick gave splendid dinners in his all-white apartment above the surgery, cooking simple dishes with style and much attention to smell (I think he relied a lot upon Elizabeth David's recipes, then revolutionary in formerly stodgy British kitchens; she was also a friend of his, one I did not meet). One evening I particularly cherish. The only two other guests were the Countess of Huntingdon and her daughter Lady Selina Hastings, just down from Oxford. The conversation became literary and turned to the Brontës. This gave me the opportunity to be fulsomely eloquent about a book I had just read called *The Brontë Story*, and I confidently announced that the best book ever written on the Brontës was by a woman called Margaret Lane. The Countess looked stunned for a moment, then saw I was guileless, and said, 'Well, that's very nice to hear, since I *am* Margaret Lane.'

To pay a compliment without knowing one was doing so was sweet indeed, and made up for the dreadful *faux pas* of my youth about Peter Daubeny's missing arm. Margaret

Lane became a firm friend, and Selina is loyal to this day, despite bluntly reproaching me for occasional vanity.

The friends I saw daily, and naturally took for granted, were the makeshift 'family' that surrounded me at Caithness Road. After Trevor's departure I had determined to live alone, and in a sense that is what I did. Yet it was far from being a life of solitude. Trevor's friends from the Crewe Repertory Theatre had become my friends, and when they needed to descend upon London, they descended upon me, as the only person they knew with a spare bed. The idea was that I should put them up for a few weeks until they found their feet and settled in flats of their own. But life was so agreeable at Caithness Road that, for the most part, they stayed for years. We were rarely less than five in the house, often six, living together as if we always had, sharing the kitchen, sharing the two bathrooms, sometimes sharing meals and taking it in turns to cook, sometimes eating separately. Nothing could have been more easy or more equable, and I never felt a stranger in my own house, nor did they give me the impression they felt themselves intruders. I recall only one daft quarrel, when Peter John, who lasted a few weeks there, wrote his initials on the eggs he had bought and made it known that he intended them to be consumed by nobody else but himself. I told him I would not permit that kind of pettiness, and that we all bought whatever was necessary when we noticed that it was necessary, without proprietary rights. It was not a row fertile enough to spread.

Brendan Price and Gwen Taylor were a couple for whom my house was their home, and their careers flourished from it. Val Phillips stayed for a couple of years in what later became the sauna room; she was a champagne communist, who delivered subversive pamphlets from her boyfriend's Rolls-Royce. Maggie Ollerenshaw was Trevor's best friend, and stayed with me between lovers. Chattie Salaman taught at the London Academy of Music and Dramatic Art (LAMDA), and was a bohemian echo of Bloomsbury with curly, dusty wild hair and a cheeky twinkle in her eye; she was Alec

Guinness' sister-in-law. Brian Staveley was the son of one of the London guides whom I employed regularly to show my tourists around – at twenty a boy of ravishing beauty but crippling shyness; he would play with his hair when he talked, hoping to distract from what he was saying. Brian stayed many years, giving up his work in order to go back to university in Manchester, during which time I kept on his room at Caithness Road for him; there was no question, it was his home and it must be whither he would return. He is now a senior producer with the BBC, married with a daughter, and still fiddles with his hair.

Another who stayed free of charge, and for many more years, was Margot. That is what she called herself, with a flamboyant theatrical and artistic past reflected in her resplendent red hair, still undyed though she must have been nearly seventy. In her favourite portrait of herself she posed like Garbo, hiding her neck on the back of her folded hands. She claimed to have connections in Venice and to have been thrown over by one husband and widowed by another. One did not know what to believe, so we accepted her at her own worth and tried to believe everything. She certainly did paint reasonably well, so there may have been some truth in the artistic story, but as details were withheld, one could not make a judgement. One thing was certain about the mysterious and glamorous Margot – she had not a penny to her name and would never improve. She refused to sign on for any state benefit, jealous that bureaucrats would find out how old she was (perhaps even *who* she was – we suspected her real name was Marjorie and teased her by saying she came from a middle-class semi-detached in Hove, which infuriated her). There was no family at her pauper's funeral many years later, so she took her mystery with her.

Many others passed through – Doreen Wells, Wayne Sleep, Alun Lewis – and I conceived the idea that, for my sixtieth birthday I would give a party for all those who had ever stayed or lived at 47 Caithness Road. I abandoned the idea when the total went above fifty persons. The point I wish to make is that, however artificial it may appear to those who have conventional families, this was a very happy house, and Brendan Price, for one (now living with wife and two children in Spain), has made no secret of his belief that it was the happiest time of his life, with or without Gwen; it was the house itself, he said, which brought the joy.

With so many people keeping the house alive and secure, I was free to take holidays whenever they were offered, and two that I took regularly brought me in touch with old-fashioned comforts and leisure that I thought had disappeared with the Second World War. The first was a visit every September to Henry McIlhenny's castle in Ireland; the second a trip to Jamaica every January to stay with Dollie Burns, only daughter of the art crook Lord Duveen.

Selina Hastings introduced me to Dollie Burns at her house in Primrose Hill. It was one of Dollie's rare outings, for she spent almost every evening of the year entertaining at her own table. A large, plump, dark woman, with iridescent crimson lipstick and unnaturally black hair, she was packed with contradictory qualities. As the only child and heir of Lord Duveen she inherited his vast wealth and watched it increase year on year, reluctant to see it squandered on wages for her staff. Yet she claimed to be militantly left-wing, even communist, and once had Marxist slogans painted on her walls. Generous and kindly towards her guests, with an ingratiating smile, she would then reprimand them if they disappointed her or said something of which she disapproved, shouting at them across the table if necessary. She claimed to admire men, but humiliated and bullied her mild little husband Bobby, a retired surgeon who was far too intelligent for her and shrugged his shoulders gamely when she went into a rant. She played bridge every day at 3:00 p.m. and lost her temper every day before 4:00 p.m. vainly kidnapping every female crony she thought she could beat and furious when she realized she couldn't. Those ladies who wished to stay in her favour and eat her meals, lost on purpose and accepted her insulting sallies as worth the price on the whole. For she was the last great hostess of London, and dinner at her Mayfair mansion was always a splendid affair.

Dollie mixed journalists with shoe designers, peers and members of parliament with provincial students, and watched the results. She was by no means a snob, inviting people who interested her whether or not they had honours or fame. She liked to celebrate achievement and was keen on spotting those who would achieve in the future. She encouraged and flattered the young. Naturally, she attracted some dreadful exploiters and hangers-on, but I suspect she always saw through them, and used them rather more than they used her. She was shrewd and smart, and though not intellectual to any degree, knew the worth of literary folk as if by instinct. Two of her regular guests, for instance, were Kingsley Amis and Peregrine Worsthorne, the former of whom never suffered fools for longer than one majestically phrased dismissive sentence, the latter a punctilious demander of good taste. They both liked Dollie, despite the fact that her taste was vulgar and her foolishness legendary.

She and Bobby spent three months of every winter at her house in Jamaica. One evening in Mayfair she told me that I *must* come to Jamaica, that I should be very welcome to stay for a fortnight. I muttered some suitable show of gratitude, but knew perfectly well that I could never afford the fare. The next day a travel agent telephoned to fix my date of travel. I said that there must have been a misunderstanding for I had not yet agreed to make the journey. 'May I respectfully point out, sir', said the suave voice smoothing its way down the line, 'that we have arranged travel for Mrs Burns' guests for some years now, and our instructions are that Mrs Burns always looks after the costs.' As I was soon to find out, Dollie did not want her dinner-parties to cease simply because she was in Jamaica, and guests being rather thinly supplied over there, she flew them in from all over the world. There were usually ten staying in the house, an undistinguished but roomy bungalow, and another ten brought in from other houses in and around Montego Bay just for dinner.

The routine was strict. We had all to go to the beach every morning after breakfast, whether we liked it or not, and fend for ourselves at lunch-time. She would have nobody in the house during the day and would have nobody absent in the evening. I once saw her reduce the Duchess of St Albans to tears because she, the Duchess, had arranged to visit friends up the coast, and Dollie forbade it on the grounds she might not be back in time for dinner. At the beach we had our own long patch of sand somehow reserved by Dollie, where we were gawped at by outsiders and spent much of the day gossiping about our hostess' latest outrage. She came down to the beach one afternoon, decked out in Victorian bathing dress and hat, to have a row with a female guest who would not vacate her bedroom to make way for somebody else. 'I'll have you know I'm the daughter of a peer', she shouted. 'So am I', said the other, hands on hips. I think Dollie lost that one.

It was on a flight back from Jamaica one year that I ran a serious risk of imprisonment. One of the black servants (to whom Dollie was appallingly rude, but whose families she often quietly supported) offered me some *ganja,* from a deliciously fresh and aromatic marijuana plant which grew in abundance in his backyard. I declined, but he brought it anyway and thrust it at me as I was packing. I seized a large brown envelope, designed to take foolscap paper (we call it A4 now), and filled it with the stuff, then put it at the bottom of my carry-on luggage.

At Montego Bay airport I was alarmed to see that every passenger was being frisked and his hand-luggage searched. Bags were being turned upside down and emptied. It was too late to turn back, and I had no idea where I could have dumped my booty, so for a few moments I faced the real prospect of months (years?) in a crowded, fetid dark cell in Kingston. I noticed a woman in a wheelchair checking in for the same flight, and walked over to her. 'How nice to see you again', I merrily chirped, 'you remember, we met at dinner with the Andrewses, at that terrible house which looked like a film-set.' 'Oh sure', she said (for she was an American lady), 'you could have placed five tennis-courts between the sofas.' We both laughed. I had never seen her before, but it was a fair bet she would have been to dinner at that garish house, and she was too polite to admit she did not remember me. I relieved the servant and took charge of the wheelchair, pushing her through a special passage which avoided the checks. We were the only two passengers on that flight whose hand-luggage was not searched.

I breathed freely for the first seven hours of the flight, then thought I should do something practical before landing. I took the envelope to the lavatory, dosed it all over with aftershave, and held it down my back under my shirt, where it rested safely on my belt. We landed. The luggage was a very long time coming. After an hour I heard a passenger say that 'they've got the dogs out, that's why it's taking so long. They're looking for drugs.' I froze for the second time, cheering myself up with the reflection that at least a prison cell in Crawley might be better than one in Kingston. Eventually the belt moved, and I took my bag. As we walked towards customs, I saw to my terror that, instead of the usual two or three officers, a phalanx of about twelve men and women were on duty, and three out of every four passengers were stopped. There was nothing for it but to push my trolley, look straight ahead, and hope for the best. I pushed, and wheeled, and went on, through the middle of a throng of customs officers busy asking questions of others, and out into the freedom of the arrivals hall. The release from tension was as sudden and snappy as a catapult, and it was only when my relief had subsided that I began to feel distinctly un-proud of myself. I gave the stuff to somebody I thought might appreciate it. Shame is a superb teller of truth.

One year I came back from Jamaica to find, amongst the pile of mail, a strange letter from the Garrick Club, informing me that the General Committee had elected me as a member. I knew this could not be correct, and read it three times before I decided what to do. I telephoned the Secretary's office and suggested that some kind of mistake had occurred, that I perhaps had received a letter intended for somebody else. No, Mr Masters, I was told with a detectable grin in the voice, there is no mistake. Please come along to the club and I shall show you around.

This was staggering news indeed. My proposer and seconder, Kenneth Timings and Roger Machell, had not told me that I was a candidate, thus ensuring that I should receive an almighty surprise. I do not know if this ruse has ever been tried upon any other candidate; it is infinitely preferable to the extreme alternative which sometimes obtains, where a candidate actively lobbies on his own behalf, flattering and enticing members to support him. By keeping my candidature secret, Kenneth and Roger could guarantee that I had twisted no arms. I had always enjoyed my visits to the club, perhaps three or four times a year, and envied those people who could call it theirs. It had never crossed my mind that I should ever belong. That kind of establishment, with its echoes of public school ethos and of armed services camaraderie, was not for the likes of me. I would not have fitted in, so it would have been pointless to aspire to membership. Suddenly, I was already there. Since the Garrick has been the solace of my life ever since, the nest to which I always return, my gratitude to Kenneth and Roger is loud enough to pierce the Neverland where they now reside.

Whenever I try to explain the singular attraction of the Garrick, its unparalleled ability to restore both energy and calm (apparent opposites), to bring cheer and instil optimism, I am driven to say that it revealed to me a third kind of friendship, one of which I had no prior experience. In youth one soon learns to divide the world into close friends, those to whom one tells one's troubles and from whom one seeks intimate advice, of which there may be three or four if you are lucky; and those acquaintances whose company you enjoy from time to time and with whom you may look forward to a chat, and of these there could be up to twenty individuals. Garrick members are neither close friends nor acquaintances, they are something beyond both. You do not pour out your heart to a fellow member as you would to a bosom friend; on the other hand you do not treat him casually, as the ordinary fare of acquaintance. He is somebody with whom you share a table, with whom you break bread, a 'companion' in etymological fact, with whom you share a home. For to many of its members, the Garrick is more like home than the place where they hang their clothes. You walk up the steps from Garrick Street knowing everything is going to be all right. You will not be bored, that's for sure, but more importantly and subtly, you will be yourself, perhaps for the first time that day wholly yourself. Distinctions and honours are swept aside as dross, and you are reduced to being just another member. But that reduction is a triumph.

There is also the harmony of proportion in the Coffee Room (so-called because all gentlemen's clubs started as coffee bars, but it is actually the dining-room), the mathematical balance of which alone makes one happy without quite knowing why, as a Bach prelude, a Mozart sonata or a Palladian façade might, soothing the soul with their sense of unalterable form. And there is the unique collection of theatrical paintings on every wall, justly famous and unfairly ours to enjoy privately. These are but bonuses. The real treat of the place is its members.

Some years after my election, a special dinner was given for Michael Williams and Judi Dench. Michael had been elected on the same day as myself, since when I have always considered him something of a brother, and Judi had been a friend of long-standing. (I was at their wedding in London Zoo, when, idly gossiping with Ian McKellen we found that we had been born on the same day in the same year, that one was about two hours older than the other.) Anyway, Michael as the member was required to give a speech in answer to the toast. What he said went something like this:

'When I was at school I was encouraged to go on stage, and told I would make it. So I applied to RADA and was accepted. There I was told that I would make it one day, that I would get there. I played the lead at the end-of-term production, and still was made to learn that I would get there one day. I joined the Royal Shakespeare Company and played Henry V, and the encouragement continued. I was assured that I would get there if I persevered. I starred in the West End with my name in lights, but I had not made it yet. I was told again that I would get there one day. Finally, I was elected a member of the Garrick Club, and I found out what "there" meant at last.'

There is no better way to put it.

CHAPTER 9

The Lure of Literature

That mischievous old bigot A. L. Rowse invited me to lunch at one of the kidney tables in All Souls, Oxford, one day in 1975, and spent his time simultaneously pawing my knee under the table and insulting the great historian E. H. Carr above it. Rowse had himself written three magnificent tomes on Elizabethan society, but his jealousy and insecurity had poisoned his good nature, rendering every other historian on the planet 'third-rate' in his eyes. 'That man sitting opposite', he said (Carr was only two feet away), 'he thinks he's an historian, but he's not. Third-rate. They're all furious at my success, because I write in a way people can understand. I know how to do it. *They* don't!' The contempt in his voice was, however, mellifluous, cheeky and naughty rather than vicious; perhaps he knew that nobody took him seriously any more. Carr himself sat in dignified silence, eating his lunch and ignoring us.

Rowse had a wonderful set of rooms at All Souls, smelling of books and learning and dust-jackets and tea and sherry, and I frankly envied them. The comfort and peace of such a life spread calm into the air one breathed. That was, of course, another bone of contention to fuel Rowse's alert wrath – the fact that he was to be deprived of these rooms and banished back to Cornwall.

It was then that he dropped into the conversation a name which I had never heard before. 'You ought to write a book about Marie Corelli', he said. 'Extraordinary woman. Dotty as a fruitcake, but what a story! Nobody's done it before. Virgin territory, just waiting for you.' I tried to elicit as much information as I could without appearing too ignorant, and soon worked out that she was the biggest-selling novelist of her day, at her peak in the 1890s, and universally mocked as a purveyor of tosh. A little like Jeffrey Archer in our own time, and suffering the fate that will inevitably befall him as well – total oblivion. I eventually discovered Rowse was wrong to suggest that Corelli's life had been untouched, for her companion Bertha Vyver had written an obsequious memoir and Eileen Bigland had attempted an objective biography in the 1940s, but both were unsatisfactory, the first because it withheld information, the second because it could discover none.

I asked Roger Machell whether Hamish Hamilton would be interested in such a subject, and met with enthusiasm and encouragement. It was only after the contract was signed that the difficulties began.

My initial enquiry was made at the National Register of Archives in Quality Court, behind the old Public Record Office in Chancery Lane. There one could look through a card index to find where archive material was deposited, whether it was accessible in public collections or in private hands, how extensive it was, and with a sentence or two giving an idea of its contents. Alas, under Corelli there was nothing. No provincial record offices, no lovely collections, no indication that she had ever led a life worthy of being remembered and recorded for posterity. I was told that she had been such a self-protective old thing, so determined that only her version of herself should survive, that she had destroyed or caused to be destroyed all her letters and all unflattering references. This was disheartening indeed, but not for long. It was impossible, I reasoned, that in an epistolary age and with a woman so eager to have her say and be heard, a woman who spilled words across the page every day of her life, that every communication from her would have disappeared. The letters were sitting somewhere; I just had to find them.

Thus began the most professionally exciting quest of my life. I felt a little like Symons in pursuit of Corvo as I gradually unpeeled the onion and found out things I am sure Marie would not have wished me to know. That is the reprehensible part of the biographer's urge – the need to sneak and divulge. Thank God there are other more laudable aspects to the job (to demonstrate general truth through a particular example, and to supply the historical record), but Marie's earnest desire to obfuscate willed me on to ever more prying methods.

If there had been letters, then after her death in 1924 they would most likely have been sent for sale by auction, especially as Bertha had nothing to live on but the dwindling royalties from a has-been. So I started with the Department of Manuscripts at the British Museum, calling up every auction catalogue of manuscript material from 1924 to 1945. There were two main auction houses which dealt in this field, but they had an average of two auctions a month, which meant reading every page of about five hundred catalogues, hoping to spot the name Corelli sooner or later. It took a while, as one might imagine, but the task was so exhilarating that I never thought to grumble. In this way I came across up to twenty sales of Corelli items, some composed of a mere dozen dull missives, others of a few hundred intimate letters. That at least confirmed my suspicion that they had existed, and that somebody had bought them, but as yet took me no further. I had then to make a note of the date of the sale and the lot number which concerned me and make a second search, in another department, into the large dusty ledger books of the auction houses. There I matched the lot numbers with the monies received, and could make a note of the purchaser. The next stage was to trace the purchaser, itself a ridiculous endeavour as every one of them must be dead half a century after their bid. Undaunted, I knew they would most likely have descendants, or if not, would have donated their hoard to the nearest university library. An awful lot of them went to the United States, where local authorities were most obliging in helping me to follow the peregrinations of families from state to state in order to track my letters (I thought of them as 'mine' already, since nobody else had ever shown any interest in them since their sell-off), and by the time I had assembled a list of likely treasure troves (none of them were certain, which made the hunt even more engaging) I knew that I would have to go to America in order to pounce. As I was far too poor to undertake such a journey unassisted, I applied to the Arts Council for a grant, and am ever grateful for the £1,000 they advanced to make the project realizable.

At the University of Illinois I found the diary of Marie's long-suffering gentlemanly publisher George Bentley, who had been stout in her defence against screaming detractors and been paid for his pains with arrogant scorn. At Yale I found Marie's entire correspondence with Bentley, from the very first letter of a hesitant hopeful tyro, begging the favour of his attention to her poor efforts and boasting the while of her Italian descent (which was invented, as was her name) and her connection with the poet Charles Mackay, which was fraudulent, up to the last, when she was rock-solid famous, berating him for hanging on to her money. Matching these with Bentley's own diary was a joy. The Bentley correspondence had been consulted by Michael Sadleir some forty years earlier, and had then disappeared. I worked out that they had to be at Yale, since their last owner was a benefactor of that university, but Yale denied all knowledge of them. They had lain uncatalogued. So I went through the manuscript deposits and sniffed them out.

Another great discovery was the collection of Marie's love

letters to the artist Arthur Severn, packed with junky baby-talk which was awkward to read, yet strangely enlivening after so many years; they brought back both her infatuation and his embarrassment. The important fact was that nobody had even known that Marie had been in love with anyone, so all this was entirely new, and helped to illuminate the devilish frustration of her fiction. Where were they? In a shoebox on a shelf at the University of Detroit; they had been put there after the war as the inaugural item in what was to be a great collection, then forgotten. The librarian had me to stay at her house, and I read of Marie's doomed love at her kitchen table in the course of a week.

There was more in California, Texas, New York and Washington, plus a great deal at home in Stratford-upon-Avon, where Marie had gone to live in order to be close to the other Great Writer of English Literature and to guard his memory from the *hoi polloi*. Her secretary's nieces were still alive, and they fetched a suitcase full of her ungrateful scribblings from a shed at the bottom of the garden. And my most wicked discovery was the large negative on glass of a photograph which I recognized as one that Marie had caused to be published in frontispiece to a novel of 1906, when she was over fifty, in which she looked about twenty-six (an age she claimed was immoveable). There were two versions of this negative, one covered in scratches. They represented the image which the camera saw, and the image which the photographer amended to suit his subject's demands; I published them both.

And so it went on. I shall not tire the reader with a list, but I must have unearthed over two thousand letters and was able, for the first time, to show Marie Corelli both as she saw herself and as revealed by her own unguarded pen. Hamish Hamilton did a handsome job of it, and I was pleased, feeling myself for the first time to be a real writer who had produced original work. The title, however, was a disaster. The actor Peter Bull had suggested it, but it was my fault for not seeing that the suggestion should be resisted.

The *Pall Mall Gazette* had reviewed one of Marie's novels, *Barabbas*, in one sentence – 'Now Barabbas Was A Rotter'. We both thought this would be a wonderfully witty title, but the trouble was it told you nothing about the content of the book. It was mystifying, a turn-off. The subtitle mentioned the name of Marie Corelli, but many browsers do not get as far as subtitles. I am still surrounded by echoes of Marie. I have her wooden tray with lifting shelf for a book to be read in bed, and her wooden letter-rack, with space for letters unanswered and letters to be sent. I also have a complete set of first editions of her work, which took me seven years to accumulate. Most of all I have her own first copy of her own first published novel – *The Romance of Two Worlds*. Anyone who has seen and held in his hands his own work in print for the first time will know how precious is this item. One cannot get any closer to Marie than that.

An unexpected consequence of this book was a new friendship. Beryl Bainbridge said on the radio that she had voted for it as biography of the year but had been overruled by her colleagues on the panel. She was good enough to voice her disappointment, and characteristically besought listeners to read it anyway. (This did not make too much difference, as the book was still anchored by that terrible title.) I was so pleased that I found her address and promptly presented myself at her front door. Her teenage daughter answered, then withdrew into the gloom, and I heard a shrill voice scream, 'What? The Marie Corelli Masters?' followed by Beryl, thin, lank and animated, teeth and eyes agleam, uncombed hair kept in place by gravity, who welcomed me warmly and asked me in. We chatted and smoked for hours, as if she had nothing better to do (which I know cannot have been true – she is very disciplined in her work), covering everything from literature to gossip with equal energy. We have never looked back, and I always cherish my friendship with Beryl for the surprising reason that she is so ordinary, so normal, so down-to-earth. I say surprising, because the common view is that Beryl Bainbridge must be eccentric; mad as a hatter, in fact.

Now, I concede that it cannot be commonplace to have a stuffed bison in the hall, so huge that nobody can get past it without squeezing sideways and holding breath the while. Nor do many dining-room tables have a life-size model of Neville Chamberlain sitting at them, eerily witnessing every conversation. Perhaps her earnest consumption of whisky in preference to wine makes her a tad unusual, and her massive intake of nicotine is probably heroic. But these are manifestations of original extravagant character, not eruptions of weirdness, and they are as endearing as her volubility and honesty. She has collected some odd things, because she sees the poetry in oddness, just as she has collected some odd people, seeing the romance in them (one was a convicted murderer who came for cups of tea and a chat). She is a woman of enthusiasm and warmth, and essentially as straight in her manner as my Aunt Ethel.

Beryl cannot be pompous or pretentious. She is a Liverpool lass who became an actress and started writing after her children had been born and her marriage foundered. There is nothing whatever grand about her, nothing forbidding or important. You never have the feeling that you are in the presence of a great novelist, and that you must watch what you say and find something interesting to report. No, you are in the presence of a garrulous neighbour, interested in everyone and everything about her, but not prone to turn everyday experience into myth before your eyes. She will giggle, she will roar, she will poke fun and whisper, she is a natural accomplice, playing the frown and the cupped hand, nudging the ribs, sliding her arm over your shoulder like a chum. She is beautiful in a lived-in way, and probably aware of it. She is a careful mother and dotty grandmother, strangely naive about the vices of children but prepared to learn, all agog with wonder. If you go out to dinner with her, she is happier with eggs and bacon at a local cafe than with a carefully crafted menu (though she does like me taking her to the Garrick Club, 'that posh place'). She is thoroughly natural.

The mystery is, of course, that she is also a magnificent novelist of quite amazing subtlety, wisdom and concealed mirth. Her writing is so pregnant with layers of meaning unexpressed that one expects her to be an egg-head, a fierce intellectual impatient of the woolly-minded and mentally soft, and she is nothing of the sort. The person who writes is kept private within her, and one rarely, if ever, catches a glimpse of that person. I have never known her to talk about her own work in depth, although I do know she may take a whole morning of three hours' solid thought to get one sentence right, and a paragraph a day is Concorde-speed for her. She also confides that she is having trouble finishing a book, and will ask advice (advice to Beryl Bainbridge!!) on how to get a point across, or how to deal with a character's change of personality. Perhaps it is that I am just not up to it, and she is too kind to say so. Much closer friends such as Michael Holroyd and A.N. Wilson see a great deal of her and may, who knows, spend their time with her discussing Kafka. But with me she keeps the mystery of her talent intact, and I prefer it to be so; she is a friend, not a literary icon.

Another friend I made at the same time was Robert de Margerie, the French Ambassador at the Court of St James's, whose elegant wife taught me what mushrooms to pick in an English forest! Bobby's official duties kept him busy virtually every evening, but when he had time off once in four months or so, he would call me and ask if we could not dine at an Indian restaurant, *incognito* as it were. Though he had been from a long line of aristocratic diplomats, his father and grandfather ambassadors before him, and knew the ropes by heart, I had the impression that he did not care for pomp and fuss and looked forward to an unceremonious conversation. Yet it was he who presented me to my Sovereign for the first time.

President Mitterand came to London on a State Visit and was royally entertained at Buckingham Palace. In return, as was the custom, he and his ambassador invited the Queen, her husband, her mother, her sister, her children, and her entire Cabinet to dine at the ambassadorial residence, a great pile in Kensington Palace Gardens which I believe had once belonged to the Dukes of Marlborough. I was not invited to dinner, thank God, but Bobby sent me an invitation to be part of the additional throng, the also-rans, who were habitually on such occasions to be present in the garden after the meal. There were about sixty of us, happily milling around and talking to one another, dressed with black-tie formality but behaving with cool relaxation as we waited for the royal party to emerge from the house. Standing right by the door through which the Queen would walk was Sir Frederick Ashton, like a stage door johnny determined not to be left out, to be the first she would greet, which struck me as odd considering that he was already an intimate of the family, had dined *en privé* with the Queen more than once, and was one of the Queen Mother's dearest toys. I suppose that's what they call insecurity; Freddy stood dutifully for half an hour while the rest of us went on drinking and chatting.

The Queen came out, and Freddy Ashton got his hand-shake. She then mingled with the crowd, and I lost sight of her, until to my alarm I saw Bobby de Margerie walking towards me with the Queen at his side. Surely not, I thought, he wouldn't do such a thing, I'm not prepared, I wouldn't know what to say. The panic rose in the three seconds it took me to realize that, indeed, I was about to be presented. I have heard it said that people who are introduced to the Queen either clam up and say nothing, or cannot stop talking. Whichever the case, it is fear which impels them to be such bores. I was one of the latter kind of bore, and I finally understood what Dr Johnson meant by his aloof remark that he would not bandy civilities with his Sovereign. Whatever else she is (nice, wicked, bright, stupid, I have no way of knowing), she is the Leader of the Tribe, the Top Person, the One beyond Whom it is impossible to go (unless to God Himself), and to meet her is (not her fault) terrifying. She had not been prepared any more than I had. 'What do you do?' she asked, harmlessly, and with a charming lilt.

'Well, Your Majesty', I began, then launched into a speech so helter-skelter with words, so packed with syllables falling over each other, so rapid in delivery, that I could hear myself and hardly believed I was doing it. I desperately did not want her to ask me anything else. I wanted to escape. The poor woman had to slide her handbag from one arm and engage it upon another, in subtle code that she really had had enough. I drew breath, and she jumped in, 'Very interesting', she said, and walked off with a winning smile in which I could detect no irritation, but some bewilderment. Still, I told myself, she must be used to it.

Another huge friend was John Ogdon, arguably the greatest pianist this country has ever produced, and certainly one of the three or four best in the world in his time. When I choose the adjective 'huge', my mind is jumping ahead of itself, for John was physically impressive as well, a giant of a man, tall, wide, fat, rolling along, but with the softest centre imaginable, so that he appeared like a grisly bear with the menace of a mouse. His unruly wavy *Boy's Own* haircut contrasted with a goatee beard he grew later, both of them yellow with nicotine, for John smoked as if untainted air was dangerous, though barely inhaling, toying with the cigarette as a device to ward off the intrusion of conversation. He was fiercely intelligent and erudite, but his best colloquy was with himself or with his piano. When obliged to 'make' conversation with other mortals, his head bounced up and down like that of a noddy-dog, he smiled sweetly, he puffed away, anything to go through the motions of human intercourse without actually engaging the real private part of himself. His voice was soft, gentle, quiescent, almost a whisper, never raised, rarely employed to impart information, redundant as a channel of disagreement of any sort. He was the most compliant man conceivable.

All too good to be true, of course, as we found out. I saw John and his wife regularly at their sumptuous though still firmly middle-class home in Regent's Park. John was utterly indifferent to his surroundings, and one could no more depict

him touring Harrods to choose chairs than dancing the lead in
Swan Lake, so the furnishings were all in Brenda's style. She
and John had met as students in Manchester, both preparing
for a career at the keyboard, when those who knew what
they were talking about already bruited the quiet young
giant's genius. They married, had a son and daughter, and
went together through John's astonishing transformation (in
the public eye only – he remained always the same) from
unknown Mancunian misfit to global sensation, winning
First Prize at the Tchaikovsky competition in Moscow to
make front-page news in London. Brenda's career went in
tandem with his, playing sometimes in duets, but for the
most part she was busy organizing him. John was so much
the archetypically vague genius that he would not know what
shirt to wear, which city he was due to play in, how to get
there, or where to stay, without Brenda's unfailing arm to
support him. She was his mainstay, his prop, his connection
with mankind. She was, as I was eventually to find out,
his sanity.

It is worth elaborating the point, for Brenda was seriously
maligned in a BBC drama documentary after John's death, in
which she was depicted as mean-spirited, greedy and vain. It
was implied that she pushed him too hard, made him earn
too much in order to give her a rich lifestyle, drove him to
exhaustion with several concerts and recitals a week, all for
her own gratification. This was untrue and malicious, and
it hurt. Brenda worked her heart out to keep John happy,
and she had tastes which were easily satisfied and by no
means extravagant. She wanted John to enjoy the fruits of
his success, and if he needed a chauffeured car to take him
to the airport, he should have one! She enjoyed his success,
too, but she never became grand or vainglorious. I like her
so much, to this day, because she has a sweet girlish giggle,
sees the funny side of life, and can be relentlessly teased by
me without either becoming shy or taking offence.

Most of all, she helped John's career because she knew,
better than anyone else, that he needed to play all the time.

The piano was the expression of his otherwise silent soul, and its music was his bloodstream. Without the piano, he was in peril. One had only to watch John Ogdon play, his great shoulders hunched in an embrace of the air which hovered over the piano, his thick, deft fingers glancing across the keyboard like quicksilver, releasing the instrument's voice, cherishing and caressing it, to know the man was possessed. He was in the grip of some power which had lain dormant through the quotidian banalities of life and which burst forth with such energy as was frightening (and thrilling) to behold. Professionals have spoken often of Ogdon's unique abilities to sight-read; he could be given music lasting a couple of hours, which he had never seen before, and would play it straight off, immediately, without rehearsal. Nobody had ever seen that before. I am incompetent to comment, except to say that such unearthly ability does seem to me just that – unearthly, aberrant, alien. It cannot be merely the product of training; that this was a man whose life was hidden from the rest of us, whose connections with music were transcendental, overwhelming and in the proper literal sense, unreal. His bond with the piano was passionate, essential; that is, the essence of John Ogdon was the pianist – the man was but a shambling shell.

The performance over, John reverted to his mild modest exterior, head nodding, smile hesitant and obedient to convention, cigarette lit. Off-performance John was a very agreeable companion, obliging and sweet-natured, but only a quarter there; you felt the rest of him was hovering in space somewhere. I went weekly to have conversations over lunch in French, which engaged a bit of his brain not exercised in domestic duties, and it amused him. One evening I asked John and Brenda to dinner at Caithness Road, and invited Barbara Leigh-Hunt to make the four (her husband Richard Pasco was on stage that night).

John was affable and cosy as usual, until Brenda left him and Bar in the front room after dinner to come and help me with the washing-up. I noticed over coffee afterwards that he was brooding, distant and aloof, fiddling with fingers and avoiding eye contact with anyone. I see now that the mood was also slightly menacing in its hint at undercurrents, but I cannot say I realized this at the time.

John and Brenda left, and later Bar went too, and I tumbled into bed. At two in the morning the telephone rang. It was Brenda, obviously in distress, asking me if she could come back to the house, telling me in fact that she must. 'I've got to leave now. I must have somebody with me, to talk to. Let me stay the night, I'll explain.' I prepared the guest-room and waited.

Brenda was indeed in a state. John had flown into a rage at home, broken a mirror in the hall, thrown a vase at her and threatened to kill her. This was so unlike the placid bear one knew that I hoped Brenda was exaggerating. She had not called the police, but she would not go back home unless I came with her. I said she should get some rest, and I would go with her in the morning. At about three o'clock John rang to see where she was. 'She's here, John', I said, 'and she wants to stay here. Wait until tomorrow.' The voice at the end was that of a chided puppy – 'Oh, all right then'. No protest, no request for explanation or even information, just mild acceptance. It did not sound like the voice of a man who had gone berserk.

When we arrived at Regent's Park after a quick breakfast on Saturday morning, John opened the door. Two lines of blood streaked down either side of his face where he had cut his temples. It must have been hours before, since the blood was dry and congealed. There was also the sign of the cross cut, presumably with a razor-blade, on his forehead. Of these strange ritual signals John was blithely unaware. It was as if they had happened to somebody else, somebody who had momentarily inhabited his body and gone away again, leaving a souvenir. Brenda asked him about them. 'Oh, yes' he said, 'I don't know. I suppose I must have done it shaving.' She then called a doctor.

I seem to remember that several doctors were consulted

during the weekend, as Brenda desperately resisted their accumulating advice that John must be admitted to hospital. While all these consultations were being held and head-holding decisions were being made, John bumbled along effortlessly, obliging everyone who wanted to examine him, not really listening to them or noticing their presence and concern. Other musical friends were called in, observed, muttered caution, and left. Ultimately it was left to Brenda to decide whether or not this man should be placed in the hands of medics, not knowing what they might do to him when her back was turned. He was not just her husband, he was one of the greatest pianists in the world. His brain was precious, her responsibility devastating. I stayed with her for the whole of the next three days.

We crossed London several times to visit hospitals in the northernmost reaches and far beyond Lewisham in the south, Brenda driving, myself in the passenger seat, John sitting behind, trying to take his clothes off and expose himself to passers-by. Brenda could only prevent him from making himself totally naked by scolding him like a child, and when she was concentrating on driving and directions, I tried to engage him in unrelated conversation; he talked rather animatedly about Marie Corelli, one subject I could keep going for an hour or more. In one hospital we were told that John was in a very dangerous mental state and needed urgent treatment. What, a lobotomy? Well, almost. He must be locked up and restrained, his bed bolted to the floor, his arms rendered immobile. We packed John into the car and went on to the next hospital.

In this, an obvious madhouse, patients passed us in drab beige-painted corridors and poked at us or bared a breast or mumbled in our faces. John was taken to see a specialist, who summoned Brenda and me into his office afterwards while John was packed off to the refectory to eat at a communal table with deranged people who would clearly find him a curiosity in their midst. The specialist again predicted disaster unless Brenda acted urgently to have John committed – it could only be done with her consent – and once more we resisted such a gruesome outcome. She said she would think about it. Meanwhile, where was John? We found him with a plate of food poured over his head, mingling with his hair and dripping on to his shoulders and into his eyes. One of the patients had satisfied curiosity by dumping on the intruder. Most depressing of all, John Ogdon did not seem to notice, to mind, to care one tiny bit. Again, we fled the place.

Brenda told me that John's father had been not only an authority on schizophrenia, but had suffered from the affliction himself, and that John had all his life dreaded the inheritance of it. In the car and back home in Regent's Park one was able, amazingly, to question John about this and elicit sensible, coherent answers. He was aware of his schizophrenic behaviour, and, being schizophrenic (or so he persuaded himself) could not do anything constructive about it. He wondered about it, objectively, himself as case study, his interest aroused but his anxiety dormant.

It was a long weekend, which terminated in Roehampton, where finally Brenda had to concede, with the most expert advice ringing in her ears, that electric shock therapy was the only hope to rescue John from the abyss which loomed before him. It was a horrible decision to have to make. 'He belongs not just to me, but to the world', she wailed. I can hear myself now saying that she had a stark choice, that between having a husband who was an undisputed genius likely to do something violent and irrevocable to himself, to her, or to both; and having a husband who was compliant, malleable, happy, and perhaps merely talented. It was none of my business, and I should not have interfered, but I knew that Brenda needed her own thoughts to be articulated by somebody else in order to confront them. The electric intervention might alter that part of the brain wherein resided John's genius. Did one have the right to permit it?

I was reminded of Alec McCowan's long speech to the audience at the end of Peter Shaffer's *Equus,* in which he, as the psychiatrist, asks whether he should cure the boy of his madness (imagining that horses could see into his sin), without having anything but banality to offer in return. It was *his* madness, the one quality which defined him, rendered him unique beside his fellows, his very own vision and solace. To cure him of it would be to make him like everyone else – flat and featureless.

The world now knows that treatment secured sanity for John Ogdon, and robbed him of life, the life that comes from a unique spark, a special private contact with the spiritual, the unknowable, the reality concealed behind appearances and empirically inaccessible. There were occasions after that when he played magically and with a stamina which would have been impossible for a mere mortal, but there were many others when he seemed to regard the piano as an instrument for noise-making, it did not much matter what style of noise. But the world does not know the agony of his wife's decision, nor her selfless devotion to his well-being in the years which followed. They sold all they had, and Brenda took to giving private lessons to unpromising teenagers to make ends meet. They went to Bloomington, Indiana, for John to take up a teaching position, and Brenda supported him when he dithered and got lost in ghostly meandering speech. It was not fun.

On a visit I made to John at Roehampton during the treatment, he stood with his back to me, gazing out of the window. 'You know, Brian', he said, 'only three people have ever got it right, have understood the meaning of the world. One was Jesus, the second was Hitler, and the third is me.' Need one doubt that he had to be delivered from this?

The trouble is, he was delivered at the same time from the empowering spark which enabled him to release the magic in music. Perhaps this spark and his skewed insights at the hospital window came from the same source, and he was merely the conduit through which they passed, in which case they both finally exhausted him. It is interesting that when one wants to praise the exuberant playing of a great pianist one often calls it, without thinking through the implications, 'demonic'. The pianist is thereby not only possessed, but possessed by forces which may be malevolent, in so far as they are exigent and careless – they require expression no matter what. The boy in *Equus* was also possessed by a force which was heedless of his physical and emotional well-being. Both this character (actually based on a true story) and John Ogdon were visionaries, that is they saw things that were denied to the rest of us, and that permitted them to understand the world differently from us. We cannot see clearly. The madman might get a better view, and that is why we fear him. This was a very popular opinion to have in the early 1960s, largely due to the now-discredited works of R.D. Laing, who proposed the notion that the schizophrenic amongst us saw into truths which we spent our lives disguising (Laing's ideas are not so well regarded nowadays only because they were based upon faulty logic, not because they have lost their attraction). But it was hardly new, versions of it abounding among the Ancients, in Pascal, La Rochefoucauld, Chamfort, Shakespeare, Proust. That John was a man touched by something special, mysterious, was undeniable.

Visionaries never suffer from *Angst*. Why should they? They cannot feel that profound uneasiness and *ennui* which comes from, amongst other things, 'thinking too precisely on th'event', because they know, they are privileged, they do not have to wonder and worry and fidget and fret; they are free from the necessity of searching. Hamlet is the most *Angst*-ridden character in all literature, a monument to the ruin of Second Thoughts. But at least he is sane. The price of sanity is confusion, disbelief, the paradoxical certainty that one will never know for sure, perpetual anxiety and recurrent unhappiness. Though Ogdon was worn out by his genius and his inherited illness, I doubt if he was ever really unhappy. His whole demeanour was that of an undisturbed, untroubled child, willing to oblige but not overly eager, responsive but only up to a point, private and self-composed. The voice was similarly marshmallic (I invent the word) and mild. If he had talked while he was playing, however, I would not mind betting a quite different voice would have emerged – deep and resonant, wild and thunderous, metallic, harsh. That is only silly speculation, of course, but I want to suggest that Ogdon did not have the hills and valleys of speech and emotion in his quotidian existence because he was simply not in touch with it. It did not matter. And you do not worry over things which do not matter. What mattered was the voice of truth which came from the piano and, after his breakdown, from his hospital window. He was safer with the piano. Once his brain had been ravaged, the truth split into fragments, like the bits of a kaleidoscope; they could not be jumbled into place again. But still he never succumbed to *Angst*. He never lost his serenity.

The causes of *Angst* are manifold: a second class mind, a tendency to regret, a disposition to lie, fear of old age (not death, since there is no point in fearing something that one will not have to live with), lack of ambition coupled with the conviction that ambition is a Good Thing, the crippling fear of making a fool of oneself. I still suffer from all of them, except the last, happily now extinct. I have always been buoyed up by the cheerfulness and gaity of Sydney Smith, whose advice is infinitely preferable to Chesterfield's or La Rochefoucauld's. In a letter to Lady Georgiana Morpeth in 1830 he listed twenty golden rules to combat low spirits. Three of them I hold very dear: to avoid long plans but take short views of the future, 'not further than dinner or tea', not to expect too much from human life, 'a sorry business at the best' and 'keep good blazing fires.'

Serenity was the very essence of the art and personality of Natalia Makarova a woman who came by surprise into my life, and stayed.

I had heard of her before we met. Who had not? After Nureyev she was the second great Russian defector of the Soviet era. Dancing with the Kirov Ballet in London, she left her dressing-room after a performance and never returned. Elaborate plans had been made with English people she knew to spirit her away, and the ensuing row with the Soviet Embassy made front-page news. What the newspapers did not report, because they did not know, was that the ballet company, no doubt on instructions from above, burnt all her belongings – clothes, papers, costume jewellery – in a determined attempt to obliterate her memory. She immediately became a non-person, and nobody in Leningrad, where her mother and relations lived, was allowed to mention her name under threat of stern punishment.

Granted political asylum (though her motives were never so shallow as to be political – she needed artistic liberty), Makarova became a guest with both the Royal Ballet in London and the American Ballet Theatre in New York, and within a very short time was acknowledged the finest *prima ballerina* then working in the world. I must leave it to ballet historians and critics to assess her genius, but I can talk of her impact. I never saw anyone on a ballet stage more ethereal, more bodyless, more able to draw wide the curtains on spiritual truth. In movement she was like liquid poetry, in shape the essence of the Perfect, and in dramatic quality the revelation of unsuspected myths. She danced in a way which brought to the audience insights they recognized with a tremble. She opened minds and massaged hearts. And, like Pavlova, she brought ballet to people who imagined they would be bored by it.

I shall jump ahead a few years to a story I have related elsewhere, and repeat it in brief. Alastair planned a ballet evening for people who lived on his estate at Wynyard, with his wife Doreen Wells as principal dancer. There were to be a number of other *divertissements* performed by members of the Royal Ballet, and quite a few stars went north for this private event. Alastair built a stage in the ballroom, converting it into a theatre. When one of the dancers was forced to drop out at the last minute, there was a scramble for a substitute. Makarova was suggested, and I was asked to persuade her. It did not need much, for she was good-hearted as well as professional. She arrived late on Saturday night, and proceeded to stay up until two or three in the morning drinking Château Palmer. On Sunday she did not come down to breakfast, and was nowhere to be seen at lunch. I went to investigate. She was not unwell, just tired, and needed rest. I pointed out that she had not even seen the stage on which she was due to dance that evening, and it might be a good idea if she took a rehearsal on it. So at four in the afternoon I took her through the grand old unused rooms to the ballroom, where workmen were still banging away at carpentry and electricians were hanging from the ceiling adjusting wires. To a recording on a cassette, and wearing leg-warmers and a T-shirt, Natasha then danced The Dying Swan to an audience of two – myself and Roy Round – and about twelve unwilling craftsmen. What happened next can only come through genius. Natasha thought she was 'marking' the steps and feeling the stage, but as soon as Saint-Saëns' music began, she ceased to be a dancer and became a creature in the last moments of life, pitifully clinging to the dignity bestowed by its natural grace, slowly subsiding as the movements of harmonious life broke and snapped into the jerkings of imminent death. The electricians and carpenters, dumbfounded, stopped in their tracks. She died amid silence.

On a personal level, Natasha following defection had to start from scratch. Georgina Parkinson found her a flat in Cromwell Gardens and helped her to furnish it. She was very shy, still wrapped in the cocoon of Soviet life where nobody talked intimately or confidentially about anything. She had taken a huge plunge, the import of which nobody but herself could comprehend. She thought she would never see her country again, never talk to her mother again, and never feel part of a family and a community by right of birth. She would have to make it all for herself. She was, I think, about thirty.

I met her backstage after a performance by somebody else. We both stood in the corridor, she an exotic bird, bone-structure sculpted by the gods, noble nose and sparkling

seductive eyes, long chiffon scarf boldly capping her tiny
head and emphasising her narrow vulnerable neck, at once
voluptuous and serene, I in a state of hypnosis. I do not
recall how, but it was I who began conversation, and I who
offered to take her home (Cromwell Gardens was on the
way towards Caithness Road). Her English was poor (and
stubbornly remained so for far too many years), but she was
anxious to exercise it and to discuss philosophical problems
rather than the daily fare of hard work. We also both liked
good red wine. Natasha showed me some paintings she had
done, and some Russians icons she had bought. I felt she
was confiding.

And that, my word, is the feeling she has kept alive ever
since. I have always been on trial, always kept on tenterhooks
by her flirting and her teasing, ever keenly aware that she
values my friendship but that I must not expect her to
demonstrate it, must not puncture her self-reliance. She tells
me that she is never bored in my company, which of course
makes me worry about boring her next time. Very clever. I
have witnessed her moments of deep distress and loneliness,
even of artistic doubt, as well as her triumphs and girlish
joys (looking back out of the window of the cab to see her
name in lights outside the Palace Theatre in *On Your Toes*,
when the world had thought she was long since secure in her
galactic position, and smiling to herself), and her gift to me
has been one of trust, that she knows I am with her, never
against, and never likely to exploit.

It is not always a comfortable relationship, because one
frequently teeters on the edge of danger, a situation which
Natasha actively promotes. Even if she does not feel angry
about something, she will pretend to be, then watch the
reaction. She likes to fire sparks. But the dangers are worth
running, for her loyalty, once gained, is solid.

She married a Lebanese businessman and American citizen,
Edward Karkar, and they had a son Andrei (Andrushka), to
whom I was assumed an unofficial godparent (the official
ones were posh, King Constantine of Greece and Jacqueline

Kennedy Onassis among them, and they paid him but scant attention). The family settled in San Francisco, with apartments in New York and London and a country estate in the Napa Valley of California. Thus the 'simple Soviet girl' (as she called herself without self-mockery) became an international woman of great style.

The change that most overwhelmed her was one she could never have predicted. Soon after the collapse of the Soviet Empire, Makarova the Outcast, the Exile, the Disgraced, was invited to return and dance once more at her old theatre, the Maryinsky in Leningrad (which reverted to its real name of St Petersburg). As her plane landed, her mother was brought out to the tarmac to embrace her as soon as she stepped on to Russian soil. People in the streets stopped her and told her that, though they had been forbidden to mention her name, they had never forgotten her. At the theatre, young Kirov dancers climbed over one another in the wings to watch the legend whom they thought they would never see. Most touching of all, she met again the woman who had been her dresser in London all those years before, and who told her that, when the men came to destroy her belongings, she managed to rescue one item, the lucky icon which she, Natasha, had been wont to hold in her palm before every performance. She had preserved it ever since and now, old and ever fonder, she was able to return it into her own hands once more.

Natasha had asked me to go with her to Russia on that visit, and I had declined, citing pressure of work. What a fool!

The *Independent* published an article in their series 'How We Met' on Makarova and myself, with a marvellous photograph taken of us at her London flat by Laurie Lewis. (Oddly, neither of us was ever allowed a copy of this picture.) In it, she said she could make me blush in an instant, and that how she did it was 'her secret'. (She adores mystification and being just beyond reach.) I think the secret is this: she alerts me to my masculinity, then watches me flounder as I wonder what to do with it. I am thrown into the water, submerge, bounce up, and am rescued in time, dripping with anxiety. I would not have it any other way.

Meanwhile, I was working on three books for three different publishers, though not with equal application. *The Mistresses of Charles II* was commissioned by Anthony Blond with the same motive that he had applied when he thought up *The Dukes*, namely that nobody had ever done it before. Though there had been many biographies of Barbara Villiers, Nell Gwynn and the rest, they had not appeared together on the same cast-list, as it were. I recall the book as entirely derivative, based only on secondary sources and gathering existing material together, but on pulling a copy from the shelf I see that I consulted a number of manuscript collections at the British Museum for details which had been but scrappily understood until then. So the book was not without merit.

Much more important to me was *Georgiana, Duchess of Devonshire*, which I wrote for Hamish Hamilton at my own suggestion. I had been utterly bewitched by this enchanting woman during my research for *The Dukes*, and amazed that her story, though often told, had never been based upon her own correspondence, carefully treasured at Chatsworth. All her letters were there, as well as many hundreds written to her, and apart from Lord Bessborough, who had long ago selected and edited a collection, nobody had bothered to look at them. Andrew Devonshire happily gave me permission to consult them, and so I was able to offer the first authentic biography nearly two hundred years after her death.

It was during those months spent at Chatsworth that occurred a number of those incidents mentioned in an earlier chapter. But they were at lunch or dinner. The rest of the time was devoted to hard labour, long hours in a special room where boxes of Georgiana's stuff were brought to me, as well as cups of coffee from On High whenever the need was exigent. Gradually I got to know her well, handling her own paper, gazing at the ink from her own ink-well (or in one case, a heart-rending letter to her son deploring her dizzy life, at the blood from her own vein), turning the pages of her own books, and walking in her own grounds. I came to feel for her and to be dismayed by the inner turmoil which wrecked her health while she was busy making everybody else happy. She had a big, undisciplined heart, and like many so blessed or cursed, she did not worry that others might take advantage of her, which of course they did. Her marriage to the 5th Duke, a cold fish if ever there was one, brought her riches and rank, but no joy. That came from her friendship with Lady Elizabeth Foster, her husband's mistress and her own best friend.

That which pleased me most in this book was my scotching of a very old rumour. Both Georgiana and 'Bess' Foster had given birth to children by the duke within weeks of one another in 1790, a boy to the duchess, a girl to the mistress. It was soon being whispered that the babies had been swapped in order to redeem Georgiana's great fault in not having presented the duke with a male heir, and that therefore the little boy 'Hart', later to be 6th Duke of Devonshire, was illegitimately conceived. The rumour was so tenacious, and so impossible of disproof, that it nipped at Hart's heels all his life, and went on to dribble down the generations. Andrew said to me, 'it would be good if you were able to sort that out once and for all.'

Picking up on a name which occurred once in parenthesis in an unremarkable letter, I worked out that the man who attended Georgiana in the weeks preceding her labour had been a young doctor called Croft. He had been summoned out to France, where Georgiana had gone for the *accouchement,* and had served as general practitioner to the whole entourage. By looking at postal and parish records, and putting more than two twos together to make a reasonable guess, I was able to track Dr Croft's home to an area in Hertfordshire, then to pore through several telephone directories in search of present-day Crofts who lived nearby. I hoped that the medical calling had remained within the family, and found a Dr Croft who might possibly fit the bill. I then called upon him. I am not sure who surprised whom the more, but Richard Page Croft was indeed the direct descendant of Georgiana's doctor, and moreover he had in a drawer a bundle of letters which his ancestor had sent to his mother from France in the late eighteenth century. We looked at them together, and I fairly shrieked when I came across one dated 21 May, 1790, written an hour or so after he had delivered Georgiana's son. There was no earthly reason why he should dissemble in a private note home, and he had no expectation that his letter would ever be published. There one had the truth from the most untainted source, hidden unsuspected in a Hertfordshire cottage while *le beau monde* went on gossiping about it for years.

The book was very well reviewed, and sold respectably, but it naturally suffered the fate of all but the rarest books and was finally forgotten. More than twenty years later Amanda Foreman visited the subject again and forged for herself a best-seller of gigantic proportions. Miss Foreman added valuable research of her own and took a novel point of view, namely that Georgiana had been politically influential. Nevertheless, she noted in a foreword that my book had relied too much on published sources, whereas she knew perfectly well that it had been the first to open Georgiana's own view on her own world, and she happily followed the lead I had given by quoting some of the same letters that I had discovered. I have never been able to comprehend the occasional ungenerosity of authors.

The third book was suggested and commissioned by Ben Glazebrook of Constable & Co., Cecil Woodham-Smith's first publishers, and one of the few houses left to be run by literate men who enjoy books instead of merely selling them. *Great Hostesses* was a celebration of those magnificent ladies who lived in order to have people to dinner, all of whom had popped up in other people's memoirs throughout the twentieth century and had been identified in footnotes, but none of whom had been afforded a whole chapter to herself. They varied from the hideous Mrs Greville to the kindly Lady Colefax, their only common denominator being a belief in negotiation through catering. For though their stories were replete with hilarious anecdote, they occasionally had tangential effect upon the nation's destiny. Mrs Greville, for whom Hitler arranged private trains, was always first on Ribbentrop's list when he came to England. She made sure that the other guests round her table would never dream of suggesting that anyone in England saw anything remotely naughty about Herr Hitler, and would assure him that England would never go to war to stop the little man. Ribbentrop was not very intelligent or discerning and would faithfully report back to Hitler the nonsense he had gathered at Mrs Greville's table near Dorking. In her tiny way then, she bore some responsibility for what transpired.

As ever, it was the research which was the most entertaining, the writing the most gruesome. (At about this time the playwright David Storey said he regarded himself as just as much a manual worker as his father had been; while dad dug coal out of the ground, David dug words out of his brain.) I quickly worked out that a number of people who had known these ladies in their hey-day before the Second World War were still alive, and so I tracked them down. One in particular serves to illustrate how much behaviour had changed since the days of their youth. Cockie Hoogterp was living alone in a cottage in Hampshire, none of her neighbours suspecting that she had lived a life close to all the great events of history (her brother had been Edward VIII's closest confidant). Cockie's dearest friend in the 1920s was the American hostess Laura Corrigan, immensely wealthy with an income of $60 million a year, immensely generous, immensely dotty with her riotous malapropisms. I found it easy enough to assemble these malapropisms for the chapter on Laura, but as tough as treacle to find out who she was. Her best friend, Cockie, did not know, because ladies in those days were never so indiscreet as to ask. She had been on countless holidays with Laura, but had never ventured to enquire where she had been born, where she had lived before she arrived in London, how she had married, where she had managed to get hold of so much money. She still paraded her framed photograph on a sitting-room table, but she simply did not know who she was. The one unfathomable mystery was her peculiar hobby. On visits to people in the country, instead of going for long walks Laura Corrigan would ask for an axe and gaily start chopping wood.

To find the truth about Laura I had to work backwards through newspaper archives, and allow one clue to point towards another. Coverage in London in the 1920s declared that she came from Cleveland, Ohio, and was the wife of Jimmy Corrigan, head of the Corrigan-McKinney Steel Company. (Jimmy, by the way, was present at most of Laura's extravagant dinner-parties, but hardly anyone noticed him. Like every husband of every society hostess, he sat at one end of the table and said nothing. Of Sir Arthur Colefax it was said that he 'bored for England'.) I then went to Cleveland and trawled through back copies of the local newspapers which predated Laura's arrival in London. They revealed an astonishing story. Laura had been engaged to marry a much older man, James Corrigan *père*, who took his private yacht on to Lake Eerie one day and sank with it. So did all his family, with the exception of Jimmy junior, a ne'er-do-well who preferred to stay at home and as a result found himself a multi-millionaire. Laura promptly transferred her affections to the heir and married him.

Another clue revealed an earlier marriage to the resident doctor of a Chicago hotel. The resourceful and ambitious Laura had found both him and the hotel rather tiresome, so she had taken a job as waitress in Saratoga Springs, where the wealthy hung out, in the hopes of catching somebody's eye. She did, and it was Corrigan's. I went to examine the newspaper archives in Chicago, which took me on the final step backwards in her history. She had come from upstate Wisconsin, born to a penniless family in a forested area, had been brought up in a caravan, and her first job had been baking cookies. Her father and the customers for her cookies had all been lumberjacks. Hence the curious wood-chopping at English country houses forty years later.

The delicious part of this story is that I was able to go back and visit Cockie Hoogterp again and tell her who her best friend had been. She was flabbergasted, and laughed in wonderment.

I also consulted Diana Cooper and Kakoo, the Dowager Duchess of Rutland, who were sisters-in-law and who separately represented, in totally contrasting styles, the best of British beauty following the First World War. While Diana had been the iconic, ice-cool, statuesque beauty of legendary perfection, Kakoo had been the sweet, cosy, comforting rose of English tradition. To lunch with the two of them at Kakoo's tiny terraced house, when they were both well over eighty, was to taste the lingering echo of their past glory. Kakoo was still pretty. Diana was never pretty; she was overwhelming. Thereafter I visited Kakoo often in her declining years, for tea and light talk.

It now seems impossible to believe, but throughout the writing of these books I was burdened with a horribly tempestuous domestic life which was entirely of my own choosing, yet which tested my resolve, stamina and endurance more painfully than any other period of my life. I was official foster-father to a disturbed and damaged adolescent boy, who made the atmosphere at Caithness Road electric with menace and was often on the brink of seriously violent eruption. Fifteen years afterwards I wrote about the experience in a book which simply bore his name – *Gary*.

CHAPTER 10

Self and Biography, Biography and Self

Of course Gary was attractive. A young adolescent full of vigour and hope, desperate for guidance (and struggling not to show it), shedding the childhood skin and not yet fitting into the new adult one, forlorn and flustered, an illiterate bombastic orphan stuffed with rage against everyone for being luckier than he, with only charm and guile to see him through. Had he been sexually cunning, or even just eager for experiment, I might not have wished to discourage him. The murk, if such it was, lay in ambush. But it required only minutes to see that Gary had a blazing need for something much more important than fun. He wanted to belong somewhere, to feel that what he said or did mattered to somebody. He wanted, in short, a father.

How dare I imagine for one second that I could fulfil such a role? Why did nobody stop me? Why was I encouraged all around, given shovels with which to dig the hole into which I was to fall? It would be vexatious, as well as unjust towards the whole truth, to repeat in summary here events which fill an entire book. I shall only say how the trap was sprung, and how I now understand my reasons for springing it upon myself.

One of the guides I hired to do London tours for my occasional groups of students telephoned the day before the job to say he could not do it, because his wife's grandson was off school and his wife, being in hospital, was unable to look after him. I begged him to think again, as it was impossible in high season to find a guide at such short notice and my students would be stranded. He was adamant. The boy was 'difficult' and could not be left alone. 'For Heaven's sake', I said, 'let me look after him for a day. He can sit here and watch television or something, and I'll give him some kind of lunch.' It was agreed that I should drive over and fetch him.

Gary needed no persuasion. He was eager to grab everything which came his way, to gorge himself on gifts. He was high with energy and vivacity, openly excited, happy and bouncy. He gave off a powerful sense of urgency, of hunger and emotional poverty, such as I had never experienced, and which weighed down all his joyous words. His response to the house was galvanizing. He appropriated it. Sniffing like a dog into every corner, he found the Guest Room and proudly announced that it would be his. He would have his name printed on the door. The fact that there were three other people living in the house besides myself (Brendan, Staveley, Margot) could not deter him. He would not say as much (or he did not analyse his own reactions – who at that age does?), but he clearly thought that he would have no trouble in claiming rights which cancelled theirs. He was buoyant with optimism, as if he had found something he had been looking for all his life. To hold him down to reality would be cruel. Let him enjoy the moment. When, at the end of the day, reality loomed as we prepared to take him home, he was suddenly plaintive, I would even say scared. 'I can come back, can't I?' he asked. I said we would see if his grandmother would let him come for the following weekend, and yes, he could have the Guest Room and put his name on the door.

Gary's mother had died in her early twenties. His father had remarried and disappeared to the Midlands, where Gary had visited him once in his life, with disastrous consequences of jealousy and hurt. He was brought up by his mother's mother, an overweight woman whose love for the child was manifested in her never demanding anything of him. He stayed away from school and she thought it unkind to pressure him, so he was uneducated. He stayed out when he felt like it, and she thought that showed character. He stole what he coveted, so she gave him as much income as he craved, which led him to steal again when that ran out or she was not immediately to hand. The food he did not care for he scraped off on to her plate as they ate. Her husband was not of Gary's family; he observed silently. Gary was wild, a chaotic jumble of needs and greeds, pathetic and unbridled, and heading straight towards inevitable delinquent adulthood, possibly even criminality. Gary's grandmother, well-intentioned perhaps (I am not even sure of that, for she may have been selfish, wishing to prolong the boy's infancy and dependence), had done her worst.

I made a deal with Gary. He could come and live at Caithness Road on condition that he went to school and did his lessons. It took great courage for him to accept this, because he would naturally always be at the bottom of any class, and would naturally want to shine to earn praise. He would have to learn to take failure as an ingredient in life, which was probably the hardest thing to ask of him. But he was so in earnest, so frighteningly worked up, that he would attempt anything. Nobody had ever been interested enough to demand anything of him. He obviously felt he could be normal at last.

I went to see the Headmaster, who approved of the experiment and promised to keep an eye on him, watching for special needs and potential eruptions. I appeared before a committee of educational experts. I was invited by the social services to become a recognized foster-parent, giving Gary the identity he craved (he signed his surname Masters after that). I introduced him to people who would not normally cross his path, in order to teach him social behaviour, and he was much fussed over by Natasha. Penelope Keith and Camilla Osborne were more circumspect. I could see that they were concerned, and worried about what might happen. As for Gary, he was most anxious to know what time he had to be home at night, if he went out with the local boys, and when I said eleven, he would make sure that he arrived, puffing and panting, at five past the hour, late enough for the fact to be noticed, not so late as to deserve reproach.

We were both in fact playing a game of make-believe, he that he had a home and a parent, I that I had a son and knew how to deal with him. I woke him up in the morning, gave him a good breakfast, tried to make his tie straight, and sent him off to school. I was there in the evening with a meal, and he was there with his homework. It was all a grotesque pretence, but I know without a doubt that at the time I believed it would work, and wanted very much for it to do so, and that Gary was full of hope. That alone was wonderful to behold, and sufficient to support the affections which such a manufactured relationship required to give it strength and life.

The experiment was tested at every turn, and with hindsight one must see that it was bound to snap. There were times when I received anxious calls from the headmaster appealing to me to go immediately to the school where Gary had gone berserk, eyes dilating, and been held down by not one, but two teachers.

Recognizing along with everyone else involved the boldness of the experiment, and not wishing to derail it, the headmaster preferred to enlist my help rather than expel a boy who was disruptive to a degree. He relied upon me to calm the situation at home, and I would then spend the best part of the evening trying to reason with Gary, to show him that people were on his side, not against him, and to guide him back to some inner peace, at least for the time being. He would frequently grip the sides of the armchair as I was talking until his knuckles went white, such was the inner turmoil he was attempting to subdue. There were terrible, disheartening discoveries of theft and mendacity, followed by more forgiveness and persuasive reasonableness on my part. On one occasion, in my absence, he lunged for a knife when somebody other than myself made as if to discipline him verbally. I took Gary to an educational therapist (in school time) who subjected him to a variety of careful tests, resulting in a ten-page report sent to me two weeks later. It said, in fine, that the boy was in a dangerous state and risked a violent future, but that the best way to avoid such an outcome was to give him precisely the full-blown attention which I and the educational authorities were trying to do. We were engaged upon a joint, last-ditch fight to save him.

One day I consulted the lady psychiatrist who had been seeing Gary weekly at my behest (he was willing for any attention under whatever guise), and told her how anxious I was at his fitful progress and how I wondered that his inner world must be a terrible place of looming shadows, when I burst into tears. I was in danger of what we used to call 'a nervous breakdown', a collapse of the psychic architecture. I had intended to consult her about Gary, and was instead laying before her my own distress and fear.

There was, I then realized, a terrible confusion of roles. For whom was I going through all this? For Gary, as I maintained? Or for myself, and if so, why? What were my aims and objectives? Who was the one seeking care here, Gary or myself? Or had we fused? What had I done to him by encroaching upon his wounded space? What had I promised that I could not deliver? What on earth was to become of him?

I could not think clearly then. Now I see better. I knew what I was trying to do well enough, but I did not know why. I wanted to give the boy a structure, a reason for living, beyond mere satisfaction of immediate needs. (In this I was constantly undermined by his grandmother, who surreptitiously gave him money when I was trying to make him budget, and who welcomed him to beans on toast and telly when he played truant, swearing that she would never tell me, in fact purchasing his loyalty.) I wanted him to learn to give as well as take, to feel pride as well as arrogance, to grow into a full human being, not a warped individual bearing permanent grudges. To this end I knew that I should maintain responsibility for him until he came of age at eighteen, or thereafter until he found a job and an income of his own. I knew that real parents did not throw out their children when they became bothersome or criminal, and that I must never give him cause to find his new home life lacking in support. What was once attempted must be seen through. There was no turning back without causing catastrophic damage. It felt like a sentence, an imprisonment from which there was no imminent escape.

But there was another central character in this experiment, another hole of attention, and that was me. What was I doing for myself?

It is blindingly obvious that I wanted to be a father, but the truth is no less worth stating for being trite. I thought all my energies were bent upon making life better for Gary, but a large chunk of them were devoted to creating a new life for myself, the life of a parent, the life of responsibility and stress, the life which I had biologically failed but could somehow construct magically out of this unexpected opportunity. It was also the life of unconditional love, of loyalty without reward, symbolized in Gary's simple requirement that I should tuck him into bed at night long after he had become a strapping lad, as token proof of peace and forgiveness, a blessing that he could sink with into sleep, that daily obliterated doubts and misgivings. With no experience at all, I was *playing* at being Father, and it now appears to me deeply reprehensible that I should have used a vulnerable boy, isolated by his profound distrust, to help me realize that part of myself which I had, for whatever reason, smothered with terrors. That it nevertheless worked in part was due as much to Gary's intuition of what was good for him as to my decisions on his behalf. He also had a canny idea of what was good for me. We were both learning and adjusting, and he emerged after two years a measurably tamed social individual with an entirely new dimension – he began to think outside of himself, to imagine what other people might feel and might want.

There was another aspect to my advantage in this adventure, and that was the tricky matter of identification. Though it is much exercised by scribblers in psychiatry who prefer textbook labels to explanations, it is actually so subtle and discreet that one cannot see it, let alone grasp it, at the time. Had anyone suggested to me that I saw myself in Gary, I should have laughed him to scorn. Our circumstances could not have been more disparate. I had never been consumed with hatred, never been violent, never known real tragedy, never felt dumped by the world. I was mild and placid against his torment and rage. Now, however, I can ever so dimly discern the lurking truths of identification. They worked in two ways. First, they underscored all the pity that I felt for Gary, by resurrecting from the deep ancient pities I had felt for myself. I, too, was Gary, craving for assistance, searching for encouragement, begging to be taken notice of for what I was, not for what I should have been. I had invented my own pride by doing well at school, in virtually everything, and so attracted that warmth and approval that had earlier been whipped out of my hands. I had been lucky. What if I had not been blessed with the intelligence to haul myself out of indifferent regard? What if I had been Gary? I saw in Gary the Brian that might have been, the Brian who might have taken the road to resentment instead of the road to renewal. I actually *felt* for Gary, as if I knew what coursed through his heart, and that can only be because I was feeling in touch once more with the self that had been Gary in embryo all those years before.

The other way in which identification operated was by proxy. I was to be for Gary the father he did not have, and to be for myself the father I wished Geoffrey Masters had been. I was to do for him all the things my father had not done for me, give him assurances, praise his little successes, forgive his big failures, accept and respect him, ease his passage through life with confiding trusts, be side by side with him. Thus I was Gary while I was being the manufactured Geoffrey, and I was Gary while I was being the resurrected infant Brian; but Gary was Brian when I was Geoffrey at his best. The splits were manifold and overlapping.

Then there was the enduring memory of what Gilbert Harding had done for me. I thought it was possible for Gary to see new horizons, to grasp new opportunities if they were offered and made available. I wanted to return that gift of unsuspected potential which I had received many years before and watch Gary become somebody else, grow into a different man from the one ordained by earlier circumstances.

I said at the end of the book that it was a cruel paradox that I had learnt more from the experience than he had, when the whole idea had been for him to gain, not me. It was a kind of hell, with great shafts of dazzling light, which I suppose more or less sums up family life anywhere. Natasha was sweet to him, flirtatious and exotic; Freddie and Elizabeth Richmond treated him with the unforced kindness any ordinary boy would expect, which was best; Iris Murdoch met him and told me that what I had undertaken was 'worthy'. My cockney neighbours and the kids in the street welcomed him amongst them and were not put off by the occasional lies and dissemblances, all part of the package of adolescence. The best summation, however, came from Gary himself.

He eventually asked if he could leave Caithness Road and go to live with the parents of his girlfriend, who were willing to take him in and who, like me, had spotted his gaping needs and responded to them. I said I would need to explain to them what they would be getting, which made him nervous, and I also resisted the notion that a new magic wand would make everything perfect; I felt he should put up with difficulties and not seek to spirit them away. I knew it was my duty to be there when the love affair evaporated, when he would surely have to move on again. But he was so keen, so touchingly anxious, that for once he found the words to articulate and to persuade. He said, 'I know you have tried to be both

Mum and Dad to me, really I do, and you've done a great job, honest. But now I've got the chance to have a real Mum and Dad for myself, one of each. You must let me take it. I'm getting old [he was sixteen] and the chance will never come again. It's got to be now or never.'

So Gary went to live in the East End of London. I saw him a few times after that, when he called to tell me how he was getting on. Tragedy befell him again, when his girlfriend died from a rare disease at the age of nineteen. He went on, took jobs painting, married and had two children, a boy and a girl, who are adults themselves now. I have never met them, and I often wonder how much like him they might be. Not, I hope, too much like.

Shortly afterwards I was asked by Yerger Clifton, one of the professors for whom I arranged student trips out of Oxford during the summer, to devise a Grand Tour around Europe in the eighteenth-century style, but without the horse-drawn carriages, the servants, and the booty bought from European collections. The idea was that students from Rhodes College at Memphis, Tennessee, and from the University of the South, at Sewanee, should spend six weeks at St John's College, Oxford, studying mediaeval architecture and Renaissance art under English professors and scholars, then go to Europe to see the buildings and the paintings *in situ* – a kind of field trip. To scoot through a museum and try to see everything (as the Japanese incorrigibly still do) would be bootless. But to study, say, the work of Carl Sluter and then spend an hour with one of his works in Dijon would be to encourage discovery and to stock the memory with something more durable than a snapshot. The universities would accept the combined courses for credit, as there would be serious work involved, with examinations at the end.

I worked out a circular programme to encompass Paris, Dijon, Beaune, Avignon, Rome, Siena, Florence, Padua, Venice, Vicenza, Munich and Amsterdam, to cover six weeks in all. It was important, I thought, to side-track air transport where possible, for I wanted the students to realize they were going somewhere, on a real journey, and not just dropping from the sky into the Piazza della Signoria. The trip across the English Channel had to be by ferry, one overnight train was included, some buses, and only one flight where the distance would otherwise have been too onerous. To make sure that all the hotel bookings, train schedules and museum appointments went according to plan, I volunteered to accompany the trip myself in the first year, planning to yield to a younger man in the future. It has not turned out so, and I have been traipsing around Europe every autumn ever since. Only now am I finally contemplating finding a replacement.

In the first year we travelled with eighteen students, Yerger Clifton, Nigel McGilchrist to do the teaching, and myself to be nanny. Now we have two separate trips, Nigel taking one to Greece and Turkey, Sally Dormer of the Victoria and Albert Museum taking the other to Northern Europe (she being the mediaeval specialist), and we select students according to their track-record and turn some away. We stand at a total of fifty-six, which we have declined to exceed for the past five years. Of the twenty-eight students with Sally and myself, one expects at least twenty of them to be unmoved by the experience, such being the cynicism and material starkness of modern American youth. The few who do respond make the effort worthwhile, and there are always three or four who are visibly shaken by what they see, changed in their habits of looking and interpreting, jostled into unfamiliar reflections. These often return to Europe to live and work the following year.

And they do get the best possible treatment, not only because Nigel and Sally are gifted teachers, able to transmit enthusiasm, but because special arrangements are made along the way. Part of their study is in the Vatican Museum, to see the Apollo Belvedere, the Torso which so inspired Michelangelo, the Raphael Stanze, and of course the Sistine Chapel. Anyone who has been to the Sistine during visiting hours knows what a scramble it is, thousands of people gawping at the ceiling for about three minutes, then hustled out to make way for more thousands. It is a profoundly dispiriting exercise, especially in such a spiritual space, as degrading in its way as buying rosaries from greedy nuns outside St Peter's. We avoid all this by giving ourselves a private visit, touring the museum for three hours when it is closed, and accompanied by just two security guards. I can be quite sure that none of our students can ever quite forget that moment, however *blasé* they might pretend to be.

I was also writing more in an occasional manner, reviews for the *Standard* and the *Spectator*, long features for the Sunday newspapers and, at one time, a series of conversation pieces with, amongst others, Frank Longford, Debo Devonshire and Robin Day. Longford had a considerable influence upon the way I see the world, as his transparent gentleness and sweet nature withstood all kinds of mockery and remained limpid despite a career in politics. He is the only person I have met who suggests what Jesus may have been like to know and to listen to. He elicits the purest kind of admiration, rooted in care for the man's well-being and love for his generous mind. I cannot imagine him ever being in a vile mood with somebody, and therefore felt sure he had never known wretchedness.

One bitter December day in 1977 I was taken by an American friend, Joe Monahan, to a restaurant in Cromwell Road called La Chanterelle for lunch. It was fortuitous indeed that I should accept the invitation, since I habitually avoided lunch as a fatal interruption of the day, preferring to have a sandwich at home and return to my desk after twenty minutes or so. Perhaps that day Joe was only in town briefly and allowed me no choice. Life would have been very different had I excused myself. How different one can never know, of course.

The waiter who took our order was short and dark, with luminous wavy black hair, olive skin, and a set of teeth so neat and white they ought to have been fashioned in Hollywood. He had a ready smile and engaging manner, and his command of English was good, but just bad enough to be charming. Having written down the main courses, he said, 'And what do you want after that?' Without control, I replied, 'Oh well, I think after that I should like to have you on toast.'

I was horrified. I tried to grab the words back and stuff them down my throat, but succeeded only in blushing furiously. I had never spoken to a stranger in that way, still less one employed to serve and therefore in no position to defend himself. It was impertinent, unmanly, rude of me, what the Americans call 'fresh' and I was mortified for the waiter's sake as well as my own. He took it in great part and flashed his winning smile with the comment, 'You wait until the end of the meal for that.' I was later to learn that such banter was hardly unknown in the Chanterelle. It meant little. Still, when he brought our overcoats I felt the need to apologize for my behaviour, and added the contradictory *coda,* 'Do you mean to say that if I asked you out to dinner, you would accept?' 'Why not?', he replied, 'call here on the telephone, and just ask for the Little One.' It was significant that he would not vouchsafe his name, but I was so green, never having made such a bold move before, that I did not give it a thought.

Two weeks passed before I dared to make the telephone call, and I was not to know at the time that he had not the faintest recollection of our encounter, or rather that he could not distinguish it from countless others of like nature. We made an appointment for the following week, and I was to meet him outside the restaurant (again, no declaration of address, all very furtive). We dined at an Italian place near Olympia, and I told him that I was quite certain we should know one another for a very long time. He, on the other hand, was equally certain that it would be a very short time; it was his custom to accept these invitations, excuse himself before dessert in order to go to the lavatory, then disappear into the night, abandoning Lothario to stew in his foolishness. Anyway, at some point in the evening he changed his mind, and Juan Melian Macias is now joint-owner with me of a house and five acres in Surrey.

Between that dinner and this house in Surrey lie many years of adjustment, conflict and resignation, which it would require several hundred pages to detail. I intend only to assess what it was in Juan's personality that landed him in Caithness Road, and why my response to this personality has caused me both fathomless distress and final peace. It must be clear already that I gravitate by instinct, almost by magnetic pull, towards the difficult and the disastrous, and Juan was to present an almighty challenge to my stamina. He will say that I got what I wanted, and I am beginning to believe he is right. I am hoping before these pages exhaust me that I shall discover why.

Juan came from a working-class family in the small town of Galdar on Gran Canaria, Canary Islands. There were lots of them, five brothers and two sisters, all brought up in an atmosphere of hardship and trial, with scarcely time in the day for affection and soft words. His father and mother worked day and night (literally, with but five hours' sleep between jobs) to make ends meet and the eldest daughter, Ana, brought up the little ones. Juan was the only member of the family to show initiative and intelligence, but these were not useful commodities when one is scrubbing for food and mean clothing, so he was not encouraged. He was on the contrary disprized, and that fed disappointment which he struggled to keep hidden. He says he never resented his family, for they did what they thought best and he admired his mother for her resilience and determination, but at the time I would not be surprised if he quietly seethed with anger and berated himself with guilty sobs for so doing. Feelings, even those of affection, were expressed by hurling abuse and insulting one another in picturesque but ultimately cruel language. Juan grew up in a tight little household loud with bruised feelings, and he has never wholly managed to shake off the habit of sneering. When his brows knit into a fierce frown, eyes darting arrows of accusation, one knows his head is back in the Canary Islands.

This has something healthy and invigorating in it; it is not all merely fatiguing. Juan was formed in an atmosphere of frank display, where feelings were candidly expressed and cautious politic repression of them never even attempted. The family is honest because it lacks the sophistication necessary for dissemblance. They are all out-front, clear and unmistakeable. Their passion does not know the subtle meanderings and insidious posturings of a Mauriac drama, wherein harm is inflicted by stealth; theirs is the direct heavy punch of Lorca, meant to make you sway without cutting you down. Lorca's world is much saner than Mauriac's. As for my own family, the Masters' spirit of avoiding trouble and making amends is feeble by comparison; we lack the red corpuscle.

Nevertheless, Juan knew that he did not fit, that he had to escape. His horizon beckoned beyond Galdar, his heart sought the solace of achievement. Once again, I can spot the process of identification edging its way in, and I wonder how much of it was going on when I first came to know Juan, and when he first proposed, four months after our meeting, that he take a room in my house. I saw much of me in him, the eagerness to earn a place for oneself and demonstrate to one's folk that one can get on. I also saw a lot in him which I had always kept so restrained within myself as never even to acknowledge it. He was the anger I never dared express, the free spirit which broke forth and spluttered its ire across the plain. He was also the power that frightened me, that would never bubble to the surface of me for fear of its destructive consequences. His power always did explode, like Vesuvius, awesome to behold, and it, too, frightened him for the opposite reason, that he was burdened afterwards with the desolation it had caused. I was to help him tame himself, he to show me my untapped emotion. It was bound to be a trying journey.

Juan's volatility was shocking; I mean literally, it announced itself without warning rumbles, bursting through the air like an electric overcharge. He could create an argument out of a stray adjective which may have had an effect beyond its deserts, and stoke it well for three or four hours, refusing to allow the embers to die. He appeared to be enjoying himself, but in fact he was tearing himself apart, asserting his worth over what he perceived to be insulting disregard for his sensitivities. Every word spoken was laden with explosive, every plan amended was the issue of a hidden desire to thwart him. It was like living with a Catherine wheel, permanently fizzing and spitting its energy into the air around us.

His character made it impossible for him to believe what he was told. He persisted in assuming falsehood long after truth had been demonstrated to the satisfaction of anyone else, and thought he was being cunningly misled; he would not allow anyone to get the better of him in that way, for he knew, he thought, how deeply hypocritical was the human heart. Like Molière's Alceste, Juan saw the black forces of deceit in everyone, and was blind to the pastel shades of compassion. He was the very epitome of the cynic, but also like Alceste, his realism afforded him no real pleasure; it confirmed and reinforced his congenital sense of dismay and disappointment.

These were profound burdens for a young man to carry, and harsh ones for me to withstand. My own faults of prevarication on the one hand, and minute examination of argument on the other, were ruthlessly exposed by Juan's directness, to whom my severe rationality was almost offensive. He countered it with raw emotion and challenged me to find truth in feeling rather than in dry fact. This has always been hugely difficult for me, as my attachment to logic intervenes. He found it correspondingly hard to stick tight to sequential thought, which made him wriggle with impatience. We certainly made an odd couple, and the fact that we survived and mellowed must be a tribute to both of us.

There were inescapable signs from the beginning that Juan would be fractious to a degree and stretch my endurance not to its limits, but way in excess of them. I knew he had an element of destructiveness within him which would test us both. To my shame, I was sometimes so perplexed and befuddled by his unyielding passion to destroy that I saw the Devil in him and told him as much, which was cruel indeed to a Catholic who, however much he may question the reliability of myth, has ingested it from birth and feels it to be part of his very flesh. I surprised myself by using the word. It indicated perhaps how useful are religious language and terms of reference for pinning concepts close to the wall.

At the same time, however (and without this I must surely have stopped the adventure at birth, unless I really am a pathological masochist), one could spot Juan's kindness and concern, his embrace of the joy and duty inherent in looking after somebody in need, his overwhelming gentleness with animals who respond by trusting him with their lives, and his quiet support, too often disguised as mockery, for my endeavours. He had infinite time for elderly people, and became a close friend of my mother, visiting her in Wales after my father's death on a regular basis, more often in fact than I did. His attachment to his own mother in the Canary Islands was beautiful to behold, for it took no account of the travails of his childhood and paid all respect to the decency and nobility of her old age. (The finest photograph I ever took was a snap of Señora Melian, which captures in her the gentleness of soul which Juan inherited along with his other baggage of emotional overcharge.)

He took several jobs after he gave up the restaurant business, and did them all well, with a thoroughness which was foreign to English staff anxious to clock off as soon as possible. But whenever promotion beckoned, he backed off and resigned rather than have his shortcomings (as he thought) exposed. He wrote a book in English, and started another, about his boyhood adventures in Gran Canaria, both of which showed that the need to climb out of his trough had not subsided. They were accomplished, though never intended for publication. Camilla was amazed that he read all the Lucia novels of E.F. Benson and caught their spirit, after which he moved on to the works of Wilkie Collins.

When I published *The Evil That Men Do* in 1996 I was conscious of gathering together the fruit of many years' reflection on the problems of moral philosophy, of the sources of goodness and the power of wickedness and how to make the former prevail over the latter. I suppose I was also trying to unravel the lessons I had taught myself in delving into the personalities of addictive murderers such as Nilsen, Dahmer and West, and that was certainly what the publishers expected me to do. Sitting here now I can see that there was another subterranean current of which I was wholly unaware at the time – a desire to secure the release of Juan from his demons. That is putting it rather dramatically perhaps, but it does make sense that I had worried for years why Juan sometimes dissolved into bleak destructiveness, when his heart was brimming with benevolence, and writing this book might have been a way of resolving the dilemma without actually mentioning him, without turning the spotlight on to him at all, but expanding it into the general. I thought I was writing about the problems of mankind; prosaically and unwittingly, I was really writing about my own.

Hindsight not only clarifies, it calms. When we consider how Juan set about emptying Caithness Road of its residents and appropriating it for himself, I no longer deplore it nor he justify it, we look upon it with wonder and amusement. Staveley moved to a flat nearby, Brendan and Gwen got themselves a flat in Shepherd's Bush, and Margot eventually moved to a room owned by the next-door neighbours. After that we had occasional lodgers on short-term. We also smile at the mighty battles and slow drip-drip of improvement towards relative tranquillity. Juan left for a while and lived in Massachusetts, tasting the independence which life with me had rendered an impossible prize (I am too keen on organizing everyone else's life as well as my own), returning each year to look in and tacitly re-state ownership. I made no objections, and finally surprised him by finding a property in Surrey which would give him the space, the grounds, the sunsets, the vegetable patch, the trees, that he had always craved, and which we then bought together. All his life he has wanted to share, even detesting the necessity of shopping by himself when there was no one around to trail after him, and now sharing is a legal as well as an emotional fact.

In addition, my brother's house is the next down the lane, which offers companionship and a nice roundness to fate.

As for me, I demand little but peace and the freedom to work at my desk. And when encroachments upon these are threatened, I can disappear to my village spot in France. I do not know or love loneliness, but I relish solitude.

That is a confession which comes as something of a surprise to those who know me and consider me to be gregarious to a fault, a man who is happiest when surrounded. That this may be true, and yet allow room for its antithesis to be true as well, confuses people who are used to blacks and whites and invariables. I love company, am possibly too garrulous and social at times, and when I am in London I could spend every evening at the Garrick Club and never be bored. There is no Garrick in Castries, the small village near Montpellier where I do most of my work, and yet I am equally content to be by myself there for many days at a time. I have heard this explained in terms of the zodiac, that an abrupt adaptation to different circumstances is typical of Gemini, the twin personality. I have never been able to take these fairy-tales seriously, if only because the fact that I was born in May is directly concerned with that other fact that I was conceived in August, and had the accident of a single spermatazoon's hitting home been delayed by a few weeks, I should have been a Cancer instead of a Gemini; I would nevertheless have been more or less the same person, wrought of my mother's character and my father's character, mixed with traces of their unknown ancestors' characters, and a new bit of my own thrown in by genetic hazard. No, my enjoyment of the company of friends and my predilection for solitude are contradictions which I must try to answer, for the stars cannot.

Having been brought up amongst buildings, I initially felt strangely bereft when I first found myself surrounded by fields, far horizons and forests. I was not able to feel my place in that wide world; it was not empty, for it teemed with vigour and spunk, plants shooting up towards the sun and competing for space, trees defending themselves against insects, insects against birds and birds against beasts, the melody of life buzzing about one's ears and the drama of it spread out every minute before one's eyes. I could admire and wonder at all this, but not know what to do with it. I could not recognize a tree or a bird (and still cannot), and was thereby denied the pleasure of familiarity which I believe enchants people who live in the country and walk miles every day, staking their route alongside the ancient tracks of the animals. I was moved to awed silence by the contemplation of vastness and richness around me. I imagine everyone has felt that moment of humility, of readjustment of proportion, when one's petty travails and jealousies and hurts as well as one's achievements spiral down to nothing against the inevitability and indifference of the world. I have felt that just as keenly on a Derbyshire hillside as in the Grand Canyon, and at such moments, grabbed quickly on the wing, one understands from inside, intuitively, the insights of the poets.

And yet I felt a visitor in the fields, an intruder wearing the wrong socks and looking through the wrong spectacles, what the French call *de trop*, in the way, unnecessary. Amongst the buildings of London I at least knew I belonged. The fact that I came late to even a smidgen of country life must mean that I can never be part of it, like the old goat-herd I see in France on the top of a hill nearby, his face brown-burnt like bark, crisp and seared by the millennia of habit that he has inherited. I was sixteen before I set eyes on a real cow, and nearly fifty when Debo introduced me to a pig, which so amazed me by its slobbering size that I thought it must have been artificially bred (it hadn't – they never were dainty creatures).

The peace of the countryside is another attraction which has its ambivalence. Long ago I was struck by the remark of a nineteenth-century scholar, one Charles Fisher, that 'peace is not perfect till you can hear a sheep cough half a mile away.' At first, it is amusing and whimsical, confident in its playful exaggeration. But spend a day on a Yorkshire dale and you see how just it is. The sounds are so eerily distant, they carry so much of the history of the planet in their muffled sharpness, that you feel lost in Time, you could go backwards or forwards and it would make no difference, for infinite peace reigns there, immutable and unconquerable despite the hundreds of daily little slaughters it conceals. And there's the rub, that's the ambivalence. It encourages one to ponder and reflect, perhaps a little too much than is good for one, as the conclusions it imposes are unpalatable. If, like me, you are exercised by the terrible briefness of the time allotted, if you worry about getting enough done before it is too late, if you wish you could re-wind and start again somewhere along the line, giving yourself those few extra years that you need, then listening to the sheep cough half a mile away will only remind you that your worries are so much flatulence in the wind. You will make no mark and leave no trace, and no amount of fiddling with words and concepts will alter that abiding truth. Your agonizing ruminations upon fate bear not the weight of a chaffinch's discarded tail-feather. The countryside shows you the face of eternity and teases you with your own ephemerality. It might sometimes be better to keep one's illusions intact in a busy London street.

Another quote: that young sceptic Chamfort wrote that the contemplative life was often a life of misery, and advised more action and less thought as the route to moderate happiness. One must not, he said, simply watch oneself living (*ne pas se regarder vivre*). In the countryside, you can do little else. Being alone on the vibrant skin of the world can be a recipe for despair.

The writer, however, must accept the danger and even embrace it, and that is why I take to the ample busyness of metropolitan life, with its discussions, its operas, its theatres and its gossip, with as much enthusiasm as I slide back into the calm waters of solitude. The one life feeds the other. In the society of one's fellows one learns; in the quietness of one's own company one thinks about what one has learnt. Everybody fashions some version of the former for himself, but only the writer wilfully moves on to bruise himself with the latter. The countryside is his ruminant cradle, liable to sway and crash as well as to soothe.

I like to begin each morning before breakfast with a brisk rock in this cradle by way of a walk in the fields, gearing up for the morning's work, taking deep breaths and sharpening the antennae. Not too long, mind, for one is not begging for inspiration, a commodity which comes but fitfully and then only as the result of hard slog. I sit at the desk at 9:30 and start. It is as simple and as demanding as that.

All writers talk about the terror of the 'block' when words will not come and even if one wrote a shopping-list it would turn out wrong. Writer's block commonly lasts at least half an hour, when precious time is wasted looking out of the window and churning irrelevant thoughts in one's head as the job in hand, the book itself, is dissipated with the morning dew and one's attempts to grab it back grow ever more defeatist. On a bad day the block can linger for a couple of hours, and then one must take evasive action, like watching the news on television or going out to buy half a dozen eggs that one does not really need. The trick is to get back to the desk with a renewed desire to launch, so that one may pretend to oneself that the lost hours were in fact a wily preparation.

I have known writers to be paralysed by this block for days or even months. In cases like those remedial action is insufficient, for the disease has spread into the soul and threatens to devour the creative urge. A man may be rendered ill by it and take to his bed; he may be tempted to give it all up and go for a less exigent profession; he may even sink into silliness and smother his memory with comforting banalities which deny that he ever wrote at all. Something like this ultimate writer's block must surely have descended upon Arthur Rimbaud, for nothing else can account, at least to me, for his abrupt fizzling out after a brief surge of creative energy. From writing the most profound and original poems in the French language at the age of sixteen, seventeen, eighteen, and then to disappear first into the Dutch army, then to a travelling circus, then take a job as works' superintendent in Cyprus, finally to dabble in the arms trade in Africa, strikes me as supremely unnatural. Biographers may come up with rational explanations dug out of psychological need or financial insecurity, but a writer who suddenly becomes somebody else is, in my view, in flight.

Nothing nearly so dramatic could ever happen to me, because I have always been of the Second Eleven team, reliant upon carefully organized swotting more than the flash of originality. Even sloggers can encounter the brick wall however, and to protect myself from it I will never begin the day with a blank sheet. At the end of the previous day's work I will make notes telling myself where I want to go next, and these will be waiting for me in the morning as a kind of menu. In this way I feel that the train slows down occasionally without coming to a complete halt until I want it to. The analogy with the train is a good one, because the first sentence of the first paragraph of the first chapter is always the most difficult; upon it seems to depend everything which follows – the tone, the pace, the energy of the story itself. So to get this right is the biggest challenge. I like to start with a paradox, to grab attention and enliven curiosity. The first sentence of my biography of Marie Corelli is, 'Stratford-upon-Avon is the birthplace of William Shakespeare', of that of E. F. Benson, 'It ought to be easy to write a Life of E. F. Benson'; and that of John Aspinall, 'As far as one knows, there is not a single zoologist among John Aspinall's ancestors.' These are not contrived openings; once they jump into one's head, they are as natural as spring water; but they may well take days to appear. With that first sentence, the train moves away from the platform. When the first paragraph has taken shape, the train is puffing along nicely. It has reached its cruising speed by the middle of the third paragraph, and thereafter it will not stop, and I will not leap off. The writing finds its own pace and enjoyment. Only when I reach the end of a chapter will I put on the brakes and turn off the engine. A few days' rest follows, during which time the first sentence of the next chapter is moving around my head, trying words in different positions and with different emphases until the right combination clicks. One can then turn on the ignition once more.

Practically all the work is done in the morning, between 9:30 and 1:00 p.m. That is quite enough to exhaust the cells. In the late afternoon, following a scrappy lunch and a nap, I will scribble my notes for the next day, then prepare to reward myself with a night out. I will never review what I have written in the morning, since the likelihood of finding it wanting is strong, and the ensuing dissatisfaction potentially very damaging – I don't want the train to break down between stations! Reviewing and rewriting takes place all the time, of course, but it does so while I am in the thick of it, in the middle of a sentence or a paragraph, not after the full-stop has been typed. The reason for this caution is not over-confidence, it is precisely the opposite, and one must not offer too many traps to a confidence which is already fragile. A real moment of satisfaction, when one feels one has got it right, that one has expressed what one had in mind as near perfection as one dare hope, might occur no more than once a month. It is rare enough to induce elation, and is always recognizable. The rest of the time one approximates; one cannot do more. Great actors and dancers hardly ever claim to have given a good performance more than half a dozen times in their lives, so a decent sentence from me once every month is above anything I have any right to expect.

There are writers who work at night (Beryl Bainbridge); others who work on the bus from Oxford to London (A. N. Wilson);

some who start with a hangover at five in the morning (Peter Ackroyd); and some who finish before breakfast (Kingsley Amis); a few who treat the job like any other, clocking on and clocking off at the prescribed minute (Anthony Trollope famously maintained that he would stop in mid-sentence if he had written the required number of words, and that if he had finished a book and another two hundred words needed to be written to meet his allocation for the day, he would open a new page and start on an entirely new book). As for me, 2,000 words a day is an aim, and 2,500 an accomplishment.

One is bound to wonder why the potent objective? Why not lean upon the whim of mood? Well, as I have said, inspiration may be all very well for Wordsworth and Cowper, but for the likes of me it may be a long time a-coming; the muse needs goading. Beyond the merely practical, there is also the working man's imperative to earn one's right to be in this world, which is why I unblinkingly used the word 'reward' to describe my wine, dinner and conversation at the end of the day. Wealth tempered with energy I could withstand, but to be both rich and idle must be onerous indeed. I need to get through those prescribed number of words per day in order to feel I have done something, that I and Time have marched together, not met and bled in conflict. It is such an exhilarating feeling that I catch myself grinning at the end of it when I might more reasonably be expected to be sighing with the effort.

There must also be that other imperative, the marrow in the bone, which is the absolute necessity of having something to say. Words by themselves can constitute delightful music and mean nothing whatever, as in some of the poems of Théophile Gautier and Leconte de Lisle, but I am no poet and have not the ear to make words sing. Nor could I lend them the warmth of colour, as the afternoon sun shafting through the stained glass at Chartres tones up the cold slabs of stone. Besides which, I am didactic by inclination, and must use words as tools towards elucidation. I do feel that I have lots to explain, and must wriggle my way through the language in order to bring that explanation out clear, sharp and unmistakeable.

It was not always so. I was not driven when young by the urge to get things across, simply because I deferred to everyone else's wisdom to understand them better than I ever could. I remained a schoolboy for a long time into adulthood. But somewhere, something occurred which ceased to be the outcome of resolute, systemized swotting and passed into insight and interpretation; I began to see behind and watch the shadows slink, attempting to escape my gaze; and it must be at that point, which I cannot identify with any precision, that my little creative component emerged and latched itself on to biography. For nobody nowadays would deny that a proper biography cannot be a cold record of facts – it must be a creative realignment of them.

In retrospect I can see that I have always been drawn to extravagant characters, by which I mean people who stretch and snap the norm. Georgiana was no ordinary duchess (and believe me, there have been dozens of those), but a vivid, lively, delectable woman who went over the top in all her endeavours. She did not just canvass for Charles James Fox at the election of 1784 (itself a bold innovation), she almost got arrested for it and exchanged kisses with butchers for votes. She did not just fritter away her allowance at the gaming-tables, she came very close to spending her husband's fortune and ruining the Devonshire Estates for ever. She did not just tolerate the duke's mistress, she welcomed and cherished her (and, I am sure, gained some very useful tips from her). Marie Corelli was not just a best-seller, she was the most outrageous producer of tosh in her day and broke all the records which preceded her. She was not just a liar, but a monumentally manufactured personage about whom not one published fact was wholly true. She did not just fall in love with Arthur Severn, she slobbered all over him with the baby-talk she had last heard in her spoilt infancy. John Aspinall was not just the creator of private zoos, he transformed the way in which zoos are conceived, in their purpose, function and style, the world over, an achievement for which he has still received only grudging praise.

All these people are more than they appear. Their personalities require careful unravelling and diffident meticulous stitching together again, so that their real selves are not transgressed by the biographer's interference but on the contrary are set forth on a clear plinth, the rubble of confusion swept from their paths. I have always chosen those most difficult to unravel, those who offered the most daunting challenge. My subjects are all mavericks in their different ways, and the maverick is notoriously unwilling to be scrutinized. The maverick is his own publicist and chief of propaganda; he is not only the star of his own story, but its script-writer and director as well. So the biographer who dares to re-write the script must tread with delicacy. But I have always known that the script needed to be re-written, that interpretation was a vital ingredient in making the story known for what it really was.

No character can be more aberrant perhaps than the addictive murderer – a maverick with the vice of slaughter in his heart – and it came to be with these kind of people that I was professionally more associated in the public's understanding. The difficulty attendant upon their stories is that the public does not want them to be interpreted (no matter how often they bleat the opposite), and that my wish to comprehend what they had done through the prism of another intelligence was deemed to be very suspect indeed. The subject of murder represented not such a leap as has been supposed. It was a progression in the line of awkward biographies, more awkward, to be sure, than any that had preceded them, but requiring the same justness of tone, calmness of purpose, precision in dissection, and objectivity of manner. In the same way that, to understand Georgiana, I had to immerse myself in the archive of her life, so, to understand a killer like Nilsen, I had to work my way through another archive, composed of police files and his own notebooks. The archives were different, the methods identical. One starts by seeing but the surface, and gradually one penetrates into the body beneath. And just as it would have been foolish to berate the social grotesquerie of being a duchess with paupers begging at the gates, or to deplore the notion of a *ménage à trois*, when the job at hand was the description of a person; so it would have been wrong, in my view, to agitate against Nilsen when it was not my job to condemn (the courts would do that), but to clarify. This insistence upon analysis would prove very unpopular.

One who warned me against involvement in the subject was a man whom I loved and admired above any other of my acquaintance at the time, a prodigious lawyer called James Crespi. He said it would be (the word bounces off the wall at me even now) 'titillating'. As I have always hated the way in which newspapers swarm upon disaster to extract from it the shallowest possible emotions with which to sell copies, and positively deter any intelligent approach, this word was worrying. Could it be that the subject was impossible to treat without descending to entertainment? I thought not, although if it were to appear on a bookshelf rather than in an obscure medical journal in Tasmania it would need to be written to alarm as well as inform. James naturally saw the court as the only place in which the subject of murder should be addressed, because for him it was the crime and not the criminal that mattered. Lawyers are not interested in people, only in indictments. Still, James was one of the most learned men I knew, and part of my aim in writing my first book on murder was to convince him that the subject could be worthy of literary as well as of legal investigation.

I wrote James' obituary for *The Times*, but the largeness of the man escaped all attempt to condense. He was the last great English eccentric, a character who looked and sounded as if he belonged in literature rather than in reality, a man shaped and delineated by a page of Dickens. He was, to start with, bulky, his body spherical, sloping majestically out from beneath a cushioned chin to a waistline which was longer in circumference than the totality of his height, a rolling tank, a big sombre presence. When he lifted himself out of an armchair it was with a grunt and a scuffle to confirm the great burden that he had to carry. His head was like an egg, balding at the front, two large black eyes, a generous mouth which pouted in repose and in reflection, and spread wide agape in loud laughter, each mood as frequent as the other. His mind was so clear and so disciplined by logical sequence of thought and choice of word that virtually nobody dared gainsay him; his argument, once presented, was irrefutable. Years as a prosecutor had made his reputation fearsome, not only for the crystal sharpness of his prose, but for his astonishing habit of addressing the court without notes. When one is used to watching barristers shuffle half a dozen files bursting with annotated highlighted pages as their 'crib' the sight of Caesar James Crespi doing it all off the top of his head, relying solely upon his sparkling memory to sort out the necessary and discard the rest, made everybody else look amateur. It was said that even the Lord Chief Justice stood in awe of his abilities. Mixed with that respect, however, was a solid amount of affection.

John Mortimer often denied that his splendid Rumpole of the Bailey was based on Crespi, but I should not be surprised if some little of James went into the cocktail, for they had the same love of the law and mischievous respect for those who got around it. James' conversation at the Garrick or at El Vino's was replete with legal stories, many so hilarious that I have repeated them dozens of times since and always drawn wild laughter. To try them here in cold print would be to lose their savour – the only way Boswell was able to capture Johnson was by doing so at the time, not in retrospect, and doing so all the time, not in snatches. I used one in an article in the *Spectator* and was told by Andrew Roberts that it was the only time that journal made him laugh out loud in the Tube. James was not averse to repeating a story twice within an hour, simply because he had forgotten the first time around. He started his day with breakfast at the

Connaught Hotel, as soon as it opened at seven, ready at the door like clockwork. He had the same table and the same menu, tea, toast, cereal, eggs, bacon, kipper, more tea, and all the newspapers. From there he would go to the Old Bailey, or whichever other court he was attending, lunch in mess, and when court rose at four, round to the Waldorf Hotel for tea (sandwiches, scones, cream, jam). El Vino's was next, and on to the Garrick for dinner. All journeys were by taxi, however short or however long, and on countless occasions he would stand in Kensington High Street and hail a cab with the words, 'Norwich, please'. Always on account. He never handled money, and never had much, all his handsome earnings being spent as they should be on giving pleasure to himself and to others. At his memorial service in the Strand half a dozen cab-drivers were present. He was so well known to the taxi fraternity that he could ask to be driven home without having to explain where; once when he gave me a lift in his cab, and had moved to new lodgings in Beaumont Street a couple of months before in order to retrench, he said to the driver, 'Home, please', and when the man, clearly new, asked where that might be, James replied, 'How the Devil should I know?'

We were the most unlikely friends, bound neither by childhood acquaintance nor profession, by identity of outlook nor common experience. We ought not, in the raw order of things, to have crossed one another's paths at all. But the Garrick brought us together, and I know he always looked forward to my arrival, as I to his, as that of an uncomplicated companion. I suspect I was the only person to tease him, to 'send him up', precisely because I was not aware, until later, of the majesty of his reputation, and he might well have found my lack of diffidence refreshing. He never lost an opportunity to put me right about something, even when he knew I had not got it wrong; he absorbed from me the habit of teasing.

He once asked to borrow my 1911 *Encyclopaedia Britannica*. Which volume, I asked? 'The lot', he said, 'you know how one thing leads to another'. I took the whole collection in a cab to Iverna Court, where he felt the least he could do was to offer me a cup of tea. He had twelve teapots, for he never washed any of them and there had to be sufficient to keep him in fresh cups until the cleaning lady came next. There was a huge American refrigerator, which must have been given to him by a well-wisher, for one could not imagine his having chosen such an object. On opening it for the milk, he revealed that it was empty save for a copy of one of John Buchan's novels.

James never shopped. Desperate for some bread, he once took a cab round the corner to Safeways and hovered by one of the check-out girls. Announcing that he needed a loaf, and seeing to his incredulous dismay that she pointed to a distant shelf, he exclaimed for all the world to hear, 'You don't expect me to get it for myself, do you?'

He lived alone, but had an eye for pretty women. He told me once that he had been married. As far as I was able to work out, he had met a girl in a nightclub, proposed to her, been accepted and marched off to the registry office the following day, and had not seen her since. So one might suppose such an arrangement did not count for much, but it was still a legal tie of some sort.

Another of his surprises was his family. He had been the son of the second resident conductor at La Scala in Milan, and his mother had emigrated to England either just before or just after his birth. He had thus grown up as an English boy, and his rotund phrases gave the impression of having been nurtured by generations of toffs. Educated at the City of London school, he had taken a Double First at Cambridge and had gone straight into the legal profession. One knew that he had a sister, because he referred to her with amusing disdain – they had not spoken for years – and one could only imagine the affection which might have been subdued; he would certainly never give any clue of it. When I came to meet his nephews and nieces at his funeral, I was amazed to hear them all speak with suburban London accents. 'Uncle James moved a long way out of our station in life', I was told.

He quoted Gibbon every day, with two or three favourite passages recurring (on the Emperor Gordian II – 'Twenty-two acknowledged concubines, and a library of sixty-two thousand volumes, attested the variety of his inclinations, and from the productions which he left behind him, it appears that the former as well as the latter were designed for use rather than ostentation'). He would say with a roar that he had made me his literary executor, and that I would one day be responsible for making sure that his History of the Second Punic War should see its way into print. I assumed this was banter, but it was true. He had written a history of the war in such pure Gibbonian prose, flowing like a noble river across the page, as to take the breath away. It took me months to read, because his handwriting (having been a sinistral forced in childhood to use his right hand) was a despair to the faint-hearted, and when I had finished I had it seen by military and classical scholars, who all agreed that it was an original piece of work. The paragraphs are numbered, the story moving effortlessly from one into the other with a tension as gripping as anything in a modern detective novel. Alas, he got half way through the war and went back to the beginning to start all over again – it must have been his replacement for a crossword puzzle – but I still hope to persuade somebody to use it. The style is as near perfection as anything I have read anywhere. And it was all written from memory – there were no classical reference books in his flat, and he had never, since university days, consulted a library.

James did not need to die at sixty-five. His health had been wrecked by asthma and being overweight, and he had been considered promising in his twenties but unlikely to survive. Nevertheless he had the resilience of a horse. He had been blown up by the IRA bomb outside the Old Bailey in 1972 (because, he said with an impish grin, 'I perceived the danger to the state and considered it my duty to place myself between the building and the bomb'). Anyone else would have been killed; James was knocked over. The doctors told him that it would take a major archaeological exploration to retrieve the bits of shrapnel that were lodged in his vast frame, so they intended to leave them, and thereafter he could not pass through the security system at the Bailey without fear of setting light to a riot.

He called me at 6:00 p.m. on a Friday evening to ask if I was going to dine at the Club. I said I would if he would be there (Friday is normally dull), and he said he would make an effort, for he had been suffering from asthma for a few days but felt better. I waited for him to appear in vain, and assumed that he must been resting at home and that I would see him the following week. He had been felled by an attack of asthma so strong that he could not reach for the telephone to call the emergency services as fast as he ought, and when he did manage it, had collapsed on the floor. Ambulance men had to break his door down to get to him, and it took more than two of them to carry him to the vehicle. There, on his way to hospital, he died of a heart attack. It was strain which killed him.

I still think how frightened he must have been that Friday evening when he realized he would not make it.

CHAPTER 11

The Lessons of Murder

Looking after three black-and-white cats to whom Juan gave the impossible names Chiquitita de Los Angeles, Pussilandio de la Montanas, and Bette Davis' Eyes, I was a long way from thinking that I should delve into another murder case.

There were in fact two more in store. Late in July 1991 I received a telephone call from Tina Brown, then editor of *Vanity Fair* in New York. A man had been arrested in Milwaukee in shocking circumstances. His flat was a charnel-house, with dead bodies on the bed and in the bathtub, skeletons in a filing cabinet, skulls in a wardrobe, and internal organs stuck to the bottom of the freezer. There was even a severed head on a plate in the fridge. The police officer who had opened the door of the fridge was undergoing therapy. The man himself was good-looking, polite, unexcited, blond and thirty-one. His name was Jeffrey Dahmer. Tina said, 'I want you to go to Milwaukee for us and do a piece about him.'

I refused without hesitation. In the first place I was busy with students at Oxford and could not simply abandon them to fly to America. More importantly, I was not a reporter. With the excessive freedom of the press which obtained in the United States it was obvious that there would already be 150 experienced reporters on the scene, that they would have been briefed by the police, and that they would have interviewed everyone who had sold Dahmer a cup of coffee. There would be nothing for me to do or find out, and I should feel positively uncomfortable trying, for I worked best with an archive and felt an intense respect for the *sub judice* rule that prevented pre-trial gossip. I said as much to Tina Brown when she telephoned again the following day. 'That's not the point', she said, 'none of the people covering the story can possibly understand it. You're the only man who could. We need you to tell us what it is really all about.' As for Oxford, 'you needn't be away for more than five days. We'll pay your fare and put you up in a good hotel. The rest is up to you.' My resistance snapped when, on the third day, she promised the payment would take account of my 'expertise'. 'How much do you want?' she asked candidly. I thought very quickly what I would be paid by a British newspaper, doubled it for a glossy magazine, doubled it again for America, and proposed an outlandish figure. It was accepted.

The first person I contacted in Milwaukee was Kenneth Smail, who I had been informed was the psychiatrist appointed to assess Dahmer's state of mind and decide whether he would be fit to stand trial. It seemed to me obvious that he would already have had private conversations with the man and was bound to have an interesting point of view. Young and amiable, Ken Smail soon overcame his circumspection in the company of a nosy foreigner and told me that I was the first person to approach him. The city was swarming with newspaper men from all corners, and not one of them had thought to interview him. He and his wife Cathy became firm friends, and I have hanging on my wall in France a tapestry which Cathy made for me.

The second important contact was not of my seeking. When it became known that I was in town, the local TV station invited me to appear on an evening programme to discuss the implications of the Dahmer case. It would be a one-to-one interview lasting half an hour, and *extempore*; it would not be recorded in advance. I talked about the Nilsen case and made what I hoped were significant comparisons. I also gave the view that Dahmer himself must have been living in a personal hell for years. Back at the hotel shortly afterwards, my telephone rang. 'Hi. This is Shari Dahmer. My husband and I have just watched you on TV, and we think we ought to meet.' Again, the exclusivity of it all was amazing, for none of the reporters had been able to get access to the Dahmers, who were heavily protected, and nobody knew where they were staying. Thereafter the three of us would meet clandestinely, and Gerald Boyle, Jeffrey Dahmer's lawyer, arranged for me to have honorary membership of the Milwaukee Club, where I could entertain Lionel and Shari without fear of detection. That, too, led to an enduring friendship.

My *Vanity Fair* article duly claimed attention, and I was commissioned to write a book about the trial. In fact, I was commissioned twice, once by Hodder and Stoughton in London, and for the United States, by Random House. This was especially pleasing, for I had never been published in the United States (*Killing for Company* had been bought for America, and the publisher had gone into liquidation the week it was due to appear); with such an American subject, and such an interesting one, I could already sniff the fame and the guaranteed fortune.

It was not to be. The tale which follows is an eloquent comment upon publishing values in the United States. I delivered the book to Random House ahead of schedule and was received rapturously by the mercurial and exhausting Harry Evans (Tina's husband) with an almost pre-dawn working breakfast. He said he would have his senior editors read it and come back to me very soon. Three of them did, and they were all keen and complimentary about the style and pace of the book, its serious tone and thoughtful analysis. But they were worried about the end, wherein I appeared to look at the world through Dahmer's eyes and to identify a *quasi*-religious element in his raging necrophilia. 'The general view', said

Harry, 'is that you need to do a re-write.' I admitted that all the wardrobes would have to be changed to closets and the pavements to sidewalks, but I could not see what else needed to be done. 'It's your attitude that needs to be altered', I was told. 'Go back to the beginning and try again. You cannot afford to make the reader uncomfortable.' I protested that Dahmer's crimes, not my treatment of them, were the true source of discomfort, and furthermore that I only had one head, and if I were to write the book again (which God forbid!) it would come out more or less the same way as before. Still, I appeared to be missing the point, which finally broke out in an immortal sentence which makes me wince even now: 'The trouble is, we in America don't *want* to understand this guy.'

In which case, I retorted rather pompously, they should look for somebody else to write their shallow books. The contract was broken by mutual consent, my not very generous advance used to set against eventual publication of *Killing for Company* (a much safer bet, for the murderer was British – no question of impugning American manhood), which they printed and bound but never advertised. It sold a few copies.

Only three years separated *The Shrine of Jeffrey Dahmer* from my book on the trial of Rosemary West, yet this, too, was undertaken at first reluctantly, although for quite different reasons. Police had found the skeletal remains of several young women beneath the basement and in the garden of a small terraced house in Gloucester. Most had died about twenty years before, and their condition indicated that they had each been gruesomely tortured before being despatched and dismembered. Disposal had been identical in all cases, the bodies cut into four pieces and heaped into a vertical shaft, usually with finger-bones, toe-bones and kneecaps missing. The house was inhabited by a gossipy journeyman builder, Frederick West, his pretty dark-haired wife Rosemary, and up to eight children. Mr and Mrs West were arrested, and variously charged with murder.

Frederick West committed suicide in custody, leaving Rosemary to face charges alone, despite the fact that three of Frederick's murders were committed before he had met her, and in one case when she was no more than thirteen years old. When it was suggested that I write a book on the subject, I demurred on the grounds that whatever I had thought about addictive killing had already been said and that I would necessarily repeat myself. It needed a fresh approach and a new kind of analysis. Privately, I also anticipated emotional fatigue, for this was a case not only dealing with necrophilia but with escalating sadism, a dismal and dangerous subject to dwell upon. But I did agree to attend the committal proceedings in the magistrates' court in Dursley, at least to discover what the case was all about.

The fact that there was a committal hearing at all indicated something unusual, perhaps suspicious, about the charges. It was generally a formality to be sent for trial by the magistrate, requiring the court sit for about five minutes. But a defendant had the right to demand that evidence be presented so that the magistrate might decide whether it was sufficient to warrant a trial. Mrs West's legal advisers clearly thought there was no case to answer, and that the charges ought to be dropped. Hence the full committal hearing.

It took nearly two weeks for everything to be said, and for part of that time there were three defendants, Mrs West and two men. Charges of rape against the two men did not go forward, but the evidence against Mrs West was heard in great and merciless detail. There were so many journalists present from around the world, that a special annex had to be established wherein the overflow could hear the proceedings relayed by loudspeaker, and I have never experienced anything like that feeling of shock as so many grown men fell into awed silence at what they were hearing. As the story was told of what had happened to Anne-Marie West (Frederick's daughter, Rosemary's step-daughter) over a period of eight years, I heard one reporter whisper, 'Now she's done for.' It did not seem to occur to anyone that there might be good reason to disbelieve what was being said. Everyone present, without exception, *wanted* Mrs West to be guilty. There was no room whatever for enquiry, no taste for dispute, no disposition towards careful thought.

When Sasha Wass, junior counsel representing Mrs West, laid out the legal and factual considerations according to which the defendant should not be sent to trial, I was reassured that my instinctive reaction had not been utterly mad. It was true; most of the evidence pointed away from Rosemary West, not towards her; the argument that she was resident in the house where remains were found did not apply, for she was less often there than were the lodgers, who heard and saw nothing; the crimes were committed when she was a girl in her teens, or a young woman, and so long ago that no possible alibi could be forthcoming, which was an abuse of process; and so on. This is not the place to set out all the arguments again, so brilliantly examined by Miss Wass, but by the time she was finished I was convinced of two matters: one, that the revolting evidence against Rosemary West which had made the journalists fall silent had nothing whatever to do with murder but related to other faults (i.e. acquiescence in incest) with which she was not charged, and that this was therefore only admitted to blacken her character; two, that following the suicide of Frederick West the police had to tamper with the evidence they had already amassed in charging him with the murder of Charmaine, his eight year-old step-daughter (daughter of his first wife, whom he also killed), in fact to change the date of the little girl's death so that Rosemary could be indicted. They sought to demonstrate that Frederick was in custody at the time, and that sixteen year-old Rosemary was therefore the only person who could have killed Charmaine. They did not say why, in that case, they had charged Frederick with her death, and not Rosemary, if Frederick could not have done it. If true, this is what in crime novels they call being 'framed'.

By this time I was feeling quite fierce, and I told the publishers, Transworld, that I very much wanted to write this book, but that it might not be the sort of book they had in mind. To their immense credit they allowed me to proceed, though they surely knew that any book which did not loudly call the woman a nasty bitch might not have the sales they would have liked. Transworld had more guts in this regard than had Random House in New York. They also agreed to publish my long-cherished project on moral philosophy *The Evil That Men Do*, as part of the deal. I doubt whether this book would have seen the light otherwise.

Throughout the Dursley hearing I had stayed with my friends Leo and Jilly Cooper nearby. They were an enormous support at the end of every day, when the burden of what I had heard was so heavy that I could not bear to repeat it, and they assuaged grim moods with lots of kitchen-chat and old-fashioned cooking. They also heard out my contention that there was prejudice against the defendant, and gave me the idea for my title, '*She Must Have Known*', being shorthand for virtually the only reason for convicting her, namely it was simply not credible that she did *not* know. Thus was Mrs West to be sent to prison for life on an assumption.

On the last day at Dursley children threw eggs at the van which brought the defendant to court. The eggs were brought there by tabloid journalists and handed to the children as the cameras prepared. I saw it happen.

The trial at Winchester Crown Court was less sensational, for we all knew by then what would be adduced. We were less shockable. But I was still amazed at what I believed was the judge's connivance with untutored public opinion, the way in which I thought he coaxed the jury into conviction, when they were clearly worried that they ought, on the evidence, to acquit; and his timorousness in the face of newspaper editors' refusal to obey his summons to appear (it certainly looked as if all the witnesses for the prosecution, save the police inspector, had been paid and in some cases rehearsed by the press).

There were three authors preparing studies of the case – Gordon Burn, Geoffrey Wansell and myself. We were colleagues, not competitors, for we each had a different story to tell. Burn's was the last to be published, and the most thoughtful. Wansell's was the most complete, as he had been given access to material which we others had to filch. Mine had only the virtue of being first.

I might add as a postscript that I have since met Mrs West and write to her from time to time as well. What I am about to say offends all my own precepts about the importance of evidence as against intuition, but in the light of my experience it might have some tangential value. Addictive murderers are cold fish. They are not tactile. They do not smile. They are interested in objects, things, dead matter, not in people, ambitions, life-giving excitements. Their emotions are arid, still-born. Their voices are monotones. Rosemary West is the opposite to all this. She is jolly, giggly, modest, sweet-natured, interested in people's lives, mad about children, with a happy disposition and a warm touch. I offer this information as a matter of wonderment only.

The Evil That Men Do is about the sources of goodness and how, once these have been located, to protect them ('goodness' in a title is a great public turn-off, apparently; only 'evil' attracts). By way of illustration there is much, of course, about the wickedness of which mankind is all too capable, but I attempt to show how and why this wickedness has been allowed to prevail, and how easy it is for people to slip into the habit of behaving grossly, especially when gross behaviour is condoned or encouraged by authority. Bernard Levin chastised me for vivid descriptions of evil acts which could infect the imagination of the reader, but he failed to note that these were the preamble to a celebration of sainthood and outward-looking benevolence, which I maintained was the ultimate expression of humanness. I was deeply influenced by the work of Iris Murdoch, whose novels are an unceasing search for the Good hidden beneath the Muck and the Mess. I introduced historical and personal examples, including my own mother, Mabel Ingledew, whose forbearance and unselfish fortitude were exemplary.

Some might think Mabel was cold. They misinterpret shyness. Isolated by deafness and frail health, my mother did not enter into colloquy with the world, but demonstrated by her quiet struggle that goodness was a positive force. Unlike evil, it does not draw attention to itself (and when it does, as with that abominable child St Theresa of Lisieux, it is suspect). It may pass unnoticed. It is nearly always taken for granted, which is its finest characteristic, and that is why so many funeral orations are fashioned in guilty shock, as the goodness of the deceased is suddenly recognized for the first time.

I have tried all my life not to wait so long. I have hunted for goodness in nature, in literature, in art, as well as in people, and have wept with frustration when I have failed to find it. My concentration upon the personalities of murderers cannot possibly be held to suggest an indifference to the sufferings of their victims. I am prostrated with grief by cruelty, to old people, to children, to those who trust and to animals alike. I cannot accept that to torture an animal is less bad than to torture a young woman, for morality resides in the act, not in the object of the act.

The desire to do good, especially in those areas where good is least likely to succeed, has landed me time and again in situations which have been near to intolerable, and which my friends have marvelled that I was willing to tolerate, manifesting (though not to me) that masochism which Selina detected. This mania to do good is arguably abnormal and sick. Still, it is there, and I must confront it, especially as I suspect that it has coloured my work as well, guiding me into choosing to write about people (Nilsen, Dahmer, Mrs West) whom everyone else regards as irredeemably wicked. It has led me to question the ubiquitous and feeble word 'evil' to describe behaviour we do not like and comprehend less, and to find other words which are not so final, closed or remorseless. 'Evil' is a brick wall of comforting ignorance which I have sought to circumvent. I suppose I have been at it quietly since the Catholics of St Alban's were so glibly sure they knew what evil was. I will curse with rage at all acts calculated to instil fear or inflict harm, and the child who torments a cat is as bad, in my world, as the child who bullies an infant. Indeed, one of the best educations available to any child, who has at hand an adult capable of seeing and showing the truth, is the study of animal behaviour. No animal could match humankind for ghastly behaviour, and the adjective 'beastly' is one of the most ironic misnomers in language. Animals are part of the circular progress of life; they kill and are killed; but they do not delight in the kill; and the concept of murder if applied to any creature other than the human would sound ridiculous.

One should watch the animals and observe how they avoid doing harm. They have much to teach. One man who did precisely that for most of his adult life was John Aspinall, whose biography I asked to write in order that I might celebrate his character and achievements. I had known him on the periphery for a number of years and thought he would accept an approach from me (he had refused all others for fear they might not understand, that they would mock and deride). Tom Maschler, once more, was big enough to welcome an idea which many a publisher might have scorned, for Aspinall was better known as a gambler and near-fascist ideologue. Tom trusted me to locate something more important.

Finding the facts of Aspinall's life, intriguing though they were, was only the beginning. I felt that I needed to spend as much time as possible with the animals in order to test the springs of his commitment, to make sure their origins were not (as the newspapers always implied) steeped in vanity. I watched him for hours. If he were accompanied, it was with one or more of the keepers, dedicated men who knew the animals even better than he because they lived with them for all the waking hours. Their conversations were specific and unemotional, concerning the well-being of a gorilla who had developed arthritis, or the exotic food refused by a rare serpent, or how to coax a mother into tending her new-born young, to whom she appeared mysteriously indifferent. The need to understand was paramount, to work out the reasons behind certain behaviour, for never was it assumed that behaviour could be merely whimsical. Aspinall and his team (he always referred to 'we' when talking about the various projects with animals) were adamant that a problem could only be solved by discovering what it meant to the animal itself, and I was quickly convinced that their success in breeding derived largely from this uncommon empathy. It may sound anthropomorphic to say so, although I still do not know why one should apologize for it, but I am sure the animals *knew* that they mattered, and that their interests were cared for. Why else should they have settled down in such obvious content, and been prepared to contemplate (another anthropomorphism) a future? Their sense of well-being, of satisfaction, of safety, even of amusement, was palpable. When the keepers left to deal with their daily chores and Aspers was alone with the mighty beasts he counted as friends, shorn of his pack of cards, unable to entertain with his stories, he was a humble guest, silent, sharing, peaceful. It was a moving experience to watch him.

At length I learned to feel a little of this companionship, with huge glorious tigers purring at me with a deep growl and lifting their tails in gratitude for a stroke or a tickle, sinuous lemurs crawling all over me, on shoulders, on head, on arms, without anxiety or hesitation, and gorillas staring deep into my eyes. I had studied the history of one gorilla in particular in order to focus attention which might otherwise become too diffuse. His name was Djala. He had been rescued as an orphan in the jungle, his mother slaughtered to make ashtrays of her hands, and as soon as Aspinall had learnt of his plight, he had been brought over to Howletts. A suite of rooms on the top floor had been prepared for him, lain with straw and made secure, and a female keeper, Julie, was entrusted with his education (I use the word literally). She remained with him in his caged apartments all day long, until he felt happy enough to move to the gorilla enclosure and join a group. I met him in the interim, when he had a section to himself in the gorilla quarters while the others sized him up and the keepers could judge whether they were ready to accept him.

Djala and I spent hours together. I might almost say we gossiped, for the degree of understanding that exists between a human and a gorilla has to be experienced to be believed. We played, we fought, we teased one another, and we displayed jealous attachment. He was always glad of company, and he delighted in pretending to scare me. Djala well knew that he was far stronger than me, and so he climbed a rope, swung, and crashed his body into me, sending me tumbling. He was careful, however, not to swing too fast, or he might cause real damage. His intuition was finely honed. I noticed also that when he sunk his huge sharp teeth into my arm, he would first make sure I was wearing thick sleeves (or he wouldn't touch), and he would control his bite so that it merely made contact. Had he wanted to, he could have torn my arm from its socket.

Trust between species of mammals is, alas, extremely rare, due entirely to human pride, hubris, exploitation. We have forgotten that we are part of a whole, and that we have duties and responsibilities as well as those privileges which derive from intelligence and ingenuity. To imagine that an animal is worth less because it cannot construct a jet engine is as myopic as Nilsen treating his victims as no more than props to his fantasies. Aspinall redressed the balance, and to my mind his achievement in this regard outweighs everything else he did, and is hardly ever acknowledged precisely because most people persist in believing that animals do not matter. Those who know the magnificence of his endeavour are the beasts he befriended, and they do not write in newspapers.

There were accidents. Three keepers were killed by tigers for no apparent reason, and one by a clumsy elephant who did not look where he was going. These fell far below the national average for fatalities in zoos, but they were the only news that newspapers found interesting. So Aspinall was perceived by the ignorant as a dangerous *dilettante*. In fact, he was more knowledgeable and more serious than most appointed zoo directors, a surprise which in time the zoo directors themselves came to recognize.

One's perspective on the phenomenon of time expands dramatically when one is in the company of a great animal. I am not sure why this should be so. A domestic cat is, or should be, as big a source of wonder as an elegant tigress, for it too has genes which ascend countless generations. So does humankind, for that matter, and the fact that our species is only a few million years old, that we began to emerge when some other species had been established long since, should not itself make any difference. The glory of it does not lie in mathematics. One begins dimly to realize that even time is not a mathematical certainty. One is so used to thinking that everything has a beginning, a middle and an end that the concept of eternity is ungraspable. It is difficult to think that the universe did not start, that it simply is. Even more difficult, then, is it to ponder eternity here on earth, in the trees, in the animals, in us. The eloquent eyes of a gorilla, which seem to suggest that it might be footling to waste thought on the impenetrable, remind one that time is not to be understood or measured. In a sense it has no existence whatever. All is mixed and mingled and repeated, the past, present and future all part of the same essence which contains and holds us. Everything carries the echo of its past and the seeds of its future, is churned in the eternal recreation of matter in different shapes. Only in that sense does reincarnation make any sense, more sense indeed than the upholders of reincarnation themselves realize. The being that is me will one day provide food for other beings that will pass into still different kinds of living tissue or sap and continue, in all logic, forever. Each of us is the vehicle of eternity; each of us holds within his flesh the history of the world.

The discovery that one is being eaten by cancer alters not only the present and the future, but the past as well. Perspectives shift, priorities tumble, time itself reverses. Little moments lost in the past now glow with a painful preciousness, for they were hitherto always ready to be recaptured and savoured, even (who knows?) repeated one day, as one usually hopes, with the mildest effort of actual intention, to revisit one's pleasures. Cancer shockingly destroys all that comfort and turns the past, which was a slowly dissolving watercolour, into a golden jewel that must be claimed before it is snatched away. One's very self, as described by the accretion of incidents, is like a possession, to be jealously vaunted and displayed in defiance of the disease which dares to tell one that there is no value either in ambition or in reminiscence, for one is no more than a piece of disintegrating tissue at the mercy of a thing which nibbles away until it is sated, then leaves the residue to rot with its fruitless memories intact.

In Thailand once, I was struck by the astonishing indifference the orientals show towards possessions. A student whom I helped get on a moving bus (they never actually stop at bus-stops, they merely slow down a bit) by holding his books as he grabbed a handrail, calmly took off his Buddha ring and gave it to me in token of gratitude. The disparity between the favour and the reward was numbing to a westerner accustomed to hold on to everything and still reach for more. The stranger did not think it odd at all. The possession of an object worn on his finger could never be important, whereas the connection between people, however transitory, could never be trivial. For weeks afterwards (and there were other similar instances of spiritual maturity in the Far East) I walked lightly, determined to break free of the drive for gain and ownership. It did not last, of course, the poison being insidious, but the lesson was never entirely unlearnt.

Now I feel that my past is my possession, and I am reluctant to relinquish it, for with it must go my soul. That, I suppose, is what death is, the last gasp of the dispossessed.

My cancer is not terminal. It was revealed at the age of sixty, as the result of a routine medical test which discovered traces of blood in the urine. The blood was invisible to me, and was accompanied by no pain or symptom of any disturbance in the body. My doctor thought it was probably nothing significant, and that little polyps frequently pop up in the bladder and have to be surgically removed. It is an easy task, over in five minutes. But further examination showed that this was not a tiny mushroom, but a spreading jam, a growth in fact. It would have to be taken out. Even that was not a huge problem, as cancers of the bladder were fairly routine; they tended to be sluggish and bored, and sit there for ten years without doing much harm. I was still not worried. Then came the laboratory report. In very few instances the bladder cancer turns out to be a majestic monster capable of gobbling up a whole body. Mine was one of those, a grade three chap, greedy and aggressive, which had already started eating away at the wall of the bladder. It was relatively young and could still be stopped in its tracks. The standard procedure was a radical removal of the bladder itself – take it out and chuck it away. Kill the dog to kill the rabies.

I resisted this stark conclusion. I did not feel ill and could trust my body to fight the intruder itself; after all, it had spent a lifetime preparing its defences. I did not trust surgery. The surgeon told me that he could not, in conscience, allow me that choice. 'If you do nothing', he said, 'within nine months you will be inoperable.' I could, in explicit words, be dead next year. That was when my past became my most precious possession.

It took me three days to decide, and three weeks in hospital to endure. I am still recovering. Indications are that the operation was curative and that the cancer has gone, but I know that indications are never more than hopes, some more reasonable than others. I must wait and see.

Now I have an external bladder which fills up willy-nilly and must be emptied all the time and changed every three days. This I do myself, hating my body as I clean the piece of raw gut which sticks out of me. My penis hangs helpless, redundant and forgotten.

Yet my body is not my possession. I have it on loan. It is my past which is mine and mine alone. I am writing of a time when I was robust and sturdy, when nibbling trespassing tumours were a ludicrous notion. I was such until a couple of months ago, long after I started on this memoir. Now that I have been restructured I see the past with more affection. It is not just a matter of reminiscence, but rather of attachment to the person one was, a person approachable by means of concentrated thought, but only really discoverable accidentally, through colours, smells, odd words, the expanse of the American sky, the sound of a New York taxi, the splash and slurp of the great river as it washes the walls of the temple in Bangkok, the changing light on the glistening elegance of the Taj Mahal. All things, but each carrying its essence, its soul, through the senses which bring them to you. One's measurable past is a sequence of events. But one's real past is a bundle of sensations.

I wonder if Yves Bertrand languishing on a bed which he can never leave in Marseilles, struggling vainly to connect with his mother and ex-wife when they visit, cruelly imprisoned in a carcass which will not function, is in touch with his past. Does he, too, feel that it is his possession, the only close treasure he has left, which he can summon and enjoy without waiting for a nurse to do it for him? Or are his courtship of Monique, his teasing of Xavier, his afternoons on horseback and his meals at home with the English teacher, are they all gone? Is it I who steal them in these pages? Is this what a writer does, in the end, as soon as he mentions anybody other than himself?

The doctors and nurses had warned me that I should be tearful when I went home. I reassured them that I had accepted what had happened to me and had worked out how to cope with it. I had determined that I should be grateful for life and not regret the mutilation which had been necessary to protect it, for I knew that I should gradually heal and grow strong. And what happened when I got home? Everything there was as I had left it three weeks earlier – the same walls and wallpaper, the same curtains, the same tread on the stair and *miaow* from the cat, the same comfortable sheets, the same cherry tree through the window, the same crockery at breakfast. All was unaltered, except myself. All was normal, except my body. I was the only misfit in the equation. And the nurses were right; I wept.

Aspers died of a cruel cancer which ravaged his face. Almost to the end he was spending quiet time with his animals, sharing their space in the long march. They did not care what he looked like. My own cancer is kinder, less florid, and as I write it may have been conquered. Good. But it too serves to give pause, not merely to indulge in fruitless lamentation, as I have too often done, and as I have been found occasionally to do in these pages, but to accept the truth of timeless essence. For what is cancer, after all? It is part of me, it is me, it is a jumbling of my own cells which multiply when they used not to multiply and lose control of their fate. My body does not attempt to fight it because my body does not recognize it as a foreign intruder. It is not. It is familiar. It is the same as it always was. And time is the same as it always was, uncontrollable and haphazard.

It is comforting to assume a linear progression, and in the obvious chronological sense there is one, within the limits of our beginning and our end. But that is a mischievous illusion, giving rise to ambition on the one hand and regret on the other. All that we were and will be is contained in our present, just as certainly as our genes determine our struggles, our conquests and our illnesses. The snotty-nosed little boy in Herring Street, Camberwell has not disappeared, though his prefab, his primary school next door, the skin and leather factories opposite have all been razed to the ground. I am still he, with his terror of team-sport and his urge to outshine competitors in his own way. He is a layer of my skin. The shame and fear he felt when Tony Merrick's little sister was invited to fellate him in the air-raid shelter at Milton Road still bring ripples to the surface and prevent sexual ease. The pubescent lad who hung around stage doors and gazed at the portals of the Savoy Hotel still hungers to lurk in the fame of others, for he does not consider his own worth remarkable. Gilbert Harding's pupil still longs to express himself properly and earn the master's praise. The Cardiff university student is still swotting his path towards a First, hoping that nobody will notice that it is all done with hard work bereft of originality. Camilla's hopeless lover still shakes in the presence of her perfect femininity, and Jean-Philippe's silent friend is still looking for his double. The teller of tales still wants to be heard, and the chronicler of Nilsen, Dahmer, Mrs West, E. F. Benson, John Aspinall, Georgiana Devonshire, still wants to be heeded, to convince. Layer upon layer of selfhood stick to me like burrs, each as present and as real as the self that is writing these words as an ageing man. Proust was so right; it is not thought that conjures up the past, for a past so imagined is nought but history re-shaped. Abandonment to the various selves which inhabit us requires a kind of radiant silence, and then there they all are, as urgent, as tactile, as sense-directed as they always were. I can smell as well as hear myself being. The past is not gone.

Nor indeed is the cancer, although the surgeons say it has been physically eradicated, chucked away with my poor bladder. I am amazed how sanguine I appear to be about it. When I was in India working on the ancestry of the ruling family of Udaipur, at the request of the Maharana, a very old man was assigned to help me decipher ancient texts written in Mewari on copper. Ghanshyamlal Sharma was a Brahmin, much respected by all generations for his extensive learning and wisdom. He spoke fluent French as well as English, Mewari and Hindi, and was ever gentle and obliging. He used to walk up the hill to the palace where I was living, slowly in the intense heat, with a stick in one hand and his other hand crooked in the small of his back. One day I suggested to him that it might be easier if I went down into town for our next meeting and consult him at his own house. 'Ah', he said, 'you have observed that I have a weak back. You are thinking I must be in pain. That is very Western. Well, let me put your mind at rest if I may. My pain is my friend. He is always with me, and will stay with me to the end. When I die, my pain will die too. We shall go together. So do not worry.'

Index